AF655404

Future of Cyber and Electronic Warfare

Future of Cyber and Electronic Warfare

Col. (Retd.) S.C. Narang

PRASHANT PUBLISHING HOUSE
DELHI-110094

Published by :

Prashant Publishing House

C-34, 28 Foota Road, Gali-3,
West Karwal Nagar, Delhi-110094
Phone : 011-22963970, Mob. : 9810396373
e-mail.: prashantpublishinghouse@gmail.com

Future of Cyber and Electronic Warfare
Reserved
First Published 2017

ISBN 978-93-80565-9-34

No part of this book may be reprduced or transmitted in any form or by any means, electronic or mechanical, Including photocoying, recording or by any information storage and retrieval system, with-out permission in writing from the Publishers.

PRINTED IN INDIA

Published by Mr. R.K. Jha M/s Prashant Publishing House and Published at H.S. Offset House Press, Delhi.

Contents

Preface

Electronic Warfare (EW) became an integral support component to more traditional warfare-offensive and defensive-in the late 20th Century. In 1973, having watched Israel jam Syrian guided missiles during the Yom Kippur War, a Soviet admiral summed it up succinctly: "The next war will be won by the side that best exploits the electromagnetic spectrum."

Cyberwarfare is politically motivated hacking to conduct sabotage and espionage. It is a form of information warfare sometimes seen as analogous to conventional warfare.

Cybernetic warfare experienced its first serious reversal with the Vietnam War, where its analytical techniques and military systems foundered in the conditions of a low-intensity conflict. James Gibson has written persuasively about the failure in the jungles of South-East Asia of 'technowar', an approach to military conflict in which war was viewed as 'a production system that can be rationally managed and warfare as a kind of activity that can be scientifically determined by constructing computer models'.

Digital war intrinsically possesses in ultimate form some of the same characteristics that traditional military planners are striving for, including low-cost precision, standoff, and stealth. Digital war threatens the ability of a nation state's military to interpose itself between its population and "enemies of the state," thereby causing a loss of sanctuary. The importance of sanctuary can be inferred by our willingness to spend significant resources on air, sea, and missile defenses to provide our citizens with a workable sanctuary with respect to territorial intrusions.

During the information age, the phenomenon is that the digital industry creates a knowledge-based society surrounded by a high-tech global economy that spans over its influence on how the manufacturing throughput and the service sector operate in an efficient and convenient way. In a commercialized society, the information industry is able to allow individuals to explore their personalized needs, therefore simplifying the procedure of making decisions for transactions and significantly lowering costs for both the producers and buyers. This is accepted overwhelmingly by participants throughout the entire economic activities for efficacypurposes, and new economic incentives would then be indigenously encouraged, such as theknowledge economy. All the matter is just compiled and edited in nature. Taken from the various sources which are in public domain.

The book takes us into the emerging arenas of war, including electronic and cyberspace. It evaluates the impact of technology and shows how dwindling resources and the scourge of global warming can precipitate conflict in the future.

—*Editor*

1

Electronic Warfare

Electronic Warfare (EW) became an integral support component to more traditional warfare-offensive and defensive-in the late 20th Century. In 1973, having watched Israel jam Syrian guided missiles during the Yom Kippur War, a Soviet admiral summed it up succinctly: "The next war will be won by the side that best exploits the electromagnetic spectrum."

EW took on new dimensions and importance in post-9/11 Southwest Asia, where the enemy used electronic means to detonate their weapon of choice-improvised explosive devices (IEDs).

The U.S. and its allies sought to combat those low-tech, but deadly, attacks with the components and capabilities arising from a technology boom that changed all aspects of warfare.

With the drawdown in Southwest Asia and the planned Pacific Pivot, EW now is entering yet another new stage of development, requirements and importance. Andrew Dunn, vice president of business development for Integrated and electronic warfare for Exelis Electronic Systems Division, calls it a "whole new mindset" for the U.S. military as the U.S. Department of Defense (DOD) shifts its focus to an area where uncontested access to the electromagnetic spectrum and physical battlespace may no longer exist. Instead, U.S. and allied forces must be ready to deal with near-peer anti-access/area denial (A2/AD) environments and a greater emphasis on the air-sea battle.

The fight against IEDs

In Southwest Asia, the Army and Marine Corps bore the brunt of low-tech attacks on the fringe of EW. That was especially true with the Army, as the internal EW capabilities they had developed during the Cold War were determined no longer necessary. It would prove to be a costly mistake the Army does not want to repeat-but fears it may. "When the USSR fell and the Cold War ended, all the organization in the U.S. Army dedicated to tactical jamming in combat EW intel battalions went away, leaving ourselves pretty vulnerable on the EW front," says Col. Rob Murray, outgoing branch chief for cyber electromagnetic activities (CEMA) at the Army Cyber Center of Excellence at Fort Gordon, Ga. "With the new challenges brought on by 9/11, going into Afghanistan and then Iraq, we found ourselves with no one responsible for EW in the Army.

The enemy quickly found that seam and ways to exploit it. IEDs at first were pretty easy to spot, then they started burying the explosives and lines to them-command-detonated by hidden observers. Every time we developed a counter to what they were doing, they kept moving to new approaches."

CEMA Deputy Branch chief Matt Cullen said the insurgents' move to radio-controlled IEDs escalated the U.S. and allied death toll: "Our challenge was to 'reinvigorate' EW as the means to counter, combat and defeat RC IEDs." The Army turned for help to the U.S. Navy, which had become DOD's lead agent for EW, but it was far from a perfect solution because the EW requirements of a ground force differ from those of the Air Force and Navy. "The Navy has a lot of its EW capability on airplanes flying off carriers and they don't turn that capability on until they are a couple of hundred miles away, so the possibility of those systems causing problems on the ship are minimal. Ships have their own EW defenses against missiles, of course, but when a missile is coming, they don't care what disruptions there may be," Cullen explains.

"But the Army has jammers in the middle of convoys in the middle of bad-guy territory-and when those jammers are turned on, they also disrupt our communications on the ground," Cullen continues. "Early in the war, the Army was buying jammers from the Air Force and Navy and support from those service's EW officers, but what they didn't understand was the jammers also disrupted our soldiers' communications."

CEMA's three pillars of EW are:

1. electronic attack;
2. electronic support-what frequencies and technologies do friendly forces use to defeat the enemy; and
3. electronic protection-keeping U.S. and friendly forces safe from fratricide and enemy EW

"The artillery guys-such as Col. Murray-take that very seriously regarding mortars. They figure out problems during planning. The same has to be done with jammers," Cullen explains. Military forces have important RF frequencies that are restricted from U.S. and allied electronic countermeasures called the Joint Restricted Frequency List (JFRL). Despite the best intention, the JFRL does not protect against accidental disruptions-especially if using a frequency that is not on the JFRL. "In a modern Army, where we have portable computing and internet capabilities that can move information around the battlefield, we should be using radio frequency engineering during the planning process, to predict the effect of jammers on our own radios." It was not until 2008 to 2010 that the Army was able to begin restoring an organic EW capability, says Lt. Col. Keith Cantrell, CEMA's incoming branch chief. That included standing up the Cyber Center of Excellence (COE), incorporating the work of the Signals COE it replaced, and slowly incorporating EW.

SHIPBOARD AND AIRBORNE ELECTRONIC WARFARE

Despite the Navy's role as DOD's executive agency for EW, its leaders are being forced to redesign the Navy's own capabilities-air- and ship-borne. That includes the Surface Electronic Warfare Improvement Program (SEWIP) to upgrade existing shipboard signals technologies used to identify, assess and analyze EM signals and EW threats. A major problem, especially with aircraft carriers, is the massive number of radars, antennas, and other electronic systems operating simultaneously in a highly complex shipboard electromagnetic spectrum.

With the prospect of near-peer EW threats in the future, carriers and other combat and support vessels will need even greater capabilities to conduct offensive and defensive EW. That includes the NGJ, designed to give the EA-18G Growler advanced technologies for offensive EW missions when the jammer goes operational by 2020.

"The vision for the future is to take what our collection, exploitation, and early warning capabilities [find] and turn them into offensive ways to use electronic attack," says Christine Fox, who recently retired from the Pentagon after serving as acting deputy secretary of defense. "If we can go after the C2 or ISR pieces of a threat instead of putting a missile against a missile, I can potentially disrupt that missile's ability to find its target."

In addition, the Office of Naval Research (ONR) in Arlington, Va., is developing a prototype technology called Integrated Topside (InTop) to extend the range and flexibility of shipboard EW. For example, InTop would integrate the current forest of antennas on a ship's deck into a shared multi-function, multi-beam aperture array that could collect signals across a wide range of frequencies, then use a central resource allocation manager to share that information with several EW processes.

Perhaps equally important is the 21st Century version of "quiet running." The Chief of Naval Operations is pushing for greater education of officers and enlisted personnel on electronic spectrum awareness and understanding all aspects of a ship's electromagnetic signature. "We have to be more mindful of how we operate in the electromagnetic domain and in cyberspace and how those capabilities come together," wrote Margaret Palmieri, director of the Navy's Integrated Fires Division, in the July 2014 issue of U.S. Naval Institute Proceedings. "We are working on better understanding how networks and signals and networks and information come together. What do we really look like to the enemy?

"Integrated-fires capabilities are a central part of the asymmetric advantage our Navy, joint and coalition forces bring to a fight. They include capabilities that disrupt adversary C4ISR systems, deliver electronic payloads that limit an enemy's freedom of maneuver and action and enhance the ability of our own forces to place ordnance on target," Palmieri wrote. "It integrates lethal and non-lethal fires, underpinned by superior battlespace awareness and assured C2, to provide commanders an expanded set of warfighting tools especially important in A2/AD environments, like Air-Sea Battle." In that same issue, Vice Adm. Ted N. Branch, deputy chief of naval operations (CNO) for information dominance, discussed the Navy's need to dominate all segments of future battlespaces-on, above, and below the sea, as well as outer space-to sustain America's "global primacy'.

"However, commanding, controlling and fighting our forces in these areas requires dominance in the information domain, to include the electromagnetic spectrum and cyberspace," he wrote. "The name we've given to this concept-information dominance-is still new and unfamiliar to some, but it's indispensable to Fleet operations, so much so that we've adopted it as a distinct warfare discipline.

"Formerly perceived by many as a collection of support activities performed by specialized restricted line officers, information dominance is increasingly recognized by Fleet operators as a critical force multiplier. It's no longer just an adjunct to warfighting. It is warfighting," Branch wrote. Navy information dominance focuses on three goals: robust and agile C2 in all operating environments; superior knowledge of the battlespace, the physical environment as well as threat capability, disposition and intent; and projecting power through the integration of kinetic and non-kinetic effects.

"We refer to these three elements, or pillars, as assured C2, battlespace awareness and integrated fires. Through them, information dominance creates decision superiority, provides asymmetric advantage and enhances the lethality of our deployed forces with non-kinetic options," Branch added. Those pillars, in turn, are designed to correspond to the CNO's three tenets: warfighting first; operate forward; and be ready.

"The critical element of the information dominance definition is integration, Branch wrote. "Blending the attributes of ISR, oceanography, meteorology, networks, cyber, and EW allows for better planning, smarter decisions and earlier results.

Aligning the related restricted-line communities of naval oceanography, information warfare, information professional, intelligence and the space cadre into the information dominance corps has likewise advanced our concept and capability development and improved data and system interoperability."

U.S. Marine Corps

While the Army and Marine Corps both are viewed as ground forces, the Marine Corps' EW requirements differ significantly from those of the Army, especially in meeting future anticipated threats. In recognition of that, the Corps has created a Marine Air/Ground Task Force (MAGTF) EW concept to develop an integrated system of distributed, platform-agnostic EW systems, including the progressive inclusion of technologies and capabilities from other services and commercial vendors.

MAGTF EW elements have several programs in development. Among them are Intrepid Tiger II (IT-2): An EW pod for communications-based targets, expandable to radar-based targets, currently deployed to CENTCOM and with Marine expeditionary units in three different versions for fixed-wing aircraft, unmanned aerial vehicles (UAVs), and helicopters.

Another program is the Electronic Warfare Service Architecture (EWSA)-an extended data exchange and hardware protocol to connect EW/SIGINT airborne nodes, via an adaptive multi-waveform network, to ground operators, Cyber/EW Coordination Cells (C/EWCCs) and other air EW nodes. The Corps also has stood up several new or redefined units, including the Cyber and Electronic Warfare Integration Division (CEWID), the Capabilities Development Directorate's integration and execution authority for all Marine Corps warfighting development activities associated with Cyberspace and EW.

CEWID coordinates with operating forces, supporting establishment and mission partners in order to identify, prioritize and integrate capability solutions across DOD's Doctrine, Organization, Training, Materiel, Leadership and Education, Personnel and Facilities (DOTMLPF) protocols. CEWID, in turn, comprises three branches: computer network attack, computer network defense, and MAGTF EW.

The General Atomics Aeronautical Systems Predator B/ MQ-9 Reaper's new electronic attack capability, using the Northrop Grumman Pandora EW system, is a major part of the Marine Corps future EW effort. The system could advance the Reaper from its existing role as a counter-insurgency ISR/ hunter-killer aircraft to a broader spectrum of EW missions, says GA-ASI President Frank W. Pace.

Pandora is a pod-based, multi-function, wideband system providing electronic attack, such as jamming, support and protection. Demonstrations at Yuma Marine Corps Air Station, Ariz., were designed to evaluate the ability of Pandora-equipped aircraft to conduct coordinated EW missions in a multi-node approach against a more capable integrated air defense system.

"Pandora brings optimal size, weight and power to current and future high-endurance platforms, opening up a new world of electronic attack capabilities," says Janine Nyre, vice president of radio frequency combat information systems at Northrop Grumman.

"We demonstrated operational concepts using a layered approach to electronic warfare with Reaper, EA-6B Prowlers, and other Group 3 UAVs," adds Brig. Gen. Matthew G. Glavy, assistant deputy commandant for Marine aviation. "By conducting multiple events, we were able to evaluate the viability of UAVs to conduct EW missions against enemy air defenses in support of tactical strike aircraft."

The 2013 Marine Corps Operating Concept for Information Operations termed information operations (IO) as a complex box of tools the Corps must incorporate and exploit within the context of its overall maneuver warfare philosophy and expeditionary culture to operate "effectively against a myriad of potential adversaries and perform multiple, diverse and simultaneous tasks across the ROMO [range of military operations]".

"In the Marine Corps, IO is not a warfighting function in its own right; it is an integrating function which facilitates the six warfighting functions of C2, fires, maneuver, logistics, intelligence and force protection. This distinction between warfighting and integrating function is key to the Marine Corps' belief IO does not-and will not-replace any of the time-tested warfighting functions. It will enable each of them," says the OCIC.

"IO is not a discrete, stand-alone capability, but is the integrated, coordinated and synchronized operational application of all information-related capabilities (IRCs), organic and non-organic, to affect decision-making by adversaries and potential adversaries, thereby creating an operational advantage. Integration is accomplished under the purview of the operations section, based upon commander's guidance, and supports achievement of the commander's end state. "IO is not synonymous with individual discrete capabilities or activities, much like fire support is not synonymous with artillery or aviation. More art than science, IO is focused on the human mind and seeks to influence behaviors to produce operational advantages."

ATTACKS ON COMPUTER SYSTEMS

While the public has perceived buildings and airplanes as the primary targets of terrorists, attacks on computers were involved in 60% of conventional terrorist acts by 1989. The pattern of criminal computer attacks, together with terrorist activity, suggest that there may be a shift toward cyberterrorism as a physically less risky means to achieve both criminal and terrorist ends.

Europe and the United States

In the 1970s the Italian Red Brigades launched 27 attacks against companies that did business in the electronics, computer and weapons sectors. In 1980, the French organization Comite Liquidant ou Detournant les Ordinateurs (Computer Liquidation and Deterrence Committee or CLODO) undertook a series of attacks on computer companies in the Toulouse region.

The organization released a statement to the press, "We are workers in the field of dp (data processing) and consequently well place to know the current and future dangers of dp and telecommunications.

The computer is the favorite tool of the dominant. It is used to exploit, to put on file, to control, and to repress."

A Belgian Group, the Cellueles Communistes Combattants (Fighting Communist Cells) conducted a series of bombings in September 1984 directed against Honeywell Controls and Litton Industries. In November 1984, the same group attacked the Brussels office of Motorola. Computers were prime targets in each of these attacks.

Similar attacks have occurred in the United States. IBM's offices in White Plains N.Y. were bombed in March1984. The group claiming responsibility for the attack, the United Freedom Front, distributed a newsletter that stated "IBM is a death merchant... The computer is an integral part of the fascist South African government's policies of racist repression and control."

The CLODO group struck again in 1983 by firebombing a Sperry-Univac computer room in Toulouse to protest the U.S. invasion of Grenada. Upon putting out the fire, the message, "Reagan attacks Grenada- Sperry Multinational is an American accomplice." was found spray painted on an interior wall.

While the attacks on computer systems failed to cause any major political victory for CLODO, they did heighten the awareness that European computers are vulnerable to attack.

A 1979 report by the Swedish Defense Ministry recommended that the government become involved in monitoring computer security of both public and private computers. While the proper role of the government in computer security remains open for debate, an article in the French daily *Le Figaro* states that computer attacks might be more harmful to national security than the assassination of random politicians.

Japan

In 1985 in Japan, the Middle Core Faction, a terrorist group consisting of approximately 300 individuals, attacked the commuter rail system to cause massive disruption during the height of rush hour. The group used C2W techniques to carry out its attack by first cutting strategic power and communications cables that fed the computer controls for the rail system. Secondly, the group jammed police and rescue radio frequencies in an attempt to hamper and delay response by the authorities.

While no one was injured in this attack, it caused a major commuting delay affecting 6.5 million commuters and cost the Japan National Railways more than $6 million in lost ticket sales. Rather than blowing up or tampering with the physical destruction of one rail, the group focused on the critical node (control circuits) and disabled the entire system by using technoterror, attacking physical targets to cause a disruption in cyberspace.

The disruption was extensive enough that the Centralized Traffic control Office of Japan National Railways (JNR) was forced to stop operation. While the attacks were successful in creating disruption, the effects were short lived, with most of the severed cables back in full service within 24 hours. This attack, while creating problems for millions of commuters, was also linked to specific objectives. The first was to show solidarity with the National Railways Locomotive Engineers' Union, which was on strike to protest the planned privatization of the JNR. The second goal may have been to influence the trial of Hiroko Nagata, the leader of the Extreme Leftist United Red Army. Her hearing was delayed because the rail shutdown prevented her defense lawyer from making it to court on time.

The combination of computer controls and energy systems raises new possibilities for terrorists. While targeting of energy systems in the past has relied primarily on the physical destruction of key assets to disrupt service, the potential vulnerability of the control systems poses an even greater risk.

Political Motivation

The rise of Information Warfare tactics may allow tomorrow's terrorists to focus their attacks on certain individuals to change their policies or courses of action. The increasing reliance on computers has opened new avenues for blackmail and political pressure. In 1984, a hacker penetrated TRW's credit report computers and obtained some incriminating information about a past small-claims court dispute involving hen incumbent Congressional candidate Tom Lantos of California. This information was passed to his opponent who further distributed the information to the press to discredit Lantos. In a second act of political computer crime, a hacker gained access to Representative Ed Zshau's computer system in Washington, D.C. and erased his data, including his correspondence and constituent database.

These events highlight the potentially selective nature of future cyberterrorism and crime. With a skilled computed operator, a terrorist group may be able to penetrate systems to manipulate a small number of people. Instead of attacking the public to affect a target audience, cyberterrorists may choose to affect the target audience to achieve their ends directly.

Environmental Groups

While "conventional" terrorist groups have targeted computer systems in the past, "eco-terror" groups, such as Earth First, have advocated attacking computer systems. In 1987, the group published a manual that advocated both physical destruction of computer equipment (conventional terrorism) and software and data manipulation/destruction (via cyberterrorism). the manual also included techniques to reduce the risk of being caught by using advance hacking techniques. The risk of cyberterrorism exists on all fronts. It is not merely limited to the "classic" conventional terrorist group. Any group with a strong interest or agenda will be able to attempt cyberterrorism.

Criminal Activity

Criminal activity directed at, or using, computers is receiving increasing attention in the press. The expansion of the Internet to include commercial ventures has sparked a debate over the correct level of security that should be afforded individuals in cyberspace. As terrorism is often crime with different intent, several criminal acts will be explored in this chapter. First, the case of a Russian hacker attempting to steal more than $10 million highlights the vast amounts of money being transferred in cyberspace. Second, the attempt to use computer viruses to hold computers hostage or attack a specific company will be examined. Finally, the possible physical risks to individuals as a result of criminal cyberspace activity are addressed in the case of a Texas professor.

Citibank. The use of computers and computer technology to perpetrate crimes has already occurred. Citibank recently "lost" $10.2 million electronically to a team of Russian hackers. A closer examination of the facts involved in this incident reveals some strengths and weaknesses of computer crime. First, the authorities can use the same technology employed by the cyberterrorist or criminal to track and capture him. Someone can, however, remain anonymous in cyberspace if they are not seeking financial gain, as virus writers have proven.

This incident, according to John Mohr, vice president of the New York Clearing House, is unique in that it utilized a personal computer. It appears that Vladimir L. Levin, a Russian computer expert employed by AO Saturn, a St. Petersburg trading company, broke into Citibank's computer system using stolen account identification numbers and passwords. With this information, he made 40 transfers from Citibank to accounts set up by accomplices in California and Israel.

These transfers occurred from June to October 1994 and were tracked by Citibank to determine who was responsible for the crime. While Citibank allowed the transfers to continue, the accounts into which he was transferring the money were frozen, While Levin attempted to transfer more than $10 million in this period, Citibank has recovered all but $400,000. Amy Dates of Citibank had the following answer when questioned about the level of security at Citibank: "We move half a trillion dollars a day through the payment system. Compare hat to the $400,000 they were able to withdraw. We think we have the right level of security." Despite these statements, Citibank implemented a new computer protocol to increase transaction security.

It is still unclear how Levin obtained the account numbers and their associated passwords, but an investigation is continuing into the possibility of inside help. Citibank, has implemented a new security system for its computer accounts that entails the use of "smart cards" that will generate a new password for each transaction. This technology helps to defeat password "sniffer" programs that allow criminals to capture passwords as they are transmitted across the network for future use. This may have been how Levin obtained his passwords. He appears to have had access to the network for some time before attempting his crime as he was careful to follow the patterns of routine transactions and kept his individual transfers to below $300,000 to avoid "built-in" security programs that would have highlighted the transaction as abnormal.

While the adoption of the smart card security system and the employment of encryption technology has, Citibank hopes, corrected the security weakness exploited by Levin and his friends, the amount of money lost in this crime is relatively small. The high level of publicity afforded this incident is due to its extranormality, not its dollar value. Each year, according to the American Bankers Association, the following amounts are lost due to crime: Check fraud- $10 *Billion,* Credit Card fraud- $712 Million, ATM fraud- $18 Million, and Online fraud (as in the Citibank case)- $5 Milllion. While Citibank could use its computers to track and eventually catch Levin, computers and high technology aided in the success of a Vietnamese check fraud ring that operated undetected for seven months. The U.S. Secret Service investigated the crime under the name, "Operation Paper Dragon" and found that the ring took in $25 Million in just over half a year.These high technology money making schemes may appeal to terrorist organizations of the future who are unable to secure, or do not desire, state sponsorship. While attractive to terrorists, the security measures put in place by the banking industry to prevent criminals will likely defeat terrorists as well.

Viruses. In an apparent attempt to extort money, the computers of several universities were infected with a virus in an attempt to make them hostages. The virus demanded a ransom for the antidote to the virus.

Computer users who found the virus were told to send $2,000 to an address in Pakistan to obtain an immunity program that would rid the system of the virus. Investigation showed that the virus was written by two brothers in a computer store in Lahore, Pakistan-they had put their names, and address, and phone number in the virus! "It's like a fantasy of being a terrorist without the blood,: said Eric Corley, editor of a national hacker newsletter, 2600, whose electronic bulletin board was also infected.

The brothers' scheme did not pay well, and the virus was eradicated without their "immunity program." The "fantasy" of being a terrorist without the blood may become reality when an organization uses cyberterror weapons in an attack.

Recently, a virus was used to attack a specific business in Germany. A virus writer, known only as "The Wizard" created then released a virus that he called the "Media Market advertising virus." Media Markt is a German home-electronics group and was not involved in the virus writing or distribution. Media Markt's lawyer claims that "this is the first time that someone has distributed a virus and tied it to a company that has nothing to do with it" To stave off negative publicity, Media Markt has distributed an anti-virus program to disable the virus on affected computers.

While the true intention of the virus writer may never be known, the principle of indirect attack (attacking the general public to influence a target audience) normally utilized by terrorists was evidenced in these tactics. The virus writer, unleashed an attack on the "innocent" computer users to create negative publicity for Media Markt. In this case, Media Markt was clearly not involved in this activity. However, the anonymous and anarchic nature of cyberspace opens the possibility of creating chaos and making it appear as if someone else is responsible. While it appears that financial gain motivated the Russian hackers in the Citibank case, the possibility exists that terrorists or criminals could perpetrate electronic attacks in the future to weaken the target company, not make money. If a terrorist group could place someone "on the inside" of a software company and infect software with a virus *before* shipment, it may call the integrity of that software company into question. While there are no reported cases of terrorists staging a concerted information warfare attack on a business, the case of Citibank might be a benchmark. Despite news that it had lost more than $10 million, Citibank stock went *up* by 1/2 a point on the day that the Russian hacker story broke.

Personal Attacks. The potential exists for terrorists to single out individuals in cyberspace. In 1994, a hacker logged into a Texas A&M professor's E-mail account and used the account to send out 20,000 racist messages. To those receiving the messages, it appeared that they had come from the professor. As a result, the professor began to receive death threats.

ELECTROMAGNETIC INTERFERENCE

Electromagnetic interference (EMI), also called radio-frequency interference (RFI) when in the radio frequency spectrum, is a disturbance generated by an external source that affects an electrical circuit by electromagnetic induction, electrostatic coupling, or conduction. The disturbance may degrade the performance of the circuit or even stop it from functioning. In the case of a data path, these effects can range from an increase in error rate to a total loss of the data. Both man-made and natural sources generate changing electrical currents and voltages that can cause EMI: automobile ignition systems, cell phones, thunder storms, the Sun, and the Northern Lights. EMI frequently affects AM radios. It can also affect cell phones, FM radios, and televisions. EMI can be used intentionally for radio jamming, as in electronic warfare.

History

Since the earliest days of radio communications, the negative effects of interference from both intentional and unintentional transmissions have been felt and the need to manage the radio frequency spectrum became apparent.

In 1933, a meeting of the International Electrotechnical Commission (IEC) in Paris recommended the International Special Committee on Radio Interference (CISPR) be set up to deal with the emerging problem of EMI. CISPR subsequently produced technical publications covering measurement and test techniques and recommended emission and immunity limits. These have evolved over the decades and form the basis of much of the world's EMC regulations today. In 1979, legal limits were imposed on electromagnetic emissions from all digital equipment by the FCC in the USA in response to the increased number of digital systems that were interfering with wired and radio communications. Test methods and limits were based on CISPR publications, although similar limits were already enforced in parts of Europe. In the mid 1980s, the European Union member states adopted a number of "new approach" directives with the intention of standardizing technical requirements for products so that they do not become a barrier to trade within the EC. One of these was the EMC Directive (89/336/EC) and it applies to all equipment placed on the market or taken into service. Its scope covers all apparatus "liable to cause electromagnetic disturbance or the performance of which is liable to be affected by such disturbance". This was the first time there was a legal requirement on immunity as well as emissions on apparatus intended for the general population. And although there may be additional costs involved for some products to give them a known level of immunity, it increases their perceived quality as they are able to co-exist with apparatus in the active EM environment of modern times and with fewer problems. Many countries now have similar requirements for products to meet some level of Electromagnetic Compatibility (EMC) regulation.

Types

Electromagnetic interference can be categorized as follows:

- Narrowband EMI or RFI interference typically emanates from intended transmissions, such as radio and TV stations or cell phones.
- Broadband EMI or RFI interference is unintentional radiation from sources such as electric power transmission lines.

Conducted electromagnetic interference is caused by the physical contact of the conductors as opposed to radiated EMI, which is caused by induction (without physical contact of the conductors). Electromagnetic disturbances in the EM field of a conductor will no longer be confined to the surface of the conductor and will radiate away from it. This persists in all conductors and mutual inductance between two radiated electromagnetic fields will result in EMI.

MISSION OF ARMY INTELLIGENCE

The mission of Army intelligence is to provide timely, relevant, accurate, and synchronized IEW support to tactical, operational, and strategic commanders across the range of military operations. In war, IEW operations support the winning of battles and campaigns. In OOTW, IEW operations support the promotion of peace, the resolution of conflict, and the deterrence of war. These operations reduce uncertainty and risk to US Forces and permit the effective application of force.

IEW in the Force Projection Army

The post-Cold War Army is a force projection Army. Continental United States (CONUS)-based with a limited forward presence, the Army must be capable of rapidly deploying anywhere in the world, operating in a joint or combined environment, and defeating regional threats on the battlefield or conducting 00TW. IEW is fundamental to effective planning, security, and execution of force projection operations.

IEW operations have changed fundamentally from those of the Cold War model. The environment in which the Army now operates requires IEW support based on the mission rather than on a monolithic threat. During the Cold War era, intelligence developed into a threat-based system upon which the Army based its doctrine, training, and modernization. For over four decades, the"threat" was the Soviet Union.

The Army developed organizations, systems, tactics, and procedures needed to conduct defensive operations against Soviet and Warsaw Pact forces attacking through central Europe.

Our defense was built upon the movement of heavy corps from in-theatre garrisons to general defense positions with follow-on forces arriving later from the CONUS, Movement and support of the corps would occur within a robust communication zone containing extensive communications and logistics infrastructures, From alert through the termination of hostilities, tactical IEW units were to be the principal sources of tactical intelligence flowing up to divisions, corps, and theatre. Intelligence, in general, would flow from the ground up to higher echelons. And, because the US focused the national intelligence effort on our nation's most likely threat, we possessed in-depth, continuous, and nearly automatic intelligence on the forces of the Soviet Union. From the two premises of tactical intelligence coming from the ground up and in-depth knowledge on the threat, we built our entire vision for IEW support.

In the force projection Army, mission-based intelligence focuses on developing broad baseline knowledge of potential threats and operational environments supporting numerous plans and likely contingency missions. From this broad baseline, commanders possess the capability to prioritize, focus, and surge the intelligence system supporting force projection operations. The commander plays a key role in mission-based intelligence and intelligence readiness. Since there is no longer one threat facing the US, command involvement is essential in ensuring that the intelligence system is focused on the commander's top contingencies. Force projection operations build force levels from the bottom up vice top down as during the Cold War.

IEW assets are tailored to meet the requirements of the mission and deployment sequence. In force projection operations, commanders depend on small, deployable teams with access to national and joint intelligence. Intelligence in the initial stages of the operation will flow from higher to lower. The size and capabilities of follow-on lEW assets will be dictated by the situation and the commander's concept of operation.

The nature of force projection operations and mission-based intelligence requires commanders to redefine intelligence readiness. Intelligence readiness means that Ml must develop broad knowledge on priority contingency areas, update those data bases daily, and be prepared to surge in support of emerging missions. Commanders and G2s (S2s) must direct the intelligence effort daily to ensure the data bases will be there upon alert to support contingency planning and execution. If our divisions, corps, and theatre forces stand ready to project force anywhere in several potential contingencies, then it is essential that their intelligence support be at the same or higher level of readiness. To maintain that level of readiness, Ml must provide commanders with routine, direct, and habitual links into the intelligence system to provide and, perhaps more important, to focus intelligence on their tactical and operational needs early.

Principles Of Force Projection IEW

Successful force projection IEW support is based on understanding five key principles: the commander drives intelligence; intelligence synchronization; split-based operations; tactical tailoring; and broadcast dissemination.

The Commander Drives Intelligence

The commander's role in IEW, not just when the crisis begins, but well before and throughout the operation, is central to the success or failure of IEW support in force projection operations. The commander must take an active role in focusing, integrating, and training the intelligence system. He must focus the effort and ensure it is responsive to his information requirements (IR) and those of his subordinates. The commander must —

- Identify, clearly articulate, and prioritize intelligence and targeting requirements.
- Understand the capabilities and limitations of the Intelligence BOS.
- Know how to leverage and employ the intelligence system to its full potential.
- Broker subordinates' information and resource requirements.
- Meld the Intelligence BOS into the total combined arms effort.

Intelligence Synchronization

Intelligence synchronization ensures IEW operations are linked to the commander's requirements and respond in time to influence decisions and operations. In the synchronization process, the G2 (S2) takes the commander's priority intelligence requirements (PIR) and backward plans to ensure that collection and production efforts are orchestrated with the operation, and deliver intelligence when required.

The collection manager ensures specific orders and requests (SORs) fully support all PIR and IR. The collection manager also synchronizes collection and reporting to deliver relevant information, on time, to support operational decisions. Intelligence synchronization ensures the MI unit commander has the time, guidance, and resources to execute IEW operations. Intelligence synchronization is a continuous process which keeps the intelligence cycle and IEW operations tied to the commander's critical decisions and concept of operations.

Split-based Operations

Split-based operations are an integral part of IEW support to force projection operations. in split-based operations, the commander deploys small, flexible, tailored IEW organizations with access to intelligence data bases and systems outside the area of operations (AO), particularly national systems. Split-basing takes advantage of direct broadcast technology from collection platforms and assured intelligence communications to provide commanders with continuous, relevant, and timely IEW support during all stages of force projection operations.

Organizations like the Deployable Intelligence Support Element (DISE) support split-based operations by bringing together communications capability, automated intelligence fusion systems, and broadcast downlink in a scalable package able to deploy with the entry force.

It is not a specific piece of equipment or a particular configuration of equipment. It is a flexible organization able to support any type of ground force commander whether from Army, joint, or combined forces. The DISE provides the commander with a link from his forward deployed force to an intelligence support base located in CONUS or other locations outside the AO.

Split-based operations allow uncommitted IEW assets, including MDCI assets, to support the deployed force through remote collection, processing and analysis, and TENCAP operations in garrison, or from secure locations outside the AO. This includes intelligence of units as they deploy from garrison to port of debarkation (POD) and onward to the AO. The support relationship established between deployment and uncommitted assets in turn facilitates the smooth integration of follow-on assets once they deploy to theatre. The deployment of these follow on assets allows the commander to transition from IEW support provided primarily by national assets, the commander can focus the intelligence effort to the resolution required for tactical operations while receiving the unique support available only from national means.

Tactical Tailoring

In force projection operations, the commander tactically tailors IEW support for each contingency. Commanders should attempt to maintain unit integrity and established command relationships to the extent possible; however, deployment of a more traditional unit such as a divisional MI battalion in full may not be the best organization for the mission. Tailoring allows the commander to build a more efficient, mission specific force by—

- Assessing IEW mission requirements. This includes determining the capabilities of remotely based and joint intelligence collection assets to support the mission; identifying the compositionof the IEW force based on mission, enemy, troops, terrain and weather, and time available (METT-T); determining communications and processing requirements; and planning the deployment sequence of IEW assets based on mission, strategic lift resources, and host nation support.
- Developing scalable IEW support packages like the DISE with communications, processing, and downlink assets for top priority contingency missions. Employment of these packages should be practiced often to refine force researching and tailoring procedures, load plans, communications connectivity, and support relationships.
- Tailoring the Intelligence BOS to ensure it provides the commander with accurate and responsive intelligence. The intelligence system should cover the entire width and depth of the battle space and area of interest (AI) throughout the duration of the operation, at the resolution required by commanders at each echelon.
- Deploying early, an IEW package that is portable, logistically sustainable, and sufficient to conduct operations for the short-term. Sufficiency in the short-term includes being prepared to provide immediate IEW support for combat operations and force protection.
- Integrating IEW assets into the deployment flow early. Depending on the availability of information and threat

capabilities, commanders must phase in intelligence personnel and, equipment that offer redundancy and that serve as the cornerstone for assets that arrive in the theatre later. These initial "building blocks" are critical to early success and follow-on capabilities. Follow-on IEW forces should enhance the capabilities of in-theatre assets and satisfy the commander's long-term concerns.

- Maintaining habitual peacetime IEW support relationships and accesses between the forward deployed intelligence element and its higher echelon intelligence organization. This allows forward deployed assets to pull from their"pull"normal intelligence sources between the predeployment and operations stages of force projection. This reduces the possibility of intelligence shortfalls which could arise from reliance on evolving intelligence organizations. For example, a CONUS-based corps may commit a maneuver brigade as part of a forward deployed joint task force (JTF). The deployed brigade could continue to receive support through a DISE from the CON US-based analysis and control element (ACE) of its parent division in addition to support from the JTF Joint Intelligence Center (JIC).
- Maximizing intelligence support from the host nation by establishing, if possible, liaison with host nation intelligence organizations in peacetime.

Broadcast Dissemination

Broadcast dissemination of intelligence and targeting information is an important element in providing commanders at multiple echelons with a common intelligence picture of the battlefield. Broadcasting facilitates the direct or skip echelon of information down to commanders in the field. Use of broadcast technology also reduces the number of collection sensors, processors, and personnel needed to support these operations. More importantly, broadcasting intelligence and targeting information directly to multiple terminals, eliminates bottlenecks inherent in point-to-point communications and provides all echelons common sources from which to "pull" information. Some of the products available through broadcast systems are TENCAP imagery and targeting information, Joint STARS radar imagery, UAV video, and Air Force RC135 (Rivet Joint) and Army GUARDRAIL SIGINT reports. Host terminals, when tied to broadcast terminals, are capable of providing filtered, processed, and tailored intelligence to satisfy specific intelligence and targeting requirements.

The ACE is the commander's primary organization for pulling information from broadcast systems and fusing it into tailored intelligence and targeting information. Through its capability to rapidly pull, process, and disseminate intelligence, the ACE provides the commander with the means to focus and synchronize the intelligence system with his intent and concept of operation. In addition, the ACEs at brigade, division, corps, and theatre form a seamless bridge linking the tactical commander with higher echelon organizations where intelligence data bases and knowledge reside.

ELECTRONICS, COMMUNICATIONS AND INTELLIGENCE

Electronics rose to prominence quickly in World War II. While prior to the war few electronic devices were seen as important pieces of equipment, by the middle of the war such instruments as radar and ASDIC (sonar) had proven their value. Additionally, equipment designed for communications and the interception of those communications was becoming critical.

Digital electronics, particularly, were also given a massive boost by war-related research. The pressing need for numerous time-critical calculations for various projects like code-breaking and ballistics tables accentuated the need for the development of electronic computer technology. The semi-secret ENIAC and the super-secret Colossus demonstrated that devices using thousands of valves (vacuum tubes) could be reliable enough to be useful, paving the way for the post-war development of stored program computers.

The United Kingdom and the United States were the leaders in electronics. The US center for basic radar development was the Massachusetts Institute of Technology Radiation Laboratory. The British developed the magnetron which is now used in microwave ovens.

Electronic and optical countermeasures such as jamming and radar absorbing material were developed.

While the war stimulated many technologies, such as radio and radar development, it slowed down related yet non-critical fields such as television and radio.

Industrial Technology

While the development of new equipment was rapid, it was also important to be able to produce these tools and get them to the troops in appropriate quantity.

Those nations that were able to maximize their industrial capacity and mobilize it for the war effort were most successful at equipping their troops in a timely way with adequate material. An outstanding German innovation was the Jerrycan which carries by its name a tribute to its success.

One of the biggest developments was the ability to produce synthetic rubber. Natural rubber was mainly harvested in the South Pacific, and the Allies were cut off from a large quantity of it due to Japanese expansion. Thus the development of synthetic rubber allowed for the Allied war machine to continue growing, giving the US a significant technical edge as World War II continued.

For the Germans it was the development of alternative fuels as in hydrogen peroxide - which would be a forerunner to the development of fuel-cell technology and synthetic fuel technology.

New Medicines

One of the most dramatic single medical advances was probably the wide spread use of penicillin to treat wounds and bacterial diseases.

ELECTRONIC WARFARE IN THE AIR

While emphasizing they "do not generally comment on EW requirements, specific technologies or capabilities of our or others' systems", the Acquisition, Science, Technology and Engineering Directorate within the office of the Secretary of the Air Force (SAF/AQRM) did provide the following statement: "The Air Force recognizes that increased budgetary constraints, coupled with widespread availability of modern electronics, requires new technology and acquisition approaches for EW. The Air Force is tackling the problem along five fronts: 1) enabling fundamental components, 2) new techniques, 3) new adaptive modular approaches, 4) early prototyping and rapid reaction developments and 5) early in-the-loop testing. "Today's EW, Communications, Navigation, Sensing and Cyber technologies require a more integrated use of the electromagnetic spectrum than ever before. The Air Force Research Laboratory (AFRL) is working on full spectrum science and technology, which includes: radio frequency EW; avionics protection; position, navigation and timing [PNT] in contested/denied environments; electro-optical/infrared threat warning and countermeasures; protected communications and robust cyber."

In its "Strategy for Spectrum Warfare", SAF/AQRM noted it is pursuing those goals through a comprehensive Advanced Components for EW (ACE) program and developing cognitive and distributed techniques, adaptive modular approaches and rapid prototyping.

AFRL issued a broad agency announcement (BAA) last fall for the Advanced Novel Spectrum Warfare Environment Research (ANSWER) program to develop adaptive spectrum warfare technologies to maintain warfighting capabilities in contested and denied environments consistent with A2/AD scenarios. AFRL encouraged industry to employ unconventional thinking on the use of advanced computing power, signals processing, modeling and simulation, anti-tamper and software protection technologies, GPS alternatives with comparable accuracies for warfighters in A2/AD environments, vision and laser-based navigation and electro-optics countermeasures.

"With an ever-changing environment between red and blue forces, the ability to control the electromagnetic spectrum is a key requirement to achieving success in warfighter operations. This is a daunting task under benign conditions and becomes even more of a challenge as adversaries are able to employ various denial capabilities," the BAA noted. "If one can conduct electromagnetic spectrum operations under A2/AD conditions, then successful operations in other less challenging environments should be achievable as well. To accomplish this, the warfighter needs to be able to control adversary use of electromagnetic spectrum, ensure friendly access to/use of electromagnetic spectrum, protect sensor/avionics end nodes, establish/maintain secure communications/data links in dense electromagnetic spectrum environments and assure the availability of accurate PNT information. The ANSWER program is designed to address these challenges."

The Post-OEF/OIF EW Environment

"When it comes to EW, it doesn't have to be a near-peer or even a known rival. Electronics that can be made to be a problem are ubiquitous throughout the world," says the Army Cyber Center's Murray. "You can find a thousand types of cell phones in Afghanistan, which I certainly wouldn't call the modern world. So a lot of technology is out there, worldwide, that, in the wrong hands, can be a very severe problem, no matter what kind of advanced weapons or armor we have.

"Technology changes so fast that what is considered SOTA today may not be in another year," Murray says. "And that's one of the challenges on things we would like to have now and in the future. But the processes we must go through to acquire the equipment we would like to have and need to have are not as agile as we need them to be. They're OK now, but if we get into a new fight, you can't wait for what you need."

The possibility of near-peer conflict is growing as the U.S. puts a greater focus on the Asia/Pacific region and Eastern Europe once again feels threatened by Russia, even as the Middle East continues increasingly tech-based rounds of ancient conflicts. In addition, the vast distances involved and the lack of U.S. land bases in the Asia/Pacific-outside of South Korea and Okinawa in the north-will mean a greater focus on the Navy and Marine Corps, especially with respect to EW.

There was a sharp reduction in the Pentagon's EW research and development budget from 2013 to 2015-a cut from $3.5 billion to $2.1 billion-more than half from the Navy and Marine Corps. Of course, an unknown-but suspected substantial-part of EW research falls under classified "black" budgets. "Although EW is declining through 2015, we expect to start seeing a resumption of spending from 2016 on," says John Hernandez, a senior aerospace and defense industry analyst at market researcher Frost and Sullivan.

"That is an area that is being underdeveloped right now, but with the potential new adversaries in the coming years, it will need to be reinvigorated. Some analysts are predicting an increase in small, even hand-held jammers, but our analysts expect to see more modularity, especially for ship-board systems. "There was a move for a while to make the F-35 the new EW platform, but I don't think the expense was worth it, given the fine job the Growler is doing.

But in the future, I can see unmanned systems doing more EW, whether that is a single platform or a flock of UAVs doing jamming or AD missions. Personally, I suspect protecting our own systems is and will continue to be a priority over offensive technologies."

Defense industry adapts

The new environment and focus on naval assets also has been reflected in industry. In February 2014, for example, Raytheon Space and Airborne Systems combined several EW efforts into a new mission area called Electronic Warfare Systems, based at the company's El Segundo, CA, campus. The new unit will focus on the Navy's Next-Generation Jammer (NGJ);; EW self-protection systems; EW communications systems; advanced EW programs; and airborne information operations.

At the Northrop Grumman Integrated Systems sector, meanwhile, airborne early warning and electronic warfare systems have seen a similar growth in importance, including the June 2014 award of a joint service (Army/Navy) contract for 18 APR-39D(V)2 radar warning receiver (RWR)/EW management system (EWMS) pre-production units.

"Our APR-39D(V)2 merges the baseline capability of previous systems with the Northrop Grumman digital receiver technology to provide advanced capability for today's and tomorrow's threat environment," says Northrop Grumman's Nyre. "This lightweight system maintains interfaces with legacy systems and includes flexibility for future growth enhancements."The company is to deliver the systems in late 2014 preparatory to hardware-software and platform integration testing in 2015.

Also next year, Northrop Grumman is scheduled to complete equipping the Navy's MQ-8C Fire Scout rotary UAV with a new external Multi-Capability Pod, providing it with "multiple EW sensors for employment in the littorals", says a DOD announcement in May 2014.

BAE Systems is leveraging advances in signals processing and machine learning under a DARPA-funded program called Adaptive Radar Countermeasures (ARC). The goal is a next-generation EW algorithm suite as a software upgrade existing EW hardware to can use to operate against emerging radar threats and help achieve and maintain U.S. air dominance in future battlespaces. Special emphasis will be on countering never-before-seen threats with unknown waveform characteristics and behaviors. "This technology will provide a revolutionary capability to EW systems on U.S. military airborne platforms to counter adaptive radar threats and significantly improve survivability," says Joshua Niedzwiecki, BAE's director of strategic development. ARC is projected to be ready for live demonstration flight tests by 2018.

Mercury Systems in Chelmsford, Mass., has been predominantly involved with air-to-air/surface-to-air systems, but Chief Technology Officer Chris Lewis says the current

SOTA for them "has been the transition from classic denial-jamming-to more deceiving your adversary". "The world today is less bifurcated between EW and Cyber, which I consider part of the same continuum," he says. "The kinds of things we're seeing starting to come on line are systems that are much tighter in their response. Where conventional systems saw a new waveform that then was captured and technology to deal with it developed in the lab, today's system is tighter, with techniques being developed in days rather than months. And the goal is be instantaneous.

"Enabling technologies for future EW include continuing improvement in the performance of FPGAs and microprocessors, the continued drive in communications and great improvement in solid state amplifiers due to gallium nitride. Further down the line is photonics for very wide bandwidth and high dynamic range. Another, not a technology so much as capability, is the adaptive learning system. Some of the SOTA things being done today are just scratching that surface and I see more of that coming online in the next few years."

Lewis sees the largest EW market for the foreseeable future being retrofits for legacy platforms DOD cannot afford to replace: "As the U.S. goes forward, there will be more and more demand to do things with less and less. And the leverage of doing that in terms of retrofits will have a lot of benefits for the country as a whole."

SPECTRUM WARFARE

Rapid advances in technology have complicated the definition of EW. The Air Force uses spectrum warfare to bring together all elements of EW with cyber warfare, information operations and essential capabilities to enable a full range of electromagnetic operations-offensive and defensive-in A2/AD environments against all levels of adversaries.

The Army prefers cyber electromagnetic activities. According to recently revised Army Doctrine for Unified Land Operations, CEMA involves "activities leveraged to seize, retain and exploit an advantage over adversaries and enemies in cyberspace and the electromagnetic spectrum, while simultaneously denying and degrading adversary and enemy use of the same and protecting the mission command system". Implementation is achieved through synchronization and integration of cyberspace operations, EW and electromagnetic spectrum operations (electromagnetic spectrum).

Terminology aside, nearly every aspect of command, control, communications, computers, intelligence, surveillance and reconnaissance (C4ISR) has (or is) a component of or dependent on 21st century EW.

Frequency-hopping radios and radar soon may be replaced by "cognitive" systems that don't rely on a set list of frequencies, but look for available "holes" throughout the full spectrum, jumping from one to the next on the fly. A primitive version of that is a smartphone that uses the best available way to connect, from nearby WiFi to 4G.

But control and unchallenged access to battlespace spectrum also is critical for navigation-from precision-guided munitions to logistics-semi-autonomous combat robots, field and battlespace medicine and more. And as spectrum becomes ever-more crucial to military and commercial communications and data transfer, two long-standing "laws" of technology continue to converge.

The more widely known Moore's Law, named for Intel co-founder Gordon Moore, states that CPU speeds double every two years (although purists note it is more accurate to say the number of transistors on an affordable CPU is what doubles).

The lesser known Cooper's Law, formulated by the inventor of the cell phone Martin Cooper, notes the number of conversations, whether voice or data, that theoretically can be conducted using a specific piece of useful radio spectrum has doubled every 30 months for more than a century. As a result, total spectrum allocation for personal communications alone has increased more than one trillion-fold in the last 90 years.

Increasingly competitive, congested and contested cyberspace and electromagnetic spectrum will be even more important as the U.S. faces potential conflict with a near-peer adversary for the first time since World War II-and as CEMA capabilities spread and grow down to the level of individual terrorist cells, criminal organizations and Third World nations, none of whom could ever hope to survive a traditional engagement with the U.S.

The services' differing views of the involved technologies are more than semantic, they also are operational. The Navy sees EW as modern warfighting, the Air Force considers it an essential and integrated component to the success of A2/AD and air dominance, but the Army continues to view it as a support component, not warfighting.

"When you talk about maneuver commanders, the objective is to seize and secure terrain. The EW mission is to support that, but EW and cyber have separate roles to play. Cyber can and is moving into a major combat role; the EW role is to control the spectrum to allow the maneuver commander to achieve his goals," says the Army Cyber Center's Cantrell.

CEMA's Cullen agrees, adding those in combat are only interested in what works: "From a maneuver commander's perspective-infantry or armor-they don't care if it is EW or cyber or whatever. There are advantages and disadvantages to both EW effects, cyber effects and kinetic effects. The requirement is to figure out which is best in a given situation."

In April 2014, the Naval Air Warfare Center Weapons Division and the Association of Old Crows held the 43rd Electronic Warfare Symposium at Point Mugu, Calif., with the theme "Enabling Collaborative EW Through Innovation and Invention."

"Staying up-to-date in EW technology is essential to supporting the warfighter, said Dr. Ron Smiley, director of the EW/Combat Systems and Avionics departments at the Naval Air Systems Command at Patuxent River Naval Air Station, Md., told the conference. "Electronic warfare is changing, becoming more challenging and has continued to become a lot more esoteric, particularly with the convergence of EW and Cyber Warfare."

Rear Adm. Mark Darrah, commander of the Naval Air Warfare Center Aircraft Division, summarized the conference discussions with a view to potential enemy developments and the changing nature of U.S. technology development. "Unlike 20 years ago, our advisories are developing similar technologies that we are-and are doing it right now," he says. "The only way we will stay ahead of the threat of our enemies is to take paper ideas and give it to our people for trial-and-error until we succeed."

INTELLIGENCE AND ELECTRONIC WARFARE SUPPORT TO MILITARY OPERATIONS

Operational Continuum

The operational continuum is a dynamic spectrum consisting of three environments: peacetime competition, conflict, and war. Within this continuum, the US can find itself in peacetime competition with one nation and at war with another nation, while in conflict with still another nation — all at the same time. Moreover, as recent peacetime contingency missions (such as URGENT FURY, JUST CAUSE, OPERATION DESERT SHIELD, and OPERATION DESERT STORM) reveal, the operational continuum is not a one-way street but rather a multi-path avenue which permits operations to flow in all directions.

The US was hoping to gain some influence over Baghdad and pull them out of the Soviet sphere. But in July 1990, Iraq massed troops on the Kuwait border and threatened to invade if Kuwait, among other things, did not cut its oil production. The US response was mostly in the diplomatic arena; however, we held some joint air defense exercises with our Persian Gulf allies which placed us on the verge of a conflict environment on the operational continuum.

When Iraq appeared to back off, the situation appeared to remain in a peacetime competition environment. However, after Iraq's invasion of Kuwait and the subsequent execution of OPERATION DESERT SHIELD, the US and Iraq entered the environment of conflict. Had OPERATION DESERT SHIELD succeeded in convincing Iraq to withdraw from Kuwait, then it would not have been necessary to move into the next environment of the continuum — war. However, when months of diplomatic and military maneuvering failed, the US and its allies initiated OPERATION DESERT STORM. At this point, we crossed over into the war environment.

Initially, the allies limited their actions to aerial bombing, hoping to persuade Iraq to withdraw. However, Iraq's failure to withdraw forced the allied move deeper into the war environment. After the NM-hour ground war, the allies called a halt to offensive operations but maintained forces inside Iraq — thus moving into the conflict phase of the continuum.

Still within the conflict environment of the continuum, the situation with the Kurdish refugees in northern Iraq caused the US to initiate OPERATION PROVIDE COMFORT. This was a disaster (manmade) relief effort under the heading of a Peacetime Contingency Operation.

Although the final chapter in the war with Iraq remains uncompleted, the allied goal is to work through the operational continuum while rebuilding Kuwait and Iraq and to reestablish a peacetime competition environment. However, it is up to Iraq whether that happens. The potential exists for the US to shift backwards through conflict and war again before achieving peace.

The ARSOF SI0 must be prepared to meet the commander's intelligence requirements for any mission and be able to anticipate what new requirements might arise as the operation flows along the continuum.

Historical Perspective

Timely and accurate intelligence and unprocessed combat information can be a significant factor in operational success. Historically, the commander who has superior knowledge of mission, enemy, terrain, troops, and time available (METT-T) factors has a critical edge in combat.

As the following examples show, the more information and intelligence commanders have, the greater their chances for success.

- In January 1945, timely and accurate intelligence enabled the 6th Ranger Battalion to rescue 511 American and Allied prisoners from a Japanese prisoner of war (PW) compound near Cabanatuan in the Philippines.
- During the Korean War the intelligence community identified enemy vulnerabilities for exploitation by psychological warfare teams. These efforts were very successful in lowering the morale, reducing combat effectiveness, and encouraging desertion and defection of communist troops. In summary, it is estimated that 65 percent of more than 150,000 communist PWs said US psychological warfare had some influence on their decision to surrender.
- In South Vietnam, the combined intelligence center's imagery interpretation (II) photographic study program provided valuable intelligence that helped SF units set up camp and hamlet security. Often these camps became isolated strongpoints astride communist infiltration routes and were a constant thorn in the side of the North Vietnamese.
- In Panama, timely and accurate intelligence enabled US forces to achieve all mission objectives within a short time. While this intelligence resulted in a quick end to the fighting, gaps in the intelligence support to post-hostilities operations (population resource control, military government) slowed the transition from combat to nation building.
- In Iraq, superb intelligence support resulted in an overwhelming victory over the Iraqi armed forces. Intelligence also played a key role in dealing with the Shiite Muslims in occupied southern Iraq. However, in northern Iraq, the US had to play catch-up to determine the direction the Kurdish rebellion was taking and was reconnoitering for suitable sites for refugee camps. This

occurred only days before the camps were to be established.

What history tells us is that the intelligence community does an excellent job of supporting combat operations. However, it is incumbent upon both the IEW system and ARSOF to identify intelligence requirements for operations across the operational continuum to include pre- and post-hostilities phases.

Combat Information

Combat information is unevaluated data. It is gathered by ARSOF elements during any combat operation or wartime environment.

This information is provided directly to the ARSOF commander which, due to its highly perishable nature or the criticality of the situation, cannot be processed into intelligence in time to satisfy the user's intelligence requirements.

Information becomes intelligence once it is collected, evaluated, analyzed, integrated, and interpreted. In other words, the distinction between combat and intelligence is in how the information is processed and used.

When information must be processed and analyzed, or if it needs to be integrated with other data and then analyzed and interpreted, it is intelligence and not combat information. Information may be both combat information and intelligence, but in sequence.

Unevaluated information collected by ARSOF units during target specific operations is considered combat information. It can be combined later with other intelligence or information as part of the all-source intelligence product. Only after the data is validated, analyzed, and processed does it become intelligence. There are two types of intelligence products: single-source and all-source.

Single-source Intelligence

If the sources of an intelligence product are from only one intelligence discipline, the final product is called a single-source intelligence product. The following are SOF-related examples of each intelligence discipline:

- Human intelligence (HUMINT) is intelligence derived from information collected and provided by human sources. ARSOF units provide the IEW system with HUMINT through SR and debriefings of units after operations. SR is explained in detail inChapter 4. MI units support ARSOF with HUMINT through controlled collection and tactical interrogation operations.
- Signals intelligence (SIGINT) is intelligence that includes all communications intelligence (COMINT), electronics intelligence (ELINT), and foreign instrumentation signals intelligence (FISINT). ARSOF units use SIGINT to prepare for and conduct infiltration and exfiltration; to locate actual or potential threat positions; and to analyze possible courses of action (COAs). ARSOF units can collect limited COMINT with organic assets.
- Imagery intelligence (IMINT) is intelligence derived from the exploitation of products from visual photography, infrared sensors, lasers, electro-optics, and radar sensors. ARSOF units use IMINT for targeting, infiltration and exfiltration, and general reconnaissance or area orientation.
- Technical intelligence (TECHINT) is intelligence concerning foreign technological developments, and the performance and operational capabilities of foreign materiel, which have or may eventually have a practical application for military use. ARSOF use TECHINT products to exploit foreign weapons. Since ARSOF units operate deep in hostile or denied territory, they are often first to discover, identify, and provide information concerning new or previously unidentified material.
- Measurement and signature intelligence (MASINT) is a highly sophisticated application of state-of-the-art technology and processing techniques to detect and identify specific foreign weapon systems based on inadvertent signatures. This identification aids in

determining capabilities and intentions. ARSOF units use MASINT for developing target data.

All-source Intelligence

All-source intelligence can be a combination of combat information, intelligence from more than one intelligence discipline, or even data from previously completed all-source intelligence products. To be called all-source intelligence, it must contain information from at least two of the intelligence disciplines.

THE NEED FOR INTELLIGENCE AND ELECTRONIC WARFARE SUPPORT

Today, ARSOF commanders depend even more on timely, accurate intelligence and combat information than did their historical counterparts. ARSOF commanders must be able to exploit METT-T factors to their advantage and to capture and keep the vital element of surprise throughout the operational continuum.

ARSOF commanders need IEW support because it is crucial in assisting the commander to make informed decisions during the decision-making process. All IEW disciplines are ARSOF operational multipliers. Each discipline provides the accurate, sensitive, and timely intelligence and combat information commanders need to complete their missions successfully. IEW supports ARSOF commanders as they plan and execute effective maneuver, firepower, force protection, and leadership.

SIGINT and EW are operational multipliers because these assets provide ARSOF commanders with passive and active means to protect C^3 systems. SIGINT and EW are employed by combining both offensive and defensive operations, as well as tactics, techniques, and procedures (TTP). Assets and products from disciplines like HUMINT and IMINT are also valuable combat multipliers because they provide information or intelligence that cannot be obtained otherwise.

Each intelligence discipline supports the final product by confirming or denying the validity of information collected by the other disciplines. IEW products are gathered and integrated into all-source intelligence products to support the commander's concept of operations.

ARSOF commanders and their staffs must understand how the IEW system works and how to integrate IEW assets and products, along with the principles of integration, synchronization, and interoperability, to support their concept of the mission. The environments and types of operations will, of course, vary. The key to effective ARSOF intelligence support is for ARSOF to fully use the intelligence system. To do this, ARSOF operators must work with supporting intelligence agencies to sensitize the intelligence community to ARSOF requirements.

2

Cyber Warfare

Cyberwarfare is politically motivated hacking to conduct sabotage and espionage. It is a form of information warfare sometimes seen as analogous to conventional warfare.

CASUALTIES OF CYBER WARFARE

That the United States and China have engaged in skirmishes in the cyber domain is no secret. Since the beginning of the 21st century, targeted cyberattacks, often with signs of Chinese origin, have attempted to penetrate the computer networks of U.S. corporations and government agencies in search of potentially valuable information. In response to this new strategic threat, the U.S. Military's Strategic Command commissioned the creation of a sub-unified Cyber Command in 2009, with one of its stated objectives being the "defense of specified Department of Defense information networks."

U.S. President Barack Obama very clearly defined the threat that cyberattacks pose to the economy, in both the public and private sectors, when he said that the "cyber threat is one of the most serious economic and national security challenges we face as a nation." Indeed, conflict in the cyber domain is still having some serious repercussions for the business world.

Civilian Involvement in Cyber Warfare

The characteristic of cyber warfare that makes it so uniquely dangerous to the corporate sector is that military power in the cyber domain must be extended through computer networks provided and maintained by non-governmental bodies. The use of these networks for cyberattacks or defense requires the conscription or cooperation of civilian resources. This creates extreme liabilities for the corporations that provide these networks, as they will quickly become the targets of suspicion and possible retaliation from the enemy state. In recent years, both Chinese and American companies have been caught in just this situation.

On October 8, 2012, the U.S. House of Representatives' intelligence committee released a report that warned of potential national security threats posed by Chinese telecommunication giants Huawei and ZTE. After conducting a year-long investigation of the suspect companies, the intelligence committee found serious vulnerabilities caused by hidden "backdoors" worked into the companies' technologies that would allow access to U.S. government and business networks.

The report advised against the purchase of products manufactured by Huawei or ZTE, and suggested that policymakers block any mergers between either of the two companies and U.S. telecommunication corporations.

These accusations have seriously hurt consumer confidence in the two companies, to the extent that in December of 2013, Huawei's executive vice president dramatically declared"we are not interested in the U.S. market anymore." While Huawei has managed to hold on to a small market share in America, the company's association with Chinese state-sponsored cyberattacks has devastated its ability to operate in the United States.

It became clear last year, though, that the United States was a perpetrator of cyberattacks as well as a victim. In June 2013, former U.S. National Security Agency contractor Edward Snowden provided the world with a look into the intelligence apparatus of the NSA, releasing thousands of classified documents to the media. The released documents revealed that the U.S., like China, was using domestic tech firms (in many cases without their knowledge or consent) as conduits for intelligence gathering cyberattacks. In May 2014, the Chinese government announced that it would no longer purchase or use two of Microsoft's main products, the Windows 8 operating system and the Microsoft Office 365 Suite. Then, in late July and early August, Chinese officials from the State Administration for Industry and Commerce (SAIC) raided multiple offices owned by Microsoft and its contractors in China. While vague statements about an anti-monopoly probe were made, the company's decision to end support for the Windows XP operating system – a move that would expose the many Chinese computers that use the operating system to security risks – was also cited as a factor in the raids.

While it is likely that the ban and subsequent raids were also intended to pave the way for new operating system technologies created in China, the Snowden revelations allowed potential U.S. espionage activities to be cited as a justification. Just as Huawei and ZTE suffered for their association with espionage activities of the Chinese government, Microsoft took a major hit because of the provocative actions of its government.

An Undefined Battlefield

On both sides of the Pacific, it is clear that both U.S. and Chinese tech firms are being caught in the crossfire of these cyber skirmishes between the two countries. Any escalation in tensions in the cyber domain could be disastrous to the private sector. Unfortunately, despite the risks that future cyberwars hold for multinational corporations, there is a marked absence of legislation, precedent, and international norms that could govern the relationships between private companies and the governments looking to use them as avenues through which cyberwar could be conducted.

For as long as these ambiguities exist, corporations that deal in the communication technology industry will exist in the gray area of an unregulated cyber battlefield devoid of any policies meant to protect the assets and infrastructures of civilian actors. It is in the interests of both countries to more clearly define, through domestic cooperation with corporate partners and with bilateral international discussion and agreement, the boundaries between civilians and the military in cyber warfare. Failure to do so could severely hamper the economic interaction that has been so lucrative for both countries and further destabilize an already fragile Sino-American relationship.

Government's Role in Domestic Cyber Security

While organizations have taken extensive measures to provide security against cybercrime, the challenges of a larger cyberwar against a capable and persistent foe require greater national organization and civilian-government cooperation. Unfortunately, in the United States, government responses to engagements in the cyber domain have been slow at best, but more often nonexistent. The cause of this is commonly the difficulty in identifying attackers and the lack of procedures in place for how a national response can and should be mobilized to address an attack on a civilian target. This lack of definition creates additional liability for the civilian counterpart because the opposing state (in this case China) does not know to what extent the civilian is involved with the defense and possible subsequent counterattacks. The lack of clarity directly increases the probability that the civilian will be the target of general suspicion and will suffer financial damage, as was seen with Huawei, ZTE and Microsoft. In broad terms, foreign attacks on domestic civilian targets can be placed in one of two categories: those that pose a national security threat and those that cause potential financial harm to the recipient of the attack. These two types of attacks require specific responses that have not yet been clearly defined by the U.S. government and the business community.

A cyberattack that directly threatens the national security of the United States might require the temporary direct use, or even the partial or complete conscription, of a civilian network. Disruptions of public utilities, theft of sensitive information from a security contractor, or the sabotage of civilian networks necessary for the operation of the military are examples of intrusions that might necessitate such a response. However, the documents released by Edward Snowden revealed that civilian networks were commonly conscripted for foreign surveillance activities, often without the knowledge of their owners. One of the largest barriers that conscription faces to becoming a transparent counter-cyberattack strategy is the ambiguity surrounding the cyber domain in warfare. Because no legislation exists that explicitly defines cyberattacks as acts of war and because the Supreme Court has never ruled on the constitutionality of conscription in any form during peacetime, no precedent has ever been set that would instruct the government on how to publicly organize a defense in the case of a cyberattack against a civilian target that threatened national security. While this does not excuse the NSA of its secrecy, it does indicate the need for legal clarification on the matter of cyber warfare. A decisive answer to the question of the legality of government conscription of civilian network assets in the interests of national security would allow a transparent strategy that involved input from both civilian and government representatives to be formed.

If a cyberattack is not a national security threat, but only threatens the financial health of the victim, the procedures for a government response are even more unclear. With traditional cybercrime, civilians are responsible for their own cyber security and the liability of unsuccessfully defending against an attempted network penetration falls on the civilian's security provider or the civilian's own security measures. However, it seems unreasonable to assume that a civilian would be able to successfully defend against the cyberattacks of a foreign state, which presumably would have greater access to technology, talent and funding.

Say, for example, a cyberattack of Chinese origin manages to steal sensitive information relating to a patented product of an American company. What response could that company expect to receive from the government? The answer to that question has yet to be explicitly defined through any official legislation or successful precedent. However, the Cybersecurity

Act of 2013, which was recommended for further consideration in July 2013, might be a step in the right direction. The bill directs the Secretary of Commerce and the Director of National Institute of Standards and Technology to work toward the, "development of a voluntary, industry-led set of standards and procedures to reduce cyber risks to critical infrastructure." While the bill does not specifically say what measures can be taken to address the problem, a dialogue between the government and the civilian sector is a necessary first step toward assuring that the government will take an active role in preventing damaging cyberattacks on civilian targets.

A Line in the Cyber Sand

The lack of adequate procedural preparation for cyber warfare and ambiguity about the government's role in protecting its civilians from cyberattacks represents a real strategic threat to the United States as well as a financial liability for civilians. Before the release of the NSA documents last year, the U.S. government was acting unilaterally to address the problems presented by aggression from the Chinese in the cyber domain. The nature of cyber warfare, however, necessitates civilian cooperation. Now there is an opening to create a partnership to more clearly define the lines between state actions that might be internationally provocative and civilian resources that, while necessary to the state's actions, do not represent the civilian's participation as an aggressor. Not only will this protect civilian assets that are not directly involved in cyber warfare efforts, it will also create procedures that will allow for a more effective and efficient strategy for the conduct of cyber warfare.

Given the very real risk that conflict between China and the U.S. in the cyber domain could escalate in the future, we need to find ways to isolate it from the vibrant economic exchange that have benefited both countries. The worst-case scenario would be the disintegration of the line between warfighting assets and civilian assets, such that the intentional targeting of noncombatants becomes a viable strategy. Both

China and the U.S. need to act to ensure that their civilians do not become casualties of cyber warfare.

THE EVOLUTION OF CYBER WARFARE

In the spring of 2007, when Estonian authorities moved a monument to the Red Army from the center of its capital city, Tallinn, to the outskirts of town, a diplomatic row erupted with neighboring Russia. Estonian nationalists regard the army as occupiers and oppressors, a sentiment that dates to the long period of Soviet rule following the Second World War, when the Soviet Union absorbed all three Baltic states.

Ethnic Russians, who make up about a quarter of Estonia's 1.3 million people, were nonetheless incensed by the statue's treatment and took to the streets in protest. Estonia later blamed Moscow for orchestrating the unrest; order was restored only after U.S. and European diplomatic interventions.

But the story of the "Bronze Statue" did not end there. Days after the riots the computerized infrastructure of Estonia's high-tech government began to fray, victimized by what experts in cybersecurity termed a coordinated "denial of service" attack.

A flood of bogus requests for information from computers around the world conspired to cripple (Wired) the websites of Estonian banks, media outlets, and ministries for days. Estonia denounced the attacks as an unprovoked act of aggression from a regional foe (though experts still disagree on who perpetrated it—Moscow has denied any knowledge). Experts in cybersecurity went one step further: They called it the future of warfare.

Cyber Warfare: The New Frontier

The attack on Estonia's "paperless government" (BBC) was one of the most publicized hacks in recent computing history. But it wasn't the first case of cyber espionage, nor the most egregious. It's the "tip of the iceberg of the quantity and quality of attacks that are going on," says O. Sami Saydjari, president of the Cyber Defense Agency, a security consultant, and a former Pentagon computer security expert. Israel, India,

Pakistan, and the United States have all been accused of launching similar attacks on adversaries.

China, however, may be the most active. Washington has accused the Chinese of hacking into government computer networks at the U.S. Departments of State, Commerce, and Defense—in some instances making off with data. But accusations of Chinese cyber-meddling reached a crescendo in June 2007, when, according to the Financial Times, hackers broke into a Pentagon network that serves the Office of the Secretary of Defense, briefly shutting it down.

Chinese electronic espionage has also been suspected against British companies (Rolls Royce is one example), as well as government agencies in France, Germany, South Korea, and Taiwan. "Chinese capabilities in this area have evolved from defending networks from attack to offensive operations against adversary networks," Deputy Undersecretary for Defense Richard P. Lawless told a House committee in June 2007. China, like Russia, denies the accusations. Both countries argue any attacks originating from IP addresses inside their countries have been directed by rogue citizens, not their governments. Western targets, however, continue to accuse the Chinese of ratcheting up their cyber attack capabilities.

U.S. Cyber Warfare on the Offensive

The United States, of course, is no innocent bystander. William M. Arkin, a defense analyst who writes the Early Warning blog for the Washington Post, says "our ability to penetrate into enemy computer networks, our ability to exploit communication networks, to manipulate digital information, is real," but little is known about the precise nature of Washington's offensive capabilities. Some details, however, have leaked. For instance, in March 2004 the Pentagon announced the formation of an Information Operations team—the Network Attack Support Staff—to streamline the military's cyber attack capabilities. The aim, senior military officials said at the time, was to create an "interface between the combatant commanders and the intelligence community."

"Our information infrastructure ... increasingly is being targeted for exploitation and potentially for disruption or destruction by a growing array of state and non-state adversaries." –Director of National Intelligence Michael McConnell

Arkin, who has reported on cybersecurity issues for over two decades, says the U.S. military also has technologies capable of penetrating and jamming enemy networks, including the classified "Suter" system of airborne technology. According to Aviation Week, Suter has been integrated into unmanned aircraft and "allows users to invade communications networks, see what enemy sensors see, and even take over as systems administrator so sensors can be manipulated into positions so that approaching aircraft can't be seen." Some speculate the Israeli military used the capability during its air raid on a Syrian construction site in September 2007. The United States made use of nascent capabilities in the 1999 Kosovo War (MSNBC.com), and built on those lessons in Iraq (Wired).

CYBER-WARFARE TACTICS

Other cyber tactics are less sophisticated. The attack that temporarily brought down Estonian networks began with a flood of bogus messages targeting government servers, called a "denial of service" attack. The approach harnesses "botnets"—massive networks of interconnected computers—to bombard targeted networks with information requests while masking the location of the primary attacker. James Lewis, a security expert with the Center for Strategic and International Studies (CSIS), says hackers in the Estonia example likely took control of tens of thousands of computers around the world without the knowledge of their owners and directed them at the government's servers. The result, he says, was a relatively minor attack that was nearly impossible to trace.

Another technique is the use of "malware," "spyware," and other malicious programs imbedded into computer systems to steal information without user knowledge. The software is designed to hide undetected and siphon information from its host—everything from secrets stored on personal computers to

Pentagon military mainframes. A December 2007 analysis of U.S. Air Force cyber vulnerabilities notes much of the Pentagon's operating systems are off-the-shelf components manufactured overseas, due to cheaper costs. But pinching pennies has potentially opened U.S. military networks to intrusion. "Foreign countries could place hidden components inside the computers, making the computers vulnerable for attack and/or spying," the analysis concludes.

> *"Our ability to penetrate into enemy computer networks, our ability to exploit communication networks, to manipulate digital information, is real." –Defense Analyst William M. Arkin*

Less common but far more worrisome are cyber attacks aimed at critical infrastructure—like nuclear-power-plant control systems, banks, or subways. In March 2007 the Department of Energy's Idaho Lab conducted an experiment to determine whether a power plant could be compromised by hacking alone. The result—a smoking, self-combusting diesel generator incapacitated by nothing more than keystrokes—sent shivers (CNN) through the private sector. The worries were apparently well-founded.

In January 2008 a CIA analyst told U.S. utilities that hackers had succeeded in infiltrating electric companies in undisclosed locations outside the United States and, it at least one instance, shut off power to multiple cities. The hackers then demanded money (AP). "The [U.S.] government is scrambling to try and protect its own systems, to try and check the Chinese from reading government email," says economist Scott Borg, director of the U.S. Cyber Consequences Unit, a nonprofit research institute that studies cyber threats. "But the focus probably needs to be critical infrastructure. That's what we need to defend."

Patching the Holes

On paper the U.S. government appears to agree. For over a decade government-sanctioned studies have delved into the subject; the Pentagon published a report on "Information Warfare-Defense" (PDF) in 1996, when public use of the Internet was still in its infancy. Saydjari says all of these studies reached the same conclusion: "The threat and vulnerabilities to our national infrastructure is serious, it's getting worse, and it's getting worse at an increasingly fast rate."

But only recently has the concern been a constant focus of attention for the security and intelligence communities. Part of the attention deficit lies with the difficulty in defining the cyber threat. A 2006 Air Force task force termed cyberspace "a warfighting domain bounded by the electromagnetic spectrum," but air force officials acknowledge "a full understanding of the domain is years away."

What is understood is how potentially devastating the loss of cyberspace dominance could be to U.S. interests. In his annual threat assessment to Congress delivered in February 2008, Director of National Intelligence Michael McConnell discussed "cyber threats" before talking about the war in Afghanistan.

"Our information infrastructure ...increasingly is being targeted for exploitation and potentially for disruption or destruction by a growing array of state and non-state adversaries," McConnell said. "We assess that nations, including Russia and China, have the technical capabilities to target and disrupt" the United States' information infrastructure.

> *"Chinese [cyber warfare] capabilities have evolved from defending networks from attack to offensive operations against adversary networks." –U.S. Deputy Under Secretary for Defense Richard P. Lawless*

The Pentagon, too, has acknowledged the threat to its infrastructure. The Defense Department is considering banning nonofficial traffic (Federal Computer Week) from its servers, and the U.S. Air Force is creating a Cyber Command to defend Pentagon networks. "When we talk about the speed range and flexibility of air power, the thing that enables this for us is the fact of our cyber-dominance," Air Force Gen. Robert Elder told United Press International. The recent flurry of high-level pronouncements also comes amid a renewed funding commitment from Washington. In November 2007 the Bush administration called on the National Security Agency to coordinate with the Department of Homeland Security to protect government and civilian communication networks from hackers. The $144 million plan, unveiled quietly in White House budget documents (PDF), aims to enhance "civilian agency cybersecurity and strengthen defenses to combat terrorism."

In January 2008 President George W. Bush signed two presidential directives calling for the creation of a comprehensive national cybersecurity initiative. According to an article by the Wall Street Journal, the White House's 2009 budget request takes the program exponentially further, with an estimated $6 billion request to build a secretive system to protect U.S. communications networks. Details of the proposed program remain classified, angering some civil libertarians who fear monitoring of civilian networks could infringe on privacy rights. Rep. Bennie G. Thompson (D-MS), chairman of the House Homeland Security Committee, has called for the program to be put on hold (PDF) until Congress can adequately review it.

Measuring the Threat

Cyber experts don't dispute that electronic espionage is a vexing problem, or that the United States is a prime target. But they do disagree on how pervasive such attacks are, who is behind them, and how disruptive they may prove to be.

According to a tally by the Heritage Foundation, a conservative Washington think tank, the hackers may already be winning: In 2007 the Department of Homeland Security logged an estimated 37,000 attempted breaches of private and government computer systems, and over 80,000 attacks on Pentagon systems. Some hacks "reduced the U.S. military's operational capabilities," the report says.

Economist Borg says the biggest threat from cyber attacks may be economic. He estimates a shutdown of electric power to any sizable region for more than ten days would stop over 70 percent of all economic activity in that region. "If you can do that with a pure cyber attack on only one critical infrastructure, why would you bother with any traditional military attack?" CSIS' Lewis takes a less alarmist view.

"The U.S. is a very big set of targets, and some of our important networks are very secure. So you could inflict damage on the U.S. but it wouldn't be crippling or decisive," he says. "I've seen people who say a cyber attack could turn the United States into a third-world nation in a matter of minutes. That's silly. We have to be realistic about this."

CYBER WARFARE AND PRESENT STRATEGIES

Crime is a social and economic phenomenon and is as old as the human society. As, Life is about a mix of good and evil, so is the Internet. For all the good it does to us, cyberspace has its dark sides too. The Internet is undeniably open to exploitation. Known as cyber crimes, these activities involve the use of computers, the Internet, cyberspace and the World Wide Web. Cyber crime is the latest and perhaps the most complicated problem in the cyber world.

Cyber crime is an evil having its origin in the growing dependence on computers in modern life. In a day and age when everything from microwave ovens and refrigerators to nuclear power plants is being run on computers, cyber crime has assumed rather sinister implications.

While the worldwide scenario on cyber crime looks bleak, the situation in India isn't any better. Cyber crimes in India are slowly evolving from a simple e-mail crime to more serious crimes like hacking and source code theft. Cases of spam, hacking, cyber stalking and email fraud are rampant despite the enactment of the Information Technology Act, 2000, the India's Cyber Law and setting up of cyber crimes cells in major cities. The problem is that most cases remain unreported due to a lack of awareness.

So, the need of the hour is to make the masses aware of the Cyber Crime itself and their rights and duties in relation to Cyber Crime. As, it is only then can this growing menace be checked.

So, in the present report an attempt has been made to describe the various types of cyber crimes and the present scenario on the cyber crime and the preventive measures that should be taken up to protect ourselves. The word CYBER SPACE was coined by Willliam Gibson in the science fiction NEUROMANCER, in the year 1984. It is used as a means of denoting the apparent or virtual location within which electronic activities take place. Of late, the word Cyber has become a loose synonym for electronics. Cyber Space therefore is a place where people meet not physically but virtually and communicate with each other electronically. Cyber Space is the aggregate of Intranets, Internet and World Wide Web.

The Internet has opened up a whole new virtual heaven for the people both good and bad, cleaver and naïve to enter and interact with a lot of diverse cultures and subcultures, geography and demographics being no bar. The rise of the Internet as one of the most significant communication and business platforms of this century has come with its own set of issues and concerns. While the Net has brought a host of benefits to the common person and to enterprises, it is also having to grapple with major challenges, primary among them security.

The very same virtues of Internet when gone in wrong hands or when exploited by people with dirty minds and malicious intentions make it virtual hell. Due to popularity of Internet, hacking or breaking into somebody into else's computer is more popular and automated than ever.

There are various frauds of computer and internet related crimes. The most common is the use of viruses to corrupt and destroy data stored in computer systems. The forms of crimes like impersonation, theft of credit card information, e-gambling, espionage, harassment, pornography are on a rise due to the growth of the medium.

CYBERWARFARE BY COUNTRY

The Internet security company McAfee stated in their 2007 annual report that approximately 120 countries have been developing ways to use the Internet as a weapon and target financial markets, government computer systems and utilities.

Cyberwarfare in China

Diplomatic cables highlight US concerns that China is using access to Microsoft source code and 'harvesting the talents of its private sector' to boost its offensive and defensive capabilities.

A 2008 article in the *Culture Mandala: The Bulletin of the Centre for East-West Cultural and Economic Studies* by Jason Fritz alleges that the Chinese government from 1995 to 2008 was involved in a number of high-profile cases of espionage, primarily through the use of a "decentralized network of students, business people, scientists, diplomats, and engineers from within the Chinese Diaspora".

A defector in Belgium, purportedly an agent, claimed that there were hundreds of spies in industries throughout Europe, and on his defection to Australia Chinese diplomat Chen Yonglin said there were over 1,000 such in that country. In 2007, a Russian executive was sentenced to 11 years for passing information about the rocket and space technology organization to China. Targets in the United States have included 'aerospace engineering programs, space shuttle design,C4ISR data, high-performance computers, Nuclear weapon design, cruise missile data, semiconductors, integrated circuit design, and details of US arms sales to Taiwan'.

While China continues to be held responsible for a string of cyber-attacks on a number of public and private institutions in the United States, India, Russia, Canada, and France, the Chinese government denies any involvement in cyber-spying campaigns. The administration maintains the position that China is not the threat but rather the victim of an increasing number of cyber-attacks. Most reports about China's cyber warfare capabilities have yet to be confirmed by the Chinese government.

According to Fritz, China has expanded its cyber capabilities and military technology by acquiring foreign military technology. Fritz states that the Chinese government uses "new space-based surveillance and intelligence gathering systems, Anti-satellite weapon, anti-radar, infrared decoys, and false target generators" to assist in this quest, and that they support their "informationization" of the their military through "increased education of soldiers in cyber warfare; improving the information network for military training, and has built more virtual laboratories, digital libraries and digital campuses.' Through this informationization, they hope to prepare their forces to engage in a different kind of warfare, against technically capable adversaries. Many recent news reports link China's technological capabilities to the beginning of a new 'cyber cold war.'

In response to reports of cyberattacks by China against the United States, Amitai Etzioni of the Institute for Communitarian Policy Studies has suggested that China and the United States agree to a policy of mutually assured restraint with respect to cyberspace. This would involve allowing both states to take the measures they deem necessary for their self-defense while simultaneously agreeing to refrain from taking offensive steps; it would also entail vetting these commitments.

Cyberwarfare in Germany

In 2013, Germany revealed the existence of their 60-person Computer Network Operation unit. The German intelligence agency, BND, announced it was seeking to hire 130 "hackers" for a new "cyber defence station" unit. In March 2013, BND president Gerhard Schindler announced that his agency had observed up to five attacks a day on government authorities, thought mainly to originate in China. He confirmed the attackers had so far only accessed data and expressed concern that the stolen information could be used as the basis of future sabotage attacks against arms manufacturers, telecommunications companies and government and military agencies. Shortly after Edward Snowden leaked details of the U.S. National Security Agency's cyber surveillance system, German Interior Minister Hans-Peter Friedrich announced that the BND would be given an additional budget of 100 million Euros to increase their cyber surveillance capability from 5% of total internet traffic in Germany to 20% of total traffic, the maximum amount allowed by German law.

Cyberwarfare in India

Cyber warfare against India has always been confused with minor cyber breaches like websites defacements and cracking into e-mail accounts. India has also been very late in recognising the need for a robust cyber security. Even the national cyber security policy of India 2013 (NCSP 2013) was declared belatedly and it is still waiting for its implementation. India has no cyber warfare policy (Pdf) till date.

International legal issues of cyber attacks, cyber terrorism, cyber espionage, cyber warfare and cyber crimes in general and international legal issues of cyber attacks and Indian perspective in particular must be understood thoroughly by Indian government to fight against cyber warfare.

The Department of Information Technology created the Indian Computer Emergency Response Team (CERT-In) in 2004 to thwart cyber attacks in India. That year, there were 23 reported cyber security breaches. In 2011, there were 13,301. That year, the government created a new subdivision, the National Critical Information Infrastructure Protection Centre (NCIIPC) to thwart attacks against energy, transport, banking, telecom, defence, space and other sensitive areas. However, there is no public face of NCIPC and some experts believe that NCIPC has failed to materialise and perform its job. It was also reported that National Technical Research Organisation (NTRO) would protect the critical ICT infrastructures of India. However, critical infrastructure protection in India has its own challenges (Pdf) that Indian government has not appreciated till now.

The Executive Director of the Nuclear Power Corporation of India (NPCIL) stated in February 2013 that his company alone was forced to block up to ten targeted attacks a day. CERT-In was left to protect less critical sectors.

A high-profile cyber attack on 12 July 2012 breached the email accounts of about 12,000 people, including those of officials from the Ministry of External Affairs, Ministry of Home Affairs,

Defence Research and Development Organisation (DRDO), and the Indo-Tibetan Border Police (ITBP). A government-private sector plan being overseen byNational Security Advisor (NSA) Shivshankar Menon began in October 2012, and intends to beef up India's cyber security capabilities in the light of a group of experts findings that India faces a 470,000 shortfall of such experts despite the country's reputation of being an IT and software powerhouse.

In February 2013, Information Technology Secretary J. Satyanarayana stated that the NCIIPC was finalizing policies related to national cyber security that would focus on domestic security solutions, reducing exposure through foreign technology. Other steps include the isolation of various security agencies to ensure that a synchronised attack could not succeed on all fronts and the planned appointment of a National Cyber Security Coordinator. As of that month, there had been no significant economic or physical damage to India related to cyber attacks.

Cyberwarfare in Iran

In June 2010, Iran was the victim of a cyber attack when its nuclear facility in Natanz was infiltrated by the cyber-worm 'Stuxnet'. Reportedly a combined effort by the United States and Israel, Stuxnet destroyed perhaps over 1000 nuclear centrifuges and, according to a *Business Insider* article, "[set] Tehran's atomic programme back by at least two years." The worm spread beyond the plant to allegedly infect over 60,000 computers, but the government of Iran indicates it caused no significant damage. Iran crowdsourced solutions to the worm and is purportedly now better positioned in terms of cyber warfare technology. No government has claimed responsibility for the worm.

The Iranian government has been accused by western analysts of its own cyber-attacks against the United States, Israel and Gulf Arabs, but deny this, including specific allegations of 2012 involvement in hacking into American banks. The conflict between Iran and the United States as been called "history's first known cyber-war" by Michael Joseph Gross mid-2013.

Cyberwarfare in South Korea

With ongoing tensions on the Korean Peninsula, South Korea's defense ministry stated that South Korea was going to improve cyber-defense strategies in hopes of preparing itself from possible cyber attacks. In March 2013, South Korea's major banks – Shinhan Bank, Woori Bank and NongHyup Bank – as well as many broadcasting stations – KBS, YTN and MBC – were hacked and more than 30,000 computers were affected; it is one of the biggest attacks South Korea has faced in years.

Although it remains uncertain as to who was involved in this incident, there has been immediate assertions that North Korea is connected, as it threatened to attack South Korea's government institutions, major national banks and traditional newspapers numerous times – in reaction to the sanctions it received from nuclear testing and to the continuation of Foal Eagle, South Korea's annual joint military exercise with the United States.

North Korea's cyber warfare capabilities raise the alarm for South Korea, as North Korea is increasing its manpower through military academies specializing in hacking.

Current figures state that South Korea only has 400 units of specialized personnel, while North Korea has more than 3,000 highly trained hackers; this portrays a huge gap in cyber warfare capabilities and sends a message to South Korea that it has to step up and strengthen its Cyber Warfare Command forces. Therefore, in order to be prepared from future attacks, South Korea and the United States will discuss further about deterrence plans at the Security Consultative Meeting (SCM).

At SCM, they plan on developing strategies that focuses on accelerating the deployment of ballistic missiles as well as fostering its defense shield program, known as the Korean Air and Missile Defense.

Cyberwarfare in the Netherlands

In the Netherlands Cyber Defense is nationally coordinated by the National Cyber Security Center (NCSC). The Dutch Ministry of Defense laid out a cyber strategy in 2011. The first focus is to improve the cyber defense handled by the Joint IT branch (JIVC). To improve intel operations the intel community in the Netherlands (including the military intel organization MIVD) has set up the Joint Sigint Cyber Unit (JSCU). The ministry of Defense is furthermore setting up an offensive cyber force, called Defensie Cyber Command (DCC), which will be operational in the end of 2014.

Cyberwarfare in the UK

MI6 reportedly infiltrated an Al Qaeda website and replaced the recipe for a pipe bomb with the recipe for making cupcakes.

On 12 November 2013, financial organisations in London conducted cyber war games dubbed 'Waking Shark 2' to simulate massive internet-based attacks against bank and other financial organisations. The Waking Shark 2 cyber war games followed a similar exercise in Wall Street.

Cyberwarfare in the United States

Cyberwarfare in the United States is a part of the American military strategy of Proactive Cyber Defence and the use of cyberwarfare as a platform for attack. The new United States military strategy makes explicit that a cyberattack is *casus belli* just as a traditional act of war.

In 2013 Cyberwarfare was, for the first time, considered a larger threat than Al Qaeda or terrorism, by many U.S. intelligence officials. Representative Mike Rogers, chairman of the U.S. House Permanent Select Committee on Intelligence, for instance, said in late July, 2013, that "most Americans" do not realize that the United States is currently in the middle of a "cyber war."

U.S. government security expert Richard A. Clarke, in his book *Cyber War* (May 2010), defines "cyberwarfare" as "actions by a nation-state to penetrate another nation's computers or networks for the purposes of causing damage or disruption." The *Economist* describes cyberspace as "the fifth domain of warfare," and William J. Lynn, U.S. Deputy Secretary of Defense, states that "as a doctrinal matter, the Pentagon has formally recognized cyberspace as a new domain in warfare... [which] has become just as critical to military operations as land, sea, air, and space."

In 2009, President Barack Obama declared America's digital infrastructure to be a "strategic national asset," and in May 2010 the Pentagon set up its new U.S. Cyber Command (USCYBERCOM), headed by General Keith B. Alexander, director of the National Security Agency (NSA), to defend American military networks and attack other countries' systems.

The EU has set up ENISA (European Union Agency for Network and Information Security) which is headed by Prof. Udo Helmbrecht and there are now further plans to significantly expand ENISA's capabilities.

The United Kingdom has also set up a cyber-security and "operations centre" based in Government Communications Headquarters(GCHQ), the British equivalent of the NSA. In the U.S. however, Cyber Command is only set up to protect the military, whereas the government and corporate infrastructures are primarily the responsibility respectively of the Department of Homeland Security and private companies.

In February 2010, top American lawmakers warned that the "threat of a crippling attack on telecommunications and computer networks was sharply on the rise." According to The Lipman Report, numerous key sectors of the U.S. economy along with that of other nations, are currently at risk, including cyber threats to public and private facilities, banking and finance, transportation, manufacturing, medical, education and government, all of which are now dependent on computers for daily operations. In 2009, President Obama stated that "cyber intruders have probed our electrical grids."

The Economist writes that China has plans of "winning informationised wars by the mid-21st century". They note that other countries are likewise organizing for cyberwar, among them Russia, Israel and North Korea. Iran boasts of having the world's second-largest cyber-army. James Gosler, a government cybersecurity specialist, worries that the U.S. has a severe shortage of computer security specialists, estimating that there are only about 1,000 qualified people in the country today, but needs a force of 20,000 to 30,000 skilled experts. At the July 2010 Black Hat computer security conference, Michael Hayden, former deputy director of national intelligence, challenged thousands of attendees to help devise ways to "reshape the Internet's security architecture", explaining, "You guys made the cyberworld look like the north German plain."

In January 2012, Mike McConnell, the former director of national intelligence at the National Security Agency under President George W. Bush told the Reuters news agency that the U.S. has already launched attacks on computer networks in other countries.

McConnell did not name the country that the U.S. attacked but according to other sources it may have been Iran. In June 2012 the New York Times reported that President Obama had ordered the cyber attack on Iranian nuclear enrichment facilities.

In August 2010, the U.S. for the first time warned publicly about the Chinese military's use of civilian computer experts in clandestine cyber attacks aimed at American companies and government agencies. The Pentagon also pointed to an alleged China-based computer spying network dubbed GhostNet that was revealed in a research report last year. The Pentagon stated:

"The People's Liberation Army is using "information warfare units" to develop viruses to attack enemy computer systems and networks, and those units include civilian computer professionals. Commander Bob Mehal, will monitor the PLA's buildup of its cyberwarfare capabilities and will continue to develop capabilities to counter any potential threat."

The United States Department of Defense sees the use of computers and the Internet to conduct warfare in cyberspace as a threat to national security. The United States Joint Forces Command describes some of its attributes:

Cyberspace technology is emerging as an "instrument of power" in societies, and is becoming more available to a country's opponents, who may use it to attack, degrade, and disrupt communications and the flow of information. With low barriers to entry, coupled with the anonymous nature of activities in cyberspace, the list of potential adversaries is broad. Furthermore, the globe-spanning range of cyberspace and its disregard for national borders will challenge legal systems and complicate a nation's ability to deter threats and respond to contingencies.

In February 2010, the United States Joint Forces Command released a study which included a summary of the threats posed by the internet:

With very little investment, and cloaked in a veil of anonymity, our adversaries will inevitably attempt to harm our national interests. Cyberspace will become a main front in both irregular and traditional conflicts.

Enemies in cyberspace will include both states and non-states and will range from the unsophisticated amateur to highly trained professional hackers. Through cyberspace, enemies will target industry, academia, government, as well as the military in the air, land, maritime, and space domains. In much the same way that airpower transformed the battlefield of World War II, cyberspace has fractured the physical barriers that shield a nation from attacks on its commerce and communication. Indeed, adversaries have already taken advantage of computer networks and the power of information technology not only to plan and execute savage acts of terrorism, but also to influence directly the perceptions and will of the U.S. Government and the American population.

American "*Kill switch bill*"

On 19 June 2010, United States Senator Joe Lieberman (I-CT) introduced a bill called "Protecting Cyberspace as a National Asset Act of 2010", which he co-wrote with Senator Susan

Collins (R-ME) and Senator Thomas Carper (D-DE). If signed into law, this controversial bill, which the American media dubbed the "*Kill switch bill*", would grant the President emergency powers over parts of the Internet. However, all three co-authors of the bill issued a statement that instead, the bill "[narrowed] existing broad Presidential authority to take over telecommunications networks".

The United States has used cyberattacks for tactical advantage in Afghanistan.

3

Convergence of Cyberspace Operations and Electronic Warfare Effects

Convergence is the foundry for new possibilities. Convergence of Cyberspace Operations (CO) and Electronic Warfare (EW) effects creates combined effects to achieve both offensive and defensive overmatch. Recently the US Air Force revealed the use of a modified EC-130 Compass Call aircraft to remotely attack enemy networks.The 24th Air Force commander, Major General Burke "Ed" Wilson, spoke of this capability enabling the ability to "touch a network that in most cases might be closed."

While the need for convergence of cyberspace operations and electronic warfare is recognized within the Department of Defense (DoD), differences between how these two capabilities are trained, resourced, organized and employed combined with the significant functional level differences between the two have hindered efforts to converge their capabilities. A concerted effort must be undertaken at the both the Joint and Service levels to closely integrate CO with EW effects to achieve combined effects, enabling comprehensive shaping of the operational environment.

The first step in this effort is for CO and EW professionals to commit themselves to professional self-development in their counterparts' field.

Description of Issue / Problem Statement

Describing the challenge of converging CO and EW effects requires first to define each and their interaction within the Open Systems Interconnection (OSI) model. The OSI model is a standard model to describe a seven-layer network protocol stack starting at the physical layer and ending at the application layer. Joint Publication 1-02, *Department of Defense Dictionary of Military and Associated Terms* defines cyberspace operations as "the employment of cyberspace capabilities where the primary purpose is to achieve objectives in or through cyberspace". JP 1-02 defines electronic warfare as "military action involving the use of electromagnetic and directed energy to control the electromagnetic spectrum or to attack the enemy". While the definitions have little in common, CO and EW are both based on three roughly similar pillars: attack, defense, and support/ operations. For cyberspace operations, the pillars are defined as Offensive Cyber Operations (OCO), Defensive Cyber Operations (DCO) and DoD Information Network (DODIN) Operations. These mission categories align well with the electronic warfare missions of Electronic Attack (EA), Electronic Protection (EP) and Electronic Warfare Support (ES). OCO projects power "by the application of force in and through cyberspace", while EA involves the use of "EM energy, DE, or antiradiation weapons to attack personnel, facilities, or equipment with the intent of degrading, neutralizing, or destroying enemy combat capability."

DCO uses passive and active cyberspace capabilities to "protect data, networks, net-centric capabilities, and other designated systems," with EP being "actions taken to protect personnel, facilities, and equipment from any effects of friendly or enemy use of the electromagnetic spectrum that degrade, neutralize, or destroy friendly combat capability." DODIN Operations are actions taken to "design, build, configure, secure, operate, maintain, and sustain DoD communications systems and networks in a way that creates and preserves data availability, integrity, confidentiality, as well as user/entity authentication and non-repudiation", whereas ES is "actions tasked by, or under direct control of, an operational commander to search for, intercept, identify, and locate or localize sources of intentional and unintentional radiated electromagnetic energy for the purpose of immediate threat recognition, targeting, planning, and conduct of future operations."

CO and EW effects are likewise overlapped within the OSI model. Both CO and EW begin at Layer 1, the physical layer. A common misconception is that EW stops at Layer 1, but the integration of Internet Protocol (IP) into a wide range of communications systems enables intelligent jamming. In intelligent jamming, knowledge of the protocol is incorporated into the jamming technique.Solid understanding each of these specific areas and their overlap is critical to achieving capability convergence and the resulting combined CO and EW effects.

In *Convergence of Electronic Warfare and Computer Network Exploitation/Attacks Within the Radio Frequency Spectrum*, David Rohret and Abiud Jimenez, members of the Joint Information Operations Warfare Center (JIOWC) / Vulnerability Assessment Team (VAT), describe how the integration of IP capabilities in systems using Radio Frequency (RF) for communication provides attackers the ability to exploit systems on isolated networks. Unlike current cyber and EW protection teams, which are focused on vulnerabilities within their respective areas, adversaries are focused on achieving desired effects and end state goals.

This threat is heightened by oversights in software and communications system developers in recognizing vulnerabilities introduced during the integration of hardware and software. This paper covers three case studies based on actual vulnerability assessments highlighting these issues.

In the first case study, an IP over radio system developed to provide high bandwidth connections from an aerial platform to users on the ground was effectively disabled through the use of intelligent jamming. The IP over radio system was protected from traditional networks attacks through the use of a proprietary secure wireless protocol, but it proved highly vulnerable to center band frequency jamming at power levels so low, the denial of service was attributed to a system error instead of jamming. In the second case, OCO and EW capabilities were synchronized in a simulated attack against a satellite communication (SATCOM) network. OCO was used to gain access and enumerate the SATCOM network to identify the ground station, which was them jammed forcing the target to use alternate communications methods, thus providing potential new avenues of attack with their own vulnerabilities. In the third case study, a coordinated CO and EW attack on a sensor network enabled the mesh network to be severely degraded, preventing data from the sensors from being received without triggering an alert from a denial of service or jamming attack. These examples demonstrate the power of synergistic effects created through the convergence of CO and EW. Combined effects dramatically increase the difficulty for an enemy to mount an effective response as they struggle to identify the source of the attack.

Our adversaries will use every tool and combination thereof to achieve decisive effects on the battlefield. Prospective near-peer adversaries, Russia and China, understand the capability of converged CO and EW effects and have long standing doctrine integrating CO and EW under the umbrella of Information Warfare (IW). Although the definition of IW and the elements of IW differ between Russia and China, both are focused on achieving combined effects. While Russian definition of IW varies depending on the agency involved, it is roughly defined as an integrated system of system for "establishing control over other states' information resources ... disrupting ... information networks and communications systems, and developing information weapons." Russian IW includes elements of "intelligence and counterintelligence gathering, disinformation, use of EW systems, debilitation of communications and scrambling of enemy data, use of psychological pressure on the enemy, and destruction of enemy computer nets and software programs." The Chinese definition of IW is more vague, but generally emphasizes three pillars, psychological operations, denial and deception.Chinese IW includes elements of precision strike warfare to destroy enemy command and control facilities, EW to "dominate the spectrum while denying the enemy's effective use of electronic equipment", computer network warfare, which covers a wide spectrum of capabilities and psychological warfare and deception to influence behavior of targeted elements. The key takeaway is that both of these potential near-peer adversaries have integrated CO and EW capabilities to achieve combined IW effects. Given their interest and investment in asymmetric capabilities to overcome US military superiority and the DoD's reliance on the availability of the electromagnetic spectrum for command and control, the threat of combined CO and EW operations poses a significant threat.

While the Air Force, Marine Corps and Navy has well established EW career fields, organizations and training programs, the Army's Electronic Warfare branch, Career Management Field (CMF) 29 was established in 2012. The Army maintained communications electronic warfare battalions during the Cold War, but were disbanded in the 1990s, causing significant deficiencies in electronic warfare capabilities, which were grimly recognized during combat operations in Iraq and Afghanistan. With less than 1,000 officers, warrant officers and enlisted personnel, the EW career field has struggled with finding its role as combat deployments have significantly decreased. As a result, when not deployed, EW personnel are often assigned to other duties, resulting in EW is often derided as standing for "extra worker".Exacerbating this problem, the Army will not field a standard electronic warfare capability, with the Multifunctional Electronic Warfare (MFEW) program not slated to reach initial operating capability until 2023. Currently the Army electronic warfare capabilities are focused on countering remote controlled improvised explosive devices, but programs are in place to develop an integrated EW Planning and Management Tool (EWPMT) to provide commanders spectrum situational awareness and enable enhanced synchronization of EW capabilities.The Army's Cyber branch, CMF 17 is now responsible for the management of the Army's

Electronic Warfare branch, CMF 29. The organization construct has the potential to spearhead CO and EW effects convergence within the DoD.

CYBERSPACE AT A GLANCE

For the most part, the Internet is built upon national and international telecommunications infrastructures, including the landlines of most public phone systems and wireless, and satellite communications. Beyond the Internet, these telecommunications infrastructures tend to be highly dependent on computing technology. Thus, by our definition, they are part of cyberspace. There are currently about 1.3 billion Internet users worldwide. The Internet now comes to ground in over 200 "countries" (Top-Level Domains, i.e. the letters which follow the dot after the domain name).

This enormous growth has been achieved since the early 90s. The only thing growing faster than the Internet is cellular telephony, with about three billion phones in use, to which 1.6 million users are added every day. The fact that soon cellular telephones will be a platform for the Internet means that at least a billion new users will have access to this resource, and this expansion will mostly be in developing countries.

(In)Security (Internet Security) at a Glance

The architecture, design, and practice of the Internet emphasize *access* (ease of use, low cost, universality). It has almost never considered security as a primary or important factor. It is an unfortunate result of the history of the way the Internet was developed that the protocols used by the Internet today are derived from those that were established in the early days of the ARPANet, where there were only a few wellrespected researchers using the infrastructure, and they were trusted to do no harm. Consequently, security considerations were not built in to the Internet. All cybersecurity measures taken today to protect the Internet are add-on measures that do not remedy the underlying security deficiencies.

The situation we have as a result is that current technology asymmetrically favors the attackers; it provides them great "nonlinear leverage", and attackers get their innovations into practice more quickly and effectively than defenders. If we make a comparison between cyber attacks and modern warfare, we would say that it is an asymmetrical conflict.

While the state, because of its capacity, has a huge technological advantage over terrorists, the problem is that the kinds of nonlinearities associated with what terrorists do in cyberspace give leverage to those with relatively little technical capability. What has always been thought of as one of the great advantages of the networks can also threaten them: They give a small number of relatively weak people extensive access to a lot of information, each other, potential recruits and sympathizers, and prospective targets. There is also a negative aspect of tightening access against terrorists or other malicious users more generally because it would compromise access and privacy for many, many more "good" users.

The functionality of the Internet ranges greatly. Of particular concern for those aware of the threat of terrorism is the fact that SCADA (Supervisory Control and Data Acquisition) systems now more commonly use the Internet to transmit data and control instructions, rather than the dedicated networks that had been used before. Additionally, very few of the "cyber" parts of the critical infrastructures were designed or implemented with security as much of a consideration, if it was considered at all. Most are riddled with vulnerabilities, which are defined as weaknesses that can be exploited through either hostile attacks or accidents. It would be almost impossible to create "patches" to protect programs from malicious people who seek to find and exploit these vulnerabilities.

Another problem to recognize is that Internet defense pushes the burden outward to the end user organizations; most of these find it difficult, and often increasingly difficult, to defend themselves.

In particular, most of the over two hundred connected countries have little or no national cybersecurity capabilities.

International Threats Arising from Globalization

One area of concern that extends broadly across all of the stages of defense is that globalization creates new populations of "insiders"—people who have authorized access with the potential for abuse that can cause great harm. Insiders still probably account for a majority of successful penetrations for criminal purposes. The problem is complicated by changes in organizational relations and technical architectures that make "inside" and "outside" more difficult even to define. The possibility that a terrorist or a terrorist sympathizer might gain employment that would enable him or her to conduct a devastating attack or to provide critical information or access to others cannot be discounted or ignored.

The two most general ways of dealing with infiltration are through deep preemployment investigations, something that most non-government entities are neither capable of doing nor permitted to do in many countries, and through stronger forms of containment and compartmentalization of access within an organization. Globalization has meant that the Internet is now less secure, with vulnerabilities resulting from new systems "intimacies". Transfer of information now takes place in unprecedented transnational contexts.

A particular problem for those who want to control or police the Internet is the spread and ownership of, and access to, transnational transportation infrastructures.

Much of the day to day running is outsourced, and offshoring (outsourcing to foreign entities) means that any attempts to control the Internet require international cooperation.

Terrorists in Cyberspace

What do we know or anticipate that terrorists want to do in cyberspace? I believe the answers to this question fall into three categories:

1. Terrorists want to support their activities and infrastructure, but not directly through an attack, using the Internet.

2. They may want explicitly to attack parts of the cyber infrastructure.
3. They may use cyberspace as a means of attacking other targets. These might include compromising transportation or other supervisory control systems to cause disasters resulting in extensive consternation and costing many lives.

It is certain that terrorists and their supporters have been engaging in extensive activities under category 1, and that they will continue to do so. This would cover communications, including encrypted communications with each other; recruiting and "advertising" (for example, via Web sites); and financial transactions such as money transfers and laundering. Training manuals for terrorists, including information about bomb-making and avoiding detection, are freely available. Terrorists are also likely to be scouring cyberspace for information on potential targets and on weapons of mass destruction.

As far as we can tell, terrorists have not been responsible for any of the major attacks or accidents that have occurred in recent years under categories 2 or 3. So much has been written about such possibilities—and they have had some prominence in the media—that it is inconceivable that terrorists are not aware of them. So far, for reasons we can only speculate about, they do not seem to have chosen to pursue these possibilities with vigor and effect, or perhaps they have tried and failed.

Systems and Networks at Risk

Should an attack be launched against systems and networks, the following would be at risk:

1. The Internet.
2. Embedded/real-time computing (e.g. avionics systems for air traffic control, SCADA systems used by the amenities, routing for shipping containers, and process control for toxic chemical production, switching of telecommunications, bank teller machines, floodgates).
3. Dedicated computing devices (e.g. desktop computers).

Each has a different role, and may be the subject of different kinds of attack. Terrorists might attack the Internet physically or "through the wires", the latter being potentially more destructive. One type of attack that we see is directed against Internet operations. Such attacks are often based on self-replicating programs (worms and viruses) that are transmitted from system to system, consuming prodigious amounts of router processing time and network channel bandwidth. In recent years, some of these worms and viruses have been transmitted without explicitly destructive payloads and yet have been able to disrupt key Internet backbone subnetworks for several days.

Another kind of attack on Internet operations seeks to corrupt the routing tables that determine how a packet should travel through the Internet. In both cases, the intent of the attack is to reduce the normally expected functionality of the Internet for some significant portion of its users—that is, a denial-of-service attack in intent, although not one necessarily based on flooding traffic. An attacker might also target the Internet's Domain Name System (DNS), which translates domain names (e.g. "example.com") to specific Internet Protocol (IP) addresses (e.g. 123.231.0.67) denoting specific Internet nodes.

A relatively small number of "root name servers" underpins the DNS. Although the DNS is designed to provide redundancy in case of accidental failure, it has some vulnerability to an attack that might target all name servers simultaneously. Although Internet operations would not halt instantly, an increasing number of sites would, over a period of time measured in hours to days, become inaccessible without root name servers to provide authoritative translation information. Physical replacement of damaged servers would be achievable in a matter of days, but changing the IP addresses of the root name servers would be more complicated.

Recommendations: Focus on Terrorists

It is only a matter of time before cyber terror attacks, at present largely a threat, become a reality. Both government and private sector need to focus on preparations. There are a number of measures that must be taken. Build Much Stronger Defenses, More Integrated Emergency Preparedness and Response Systems, and Improve the Processes for Their Use. The first order of business is to provide indications and warnings that an attack is taking place. This is a difficult area, and intrusion detection has become a particularly active area in research and development. Not surprisingly, detection and notification are more difficult and prone to false positives during the early stages of an attack, before significant damage has been done.

To prevent penetration of the system at risk from the outside, we try to erect barriers and otherwise harden it. Both cyber and physical approaches are necessary. Passwords are the oldest, and still most widely used, cybertechnique. More recent and somewhat widely used techniques are firewalls and proxy servers. Like all forms of cyberdefense, these can be defeated, although it is possible to make them real barriers against many attempted attacks. Physical protection needs to consider several forms of penetration or attempts to isolate the system. These include attacks on electronics using electromagnetic pulses, and attempts to cut cable endings. A wide variety of forms of physical protection are possible, ranging from fences to biometrics.

In the event of an attack there needs to be a system for incident management, mitigating an attack, and damage limitation. A next line of defense is internal compartmentalization and containment. In this instance, the goals are to limit penetration and damage, protect surviving assets, and protect and gather information to help with recovery and response after the attack. Approaches include creating internal physical barriers and cyberbarriers through compartmentalization and need-to-know access controls, intrusion tolerance schemes, setting up decoys, maintaining protected redundancies, and hiding assets. All have both static (pre-positioned and unchanging during the attack) and dynamic variants.

Another approach is automatic or partial shutdown and reallocation. A system that senses it is under attack would start erecting internal barriers that would not be tolerable during normal operations, in an attempt to isolate those parts of the system that had been compromised. It would also involve load-shedding strategies to reallocate surviving capabilities to the most important functions required by the organization. All of this amounts to various forms of real-time reassignment and reconfiguration under rapid degradation. Particular attention needs to be given to preserving and collecting information during an attack. This is done most easily if the attack has a clear and precise starting time and backups are made regularly, or if the organization maintains a redundant "shadow" system. More insidious attacks that build up slowly present a much more difficult problem in identifying a state where the system is free from inserted malicious code. It is also important to have strong audit functions to identify when an attack starts and to collect information that might assist in the identification and apprehension of the attacker and help the organization better defend itself against similar attacks in the future.

Organizations should establish security policies and plans for defending against attacks. Special attention should be given to preventing and dealing with insider attacks. Staff should know who to call for help. It might be a good idea to test the plan through the use of exercises. However, most organizations avoid live "fire drills" because they can be expensive, disruptive, and risky in their own right. Many information systems are delicate and their owners are afraid something will go wrong, resulting in the selfinflicted equivalent of a serious attack.

Improve the security of systems that control physical processes (e.g., SCADA).

From the standpoint of counter terrorism, we would imagine that attacking physical targets via control and management systems would result in the kind of mass casualties, damage, fear, and loss of confidence that terrorists favor. Many of these systems are vulnerable to tampering with control signals, especially by insiders.

Increasing the security for DC/SCADA systems poses particularly difficult problems. These systems are often small and self-contained, and have constrained power needs (including backup). Security may not readily fit with the space, real-time, or power requirements.

Security measures could also reduce performance or be problematic in the synchronization of other more extensive processes. Additionally, most of these systems are in the private or mixed sectors (for example, airports). Their owners and operators may not have sufficient resources to secure them more effectively. National governments that are in positions to do so should give priority to protecting the small percentage of cyberspace users who are private owners and operators of digital control and management systems.

This would include providing them with various forms of assistance and technology. Particular attention should be given to transportation systems because for decades they have been highly favored by terrorists both as targets and as the means of delivering an attack.

This kind of defensive work is essentially "target hardening". This can be defined as the use of various technologies and products and procedures (for example, those governing outside dial-in or reconstitution and recovery) to protect the information technology (IT) assets owned or operated by an individual or organization.

It is important to notice that many of these recommendations would have more general value than just vs. terrorists (e.g., they would help against accidents, natural disasters, serious crime, and non-terrorist forms of conflict). However, as defense does not involve serious risk or impose a penalty on the attacker, there is also the need to develop deterrents. For this we need laws:

Design and Implement a Stronger "System of Justice", Especially Its International Dimensions

International cooperation should concentrate on effective intelligence operations. This is an area where a considerable amount of success could be expected, which would create the atmosphere for a long-term international legal framework.

The problems of jurisdiction are greatly compounded by the easy transnational access provided by many components of cyberspace, most notably the Internet.

What may be perceived as serious in one country whose cyberinfrastructure may be used as part of a terrorist action may not even make the legal radar screen of others that are part of an attack that crosses multiple sovereign physical jurisdictions. Most countries have given little or no thought to making serious crimes of the various forms of cyberattack, and "without law there is no sin".

Seeking widely adopted national laws at least criminalizing attacks against or using the networks is an important objective. Legislating against the support functions to which terrorists put the Internet would be a more distant prospect. The enforcement and prosecution of these laws are also critical elements of cybersecurity.

Given the many technical and evidentiary problems of identifying cybercriminals and prosecuting them, nobody has any delusion that such laws would end criminal or terrorist activities in cyberspace. Nonetheless, they might reduce the enormous amount of malicious "noise" in cyberspace, and this would help make it easier to more readily identify more serious activities. They would also provide a necessary basis for encouraging people to report malicious cyberactivities, and for international cooperation in dealing with several kinds of problem.

CIIP at Every Stage

Security must become a criterion for any system used for CII from the design stage onwards. The priorities in design have been access and throughput. Added security is not just costly; it may also result in reduced efficiency and functionality. Furthermore, so far there does not seem to be much incentive for people to design or redesign systems to be much more secure.

There has been much speculation that the design or redesign of systems will occur only in the aftermath of a "digital Pearl Harbor" or in response to the forces of legal liability or insurance necessities and standards. Even better, security should be a factor to be considered over the entire life cycle of such systems. Organizations should build cadres of capable defenders, and contingency plans (including internationally) for crisis and emergency conditions need to be in place. There could be national-level CERTs or CSIRTs (Cybersecurity Incident Response Teams). A postdesign and implementation variant is to try to prevent attacks by finding and fixing vulnerabilities before an attacker can try to exploit them. Red teams, test beds, or simulations may be used to do this. Another approach, at least to the often-serious threat of possible insider attacks, is to more thoroughly screen employees with potentially sensitive access. It is clear that for a number of these measures operational contingencies among owners and operators and their governments need to be established.

EFFECT OF CYBER-ATTACKS ON STOCK PRICES

Thus far, reported cyber-attacks have been relatively limited in scope, and have not yet been on a scale that would have significant macroeconomic consequences. Individual firms, however, may have suffered significant losses as a result of past attacks. An examination of the effects of those attacks might be illuminating. Most estimates of the cost to companies of cyber-attacks are based on surveys. Survey responses are often expressed in such a wide range as to indicate considerable subjectivity and thus they may be of limited use. There may, however, be a more objective measure of the effect of cyber-attacks on individual firms.

In theory, the price of a company's stock is primarily determined by the present discounted value of the cash flows expected to result from that firm's output. That cash flow is what contributes to the wealth of the stockholders, either in the form of dividends or in the expansion of the firm's stock of productive capital. Any event that changes investors' expectations about that future stream of income is likely to affect the price of the stock.

Four recent studies have examined a number of actual cyber-attacks in an effort to see if any of those attacks could be linked to a change in the stock prices of the affected companies. In some cases, the studies attempted to measure if any stock-price effect depended on the different characteristics of either the firm or the attacks.

It seems at least intuitively obvious that some firms are more exposed to cyber-attacks than are others. It is conceivable that firm size may affect vulnerability to attack, but more to the point some firms are more dependent on computer networks than others to conduct business.1 Conventional firms, which have been referred to in this context as "brick and mortar" firms, might be expected to be the least vulnerable to cyber-attacks as they are the least dependent on the Internet to conduct business. Some firms, characterized as "click and mortar," conduct business both off-line and over the Internet. These firms face an increased vulnerability because of the risk that the business they conduct via the Internet might be interrupted.

Finally, there are firms whose business is conducted almost exclusively over the Internet. These firms would seem to be most at risk. The extent to which a business is affected might reasonably be expected to depend on the type of attack. Most attacks have fallen into one of two categories. The first is a "denial-of-service" attack (DoS). A DoS attack renders a firm's Internet portal inaccessible and interferes with its ability to conduct on-line business. For the most part, this kind of attack causes no lasting harm. The more serious category of attacks are those that involve the theft or destruction of secure information. This kind of security breach is more likely to have lasting effects on the targeted firm.

Other things being equal, the more dependent a firm is on the Internet, and the more intrusive an attack is, the more likely it is that any attack will have significant consequences for the financial health of that firm.

In contrast, firms that provide computer security might be expected to benefit from cyber-attacks (unless their products were publicly blamed for an attack's success). An increase in the apparent vulnerability of computer networks could be expected to raise future earnings of those companies and thus boost their stock price.

Cavusoglu, et. al., examined five specified hypotheses regarding the consequences of cyber-attacks. To do so, they identified 66 distinct security breaches that occurred between 1996 and 2001. Of those 66 events, 34 were availability (DoS) attacks. Of the 66 events, 31 affected firms whose business was conducted almost entirely over the Internet.

The attacks were divided into four distinct types: simple web site defacing; DoS; theft of credit card information; and theft of other customer information. In the case of web site defacing, the average loss in stock value was 2% on the second day, which rebounded somewhat to a 1.1% loss on the third day. DoS attacks resulted in a 2.9% drop on the second day, and a 3.6% decline on the third day. For attacks that compromise non-financial information, there was an average drop in stock value of 0.5% on the day of the attack, and a total decline of 1.5% on the third day.

Attacks which compromised financial information, chiefly credit card data, caused the largest declines. On the day of the attack, stock prices of affected firms fell a average of 9.3% and by the third day the decline reached 15%. The authors also found that there was a correlation between the number of credit cards that were compromised and the magnitude of the stock price hit.

All the studies found that there was a significant decline in stock prices of affected firms in the days immediately following a cyber-attack. The time frame is necessarily restricted in an effort to isolate the effects of the attack. To extend the time horizon would increase the likelihood that any variation in stock prices was due to other events. Therefore, the studies do not attempt to determine if there is any persistent change in stock prices, or if the drop in stock prices is temporary.

Two of the studies determined that the drop in stock price was related to the type of attack, with DoS attacks generally having a smaller effect than attacks which compromised confidential information. One of the studies found that there was no significant correlation between the kind of attack and the magnitude of the effect on stock prices. The fourth study found that the magnitude of the drop in price of stock was correlated with managers' assessments of the firm's exposure to the risk of cyber-attacks.

Cyber-Attack Costs

In 2003, the Computer Security Institute (CSI) and the Federal Bureau of Investigation (FBI) published their eighth annual survey on computer crime and security. Computer security practitioners in 530 U.S. corporations, financial institutions, government agencies (federal, state, and local), medical institutions, and universities provided information about their organizations' experience with computer crime over the previous year.

In 2003, 56% of respondents reported some unauthorized use of computer systems within the last 12 months. No such unauthorized use was reported by 29%, and 15% did not know. The 2003 data on the percentage of respondents reporting various types of misuse and attacks, and the expected dollar value of losses by type attack.

The distribution of losses by type of attack has not been consistent over the years that the survey has been conducted. In the 2000 survey, for example, theft of proprietary information was the most expensive type of attack, as it was in 2003. However, financial fraud accounted for 21.1% of all losses reported in 2000, as opposed to only 5.0% in 2003.

There is no consistent trend in total reported financial losses to computer crime It is likely that the results are skewed from year to year by a small number of relatively large loss reports. In addition, the number of respondents varies from year to year. The survey also presents data on the reported costs of individual attacks, with highest, lowest, and average values, by type of incident. For 2003, the lowest cost reports drop into the hundreds of dollars; the highest values range up to $35 million (theft of proprietary information) and $60 million (denial of service).

Besides the cost and frequency of attack data summarized here, the CSI/FBI surveys include information on incidents related to web sites, computer security practices, and the sources and methods of attacks.

What do the CSI/FBI survey results have to tell us about the overall costs of cyber-attacks in the United States? Unfortunately, not much. The survey's authors do not claim that their respondents are a representative sample of the businesses, organizations, and other entities that are exposed to cyber-risk. Survey recipients are not randomly chosen, but are self-selected from among security professionals. As a result, there is no rigorous, statistically sound method for extrapolating the loss reports of the 530 respondents to the national level.

Secondly, the cost data reported are incomplete even for the sample. As noted above, 15% of respondents to the 2003 survey did not know whether there had been unauthorized use of their systems. More significantly, while 75% of respondents reported financial losses, only 47% could quantify the losses. Thus, the figures in the charts above represent only measurable losses, and substantially understate total losses, though no one can specify the degree of understatement. Furthermore, if less than half of respondents reporting losses can put a dollar figure on those losses, the clear inference is that there is no standard technique for quantifying the amount of loss.

The survey does provide numerical support for a number of propositions that are generally accepted in the computer security literature: that insiders are the source of a substantial percentage of attacks; that many attacks are unreported; and that there is no simple, standardized method for quantifying the costs of cyber-attacks. Although limited as a statistical tool, the surveys usefully provide, in the authors' own words, "a series of snapshots of how the people in the trenches viewed their situation at a given time."

Measuring Costs

While organizations may have good reasons not to make public disclosures regarding security breaches, one would expect their incentives to measure the costs of such incidents internally to be strong. Without accurate cost data, how would organizations assess the cyber-risks they face, make rational decisions about how much to spend on information security, or evaluate the effectiveness of security efforts? In fact, there are no standard methods for measuring the costs of cyber-attacks. Attacks produce many kinds of costs, some of which cannot be quantified easily, if at all. As a result, there is a presumed gap in private, internal data that mirrors the absence of public data on cyber-attack costs.

The costs associated with cyber-attacks can be divided into direct and indirect costs. Direct costs include the expenses incurred in restoring a computer system to its original, pre-attack state. Recovery from an attack will typically require extra spending on labour and materials; these are the easiest costs to measure. But even at this basic level of cost accounting, complexities may arise. If an attack leads to increased spending on IT security, to what extent are those costs attributable to the attack? If a planned upgrade in hardware or software is accelerated after an attack, should the upgrade be classified as a security cost? Measurement of productivity loss is not always straightforward or uniform. Generally, this is not an added dollar cost: the workers are paid what they would have been paid anyway. Assigning a value to lost time depends on each individual organization's estimates of its own costs related to business opportunities forgone (during the disruption) or diversion of resources (during the recovery effort).

Another direct cost may involve the loss of value in information assets that are stolen, compromised, or otherwise degraded during an attack. Hoo summarizes the difficulties in measurement that may arise here:

The value of an information asset is highly dependent upon who possesses the information. Sensitive commercial R&D

information in the hands of a competitor is significantly more problematic than if it were in the hands of a Netherlands teenager. Time sensitivity can also complicate the valuation problem. For example, a password that expires in ten seconds is worthless after it has expired, but it is quite valuable during the ten seconds that it could be used to gain system access. Add to these difficulties the quantification challenges posed by intangible values, such as reputation, trust, embarrassment, etc., and the task of valuation quickly becomes a highly uncertain and potentially contentious enterprise.

Attacks also have indirect costs, which may continue to accrue after the immediate damage has been repaired. Many indirect costs flow from loss of reputation, or damage to a firm's brand. Customers may defect to competitors, financial markets may raise the firm's cost of capital, insurance costs may rise, and lawsuits may be filed. Some of these cost factors are readily quantifiable, but other aspects of loss of trust or confidence are intangible and difficult to measure.

Some analysts regard these indirect, intangible costs as more significant than direct costs. Cavusoglu, Cavusoglu, and Raghunathan conclude that the inability to measure intangible costs leads many firms to grossly underestimate the costs of security breaches, and that this explains why estimates of incident costs reported in the CSI/FBI survey are much lower than the price of an attack on a major company would be in terms of stock market capitalization.

Indirect costs of cyber-attacks may also include economic harm to individuals and institutions other than the immediate target of an attack. An attack on one firm's computer networks may affect other firms up and down the supply chain. When credit card data is hacked, or an internet service provider goes down, consumers suffer costs. From an accounting perspective, these do not count as costs to the target firm, but from a policy perspective they can be significant. The possibility of cascade effects–disruption spreading from computer to interlinked computer–is well-known, but we are far from being able to quantify the economic impact of an event of this type. To a profit-seeking business, measurement of costs already incurred is useful primarily to the extent that it facilitates prevention or mitigation of future losses. In the cyber-security field, as elsewhere, risk assessment is primarily a forward-looking activity. It is no less important or necessary because certain costs cannot be quantified.

IMPACTS OF INFORMATION AGE TECHNOLOGIES

To understand the future one needs to develop at least a broad conceptual understanding of the nature of the impacts that these technologies are likely to have. The impacts that these technologies are projected to have can be grouped into the following six areas.

First, the speed at which information can be transmitted, managed, manipulated, and interpreted will increase significantly. Information flows within and between organizations and among organizations and international actors will also accelerate, although at differing rates depending upon a host of factors. Increased speed will matter more for some uses than for others, and some international actors will benefit more from more rapid information flows than will others. But in general, the increased speed of information flow will increase the tempo of interactions within and between international actors.

Second, the capacity to transmit information will also increase significantly. Again, increased capacity will become available at different rates to different international actors. As with increased speed, greater information and communication capacity will benefit some organizations and international actors more than others. Here, however, the point to stress is that for many international actors, the ability to transmit and interpret greater amounts of information will mean that decision makers could have a greatly enhanced picture of the world, themselves, and others upon which to base their decisions.

Third, Information Age technologies will enhance the flexibility of information flows. Those needing information will be able to reach out and get it from more sources. Those needing to communicate with someone will find it ever more easy to do so quickly and directly. Put differently, these technologies will decrease the location-dependence of information and communication transactions. This greater flexibility will be available to some more quickly than to others, will matter more for some than for others, and will be embraced more quickly by some than by others.

Fourth, these technologies will provide more and more individuals greater access to more and more people, organizations, and information than ever before. This, some observers have argued, will lead to the democratization of information and communication flows throughout the world, that is, a decreased ability of a few (e.g. governments, businesses, and the other "haves") to dominate information and communication channels. This will free information from the hierarchy, or in the case of the military, from the chain of command. Although this may be true, improved access will not occur—or in some cases, be permitted—at the organizations, societies, and international actors.

None of these anticipated impacts means that time, distance, or location no longer matter—they still do. Indeed, as pointed out several times above, Information Age technologies will be absorbed, diffused, and operationalized by different international actors in different ways and at different speeds. This will lead to different types and rates of change in different international actors. Factors that will influence the way and rate in which advanced technologies will be absorbed, diffused, and operationalized include but are not limited to:

1. purchase and upkeep cost;
2. age and utility of in-place technology;
3. an actor's social and cultural receptivity to new technology;
4. degree of insularity within an actor;
5. level and reliability of an actor's human, technical, and economic support infrastructures;

6. level and strength of traditional values and outlooks within an actor;
7. levels of concern over sovereignty on the part of states, and over control of decision-making processes on the part of the actors; and
8. many political, social, and economic factors idiosyncratic to each actor and therefore impossible to detail.

Despite these constraints on adoption, Information Age technologies are indeed lessening the role that time, distance, and location play in human interactions. It is also noteworthy—and fraught with implications for national security—that this process is uneven and will create new "gaps" and a new power relationship among players on the world stage.

INFORMATION AGE

The Information Age (also known as the Computer Age, Digital Age, or New Media Age) is a period in human history characterized by the shift from traditional industry that theIndustrial Revolution brought through industrialization, to an economy based on information computerization. The onset of the Information Age is associated with the Digital Revolution, just as the Industrial Revolution marked the onset of the Industrial Age.

During the information age, the phenomenon is that the digital industry creates a knowledge-based society surrounded by a high-tech global economy that spans over its influence on how the manufacturing throughput and the service sector operate in an efficient and convenient way. In a commercialized society, the information industry is able to allow individuals to explore their personalized needs, therefore simplifying the procedure of making decisions for transactions and significantly lowering costs for both the producers and buyers. This is accepted overwhelmingly by participants throughout the entire economic activities for efficacypurposes, and new economic incentives would then be indigenously encouraged, such as theknowledge economy.

The Information Age formed by capitalizing on computer microminiaturization advances.This evolution of technology in daily life and social organization has led to the fact that the modernization of information and communication processes has become the driving force of social evolution.

Internet

The Internet was conceived as a fail-proof network that could connect computers together and be resistant to any single point of failure. It is said that the Internet cannot be totally destroyed in one event, and if large areas are disabled, the information is easily rerouted. It was created mainly by DARPA on work carried out by British scientists like Donald Davies; its initial software applications were e-mail and computer file transfer.

Though the Internet itself has existed since 1969, it was with the invention of the World Wide Web in 1989 by British scientist Tim Berners-Lee and its introduction in 1991 that the Internet became an easily accessible network. The Internet is now a global platform for accelerating the flow of information and is pushing many, if not most, older forms of media into obsolescence.

STRATEGIC IMPACT OF THE INFORMATION AGE

The arrival of the new millennium not only marks a milestone in the Christian calendar but also signals a technological watershed for mankind. This happens to be a coincidence, not planned by man or nature, yet it provides us with a rare occasion to pause and reflect.

The reason I say we are approaching a technological watershed is that many believe, and I agree, that we are passing from the industrial age to the information age, driven by rapid and remarkable advances in information and communication technologies. New products and services based on these advances are everywhere. Although they are not always visible to us as consumers, they have permeated our lives as if we were living in an infon-nation-communication ether.

Management of industrial R&D in the next 10- 15 years will be profoundly influenced by the all-connecting, all-pervading nature of this information-communication ether. The impact will be felt in many ways, some obvious, some not so obvious and some not yet foreseen. In my view, there are at least five significant impacts with strategic implications for R&D leaders in industry:

Shrinking Time and Distance

This is the most direct and obvious impact of the information-communication revolution. Members of an R&D project team can now be dispersed around the world yet work together around the clock as if they were next-door neighbors, thanks to innovations like videoconferencing and on-line meetings. Multi-site videoconferencing with high-fidelity document transfer is bringing together technology users and suppliers on short notice and overcoming the inconvenience of time zones. Real-time (or near real-time) on-line meetings involving many individuals from as many locations are becoming fairly routine.

Such cybermeetings are being organized and run just like traditional, face-to-face get-togethers. On-line brainstorming sessions are gaining particular popularity. In some companies, videoconferencing is being combined with simultaneous on-line meetings to provide a truly powerful tool. For example, British Petroleum technologists were reportedly able to see, analyze, diagnose, and solve equipment malfunction problems on off-shore oil-drilling equipment-from their comfortable offices and laboratories in England!

Lowering Cost and Increasing Output

In addition to saving travel expenses and time, R&D people everywhere are reducing activity cost and increasing work output through intelligent use of information and communication technologies. Computer-aided design tools, laboratory information management systems, molecular modeling techniques, process modeling and simulation exercises, and electronic submission of new drug applications (NDAs) to regulatory agencies are just a few examples. R&D and engineering managers are making use of computer-aided project management to reduce product development cycle time. And use of computers and robots in conjunction with statistical planning of experiments is reducing the amount of trial-and-error in R&D.

Enhancing Organizational Networking/Learning

Even five years ago, most individuals in an organization depended on face-to-face interactions to build linkages, share knowledge, and generate ideas. Telephone and paper exchange complemented these face-to-face interactions. Because of widespread availability and use of network-based tools and systems such as electronic mail, groupware, search engines, web crawlers, etc., organizational networking and knowledge-sharing have now become much easier and more widespread within (and outside) R&D. Thanks to Internet and e-mail, opportunities to access external information rapidly and communicate with individuals at distant places have multiplied by several orders of magnitude.

Secure Intranets (and Extranets) are not just opening doors to similarly rapid access and exchange internally (and externally with selected partners) but also creating computerized information archives as lasting knowledge legacies for R&D organizations. Push technologies are allowing individuals and groups to broadcast information to wide audiences yet reach targeted groups and individuals to meet their specified interests. Last but not least, distributed information systems are providing the opportunity for every user to become a provider as well. Thanks to such self-managed networks and systems, organizational knowledge is building up within companies at a rapid rate, without bureaucratic and costly involvement of librarians, screening agents ("gatekeepers"), or editors.

Bringing Technologies Together in Novel Ways

Because information and communication advances are able to find their ways into so many applications, they are proving to be catalysts for converging multiple technologies that create new products, new services, and even totally new markets and channels. Although early examples were seen in the 1970s (e.g., computerized axial tomography) and in the 1980s (e.g., video games, industrial robots, VCRs, etc.), the 1990s have witnessed a truly dramatic rise in the number of such innovations. Examples are all around us: video camera, ATM, PC-TV, digital phone, DVD, Internet and e-commerce, and the list goes on.

In BOC, for example, we have combined advanced telemetry systems (to remotely monitor levels of our liquified gas products in storage vessels at customer sites) and predictive modeling techniques (to forecast timing for fresh product supply) to schedule timely delivery and eliminate product "run out." Taking a cue from other industries, we have initiated use of "smart tags" to track movement of our gas cylinders within our operations and at our customers' sites. Our vacuum pumps and related products for the semiconductor industry have built-in networking and diagnostic/predictive capabilities—capabilities that were virtually unimaginable 10 years ago. Looking 10 years ahead, I can only see an explosive proliferation of intelligent devices and components ranging from smart refrigerators (e.g., recently announced by GE) to intelligent lawnmowers.

Blurring of Traditional Boundaries

Last but not least, the information—communication revolution is blurring, if not eliminating, many of the traditional boundaries to which we have grown accustomed. We are witnessing not only the shrinking of time and distance and the merging of multiple technology streams but also an increasing level of cross-functional and cross-organizational collaboration. While the harsh realities of globalization and competition may have driven most firms to promote internal and external collaboration, the widespread availability and use of information and communication tools and systems has clearly accelerated the phenomenon. It is no longer rare for a salesperson to interact with his R&D counterpart on a real-time basis to clinch a deal, or for R&D in one division to directly access market research done in another, or for a general manager to hook up to the company's Intranet to review the latest status of a new product development effort. Finding an expert across the globe to answer someone's burning question, without many frustrating phone calls, is now relatively easy in many companies. Employees, whether they are in R&D or Planning or Finance, can now log-in their ideas, technical and non-technical, on their company-wide network, get feedback from familiar as well as unfamiliar individuals and may even be able to secure management approval for exploratory efforts. Ideas no longer carry national or ethnic tags of origin as they can move across geographic and other boundaries almost instantaneously.

Probably the strongest indication of the move away from traditional functional mindsets is found in the new enterprise resource-planning (ERP) systems being rapidly adopted by large corporations everywhere. The modules and elements within these systems are designed around work processes, not traditional functional responsibilities and requirements.

Silently, invisibly and usually without fanfare, information and communication networks and systems are bringing together people from different organizations, backgrounds and responsibilities. Thus, the traditional organizational silos are slowly but surely being eroded to create a more integrated and efficient work environment. At ABB, for example, Percy Bernavik and his senior management team were able to run over 1,000 companies in more than 100 countries with a headquarters staff of only about 100!

Advice to R&D Leaders

In view of these significant impacts, how should R&D leaders in industry adjust their management strategies and processes as they approach the new millennium? The exact answer, as always, will depend on individual circumstances. With that in mind, I offer a few suggestions: There is no turning back for the forces unleashed by the information-communication revolution. We should, therefore, embrace and leverage them to the fullest for the benefit for our organizations. At the very least, we must take full advantage of the many time- and energy-saving features of information and communication advances to reduce cost of operation and increase output quality and quantity. However, we should not be satisfied with such a reactive and minimalist mindset. Instead, we must continually push toward a more proactive and expansive approach.

In almost every industrial firm, R&D was the first function to welcome and exploit "computing." Yet, with time, R&D seems to have fallen behind. The adoption of manufacturing and logistics planning systems (MRPs) and ERPs by other functions has positioned them as the more imaginative and influential proponents of information (and communication) technologies. R&D management should pursue aggressively every opportunity to utilize information and communication technologies to support and enhance all aspects of the innovation process.

One area in which R&D should be able to take a legitimate lead is "knowledge management" for the corporation. Knowledge management, of course, refers to an actively managed process of capturing, disseminating, leveraging, and enriching knowledge within an enterprise, both explicit knowledge that is documented and implicit knowledge that is embedded in the experience and expertise of its people in informal and unwritten forms. Technical know-how often forms the largest (and probably the most valuable) part of an organization's knowledge assets. For R&D to assume the leadership role in knowledge management would appear logical, provided R&D takes a broad-based, enterprise-wide approach and does not limit the scope to technical matters.

R&D leaders should not just recognize the phenomenon of multiple technology convergence but capitalize on it. They should proactively look for opportunities to marry information and/or communication technologies with advances in their own areas of interest and competence to create innovative products and services. If they do not, their competitors will do so and gain the advantage.

Blurring of traditional organizational boundaries gives R&D leaders the opportunity to establish truly close working relationships with Marketing, Manufacturing, Finance and the other key stakeholders in their companies. Additionally, R&D leaders should take advantage of this general trend and aggressively pursue and develop strategic collaborations with external sources of technology and innovation. In thus moving away from the traditional "make" model of R&D to the more balanced approach of "make or buy," R&D leaders will serve their organizations well in the future.

In conclusion, the new century will no doubt witness numerous innovations, and some will probably be more breathtaking than even the most spectacular innovations of the 20th century. R&D managers will certainly play critical roles in bringing about many of these innovations. Advances in information and communication technologies will provide invaluable support to future generations of R&D managers, especially those who aggressively institutionalize timely absorption and exploitation of such advances.

THE IW IMPACT ON MILITARY ORGANIZATIONAL STRUCTURE

Wars during the industrial age have had military structures determined by the "firepower casualty system" base, but wars in the information age will require an "information-based" troop organization. With a changed base, the military system establishment will also be bound to change significantly.

Alvin Toffler noted recently that in the information age, "as the winning of wars will rely on military quality, not quantity, the military will shrink in size." Therefore IW in a certain sense is "precision warfare," with objectives achievable without using large amounts of troops or arms.

The military makeup will change. To adapt to IW needs, changes in military makeup will experience the following trends: In the balance of army, naval and air force might, the ratio of army troops will decline, while that of naval and air force troops will grow; in support units, technical support will grow, while logistics support will decline; in the officer-to-men ration, there will be more officers and less men; in the officer makeup, there will be more technical officers and less commanding and ordinary staff officers. Also, there are likely to be new service arms such as a space force and computer soldiers.

The unit establishment will tend to be smaller, more integrated, and more multifunctional. While Western nations have not yet determined the IW unit establishment, they hold that these units will have the following features: "The best combination of men and machines," with quality personnel and high-tech arms both being as efficient as possible; flexible mobility suited to command, control, and information flow; light equipment that is easy to deploy; high combat effectiveness, fewer command levels, multifunctional commanders, and crack commanding organs.

There are two implications for smaller units. 1) Unit might at all levels will be smaller. For instance, U.S. Army divisions will be cut from 18,000 to 12,000 troops each, with British and French Army divisions likely to be reduced from 12,000 to under 10,000 troops each; 2) The status and role of units at all levels will be obviously higher. For instance, the U.S. military plans to raise the role of the army in campaign planning to the group army level, replacing the division with the brigade as the basic tactical operations unit equipped with all sorts of combat and support platoons. The Russian military is also planning to institute an "army brigade system." The factors in the appearance of such a situation include higher-quality officers and men, weaponry advances, and robot-equipped units.

Unit integration means that composite units will reach new heights, with a transition from composite service arms to composite armed forces. For instance, the U.S. military is considering the establishment of two units, one being a composite army-air force unit the "flying tank" or "air mechanized unit," and the other a land, sea and air "joint task force." This latter unit will be made up of an army brigade task force, an air force fighter squadron, a naval fleet unit, and a marine expedition platoon, suited to countering low-force conflicts and breakouts overseas. Multifunctional units will mean that units at all levels will have to fulfill diverse combat missions in wars on all combat terms and all degrees of force, including "noncombat operations." Meanwhile, army, navy, and air force combat units are also likely to break the traditional service arm operating limits, and perform the combat operations of other service arms. For instance, land units will fight naval and air battles, with naval and air force units fighting land battles. Therefore, some Western military experts predict that as units diversify, unit establishment categories will decrease.

The IW Impact on Organizational Structure

Because of the "effects" of IW and military spending shortages, developed nations are adopting an equipment establishment policy of "more research and new technology, and less production and arms purchases." To implement this policy, they are taking three steps:

- Terminating and adjusting preset unit development projects and purchase plans. For instance, the United States has eliminated over 150 arms production plans, and delayed over 20 equipment purchase plans; Germany has eliminated and postponed over 40 arms purchase plans.
- Increasing their research input. In the past decade, the defense research outlays of Japan, the United States, France, and Germany have increased, respectively, by 120 percent, 67 percent, 66 percent, and 56 percent. Most of this outlay is going to develop the "crucial technologies" of smart ammunition, smart weapons platforms, and the C3I system.
- Upgrading their existing weapons. While the Western nations are slowing their rate of production of new weapons, they are paying more attention to the use of electronic information technology to modernize and upgrade their existing equipment. For instance, the U.S. Air force is planning to upgrade its B-52 bombers by outfitting them with high-tech systems such as new

radar, global positioning systems, and cruise missile launching units, to keep them in service until the year 2000.

To be able to fight IW in the next century, developed nations such as the United States will place priority on the development of equipment such as the C4I system (command, control, communications, computers, and intelligence system), personal digitized equipment, and stealth weapons.

RECOMMENDATIONS

The Army should serve as a proving ground for CO and EW effects convergence due to several factors that minimize the friction to achieve effects convergence. These advantages include established doctrine converging CO and EW, unity of command at the force proponent level for CO and EW career fields and combined research and development efforts in these fields. In February 2014, the Army published FM 3-38 *Cyber Electromagnetic Activities.* This document provides doctrinal guidance and conducting cyber electromagnetic activities (CEMA) and the procedures and tactics for commanders and their staffs for planning, synchronizing and integrating CEMA. Due to the Army's recent creation of both the Electronic Warfare Branch (29) and Cyber Branch (17), it is in a unique position to develop the force structures, capabilities and tools for converged CO and EW operations and effects. Both branches also currently fall under the Cyber Center of Excellence, the force modernization proponent (FMP) for cyberspace operations, signal/communications networks and information services, and Electronic Warfare. Furthermore, a single organization, the Army's Intelligence and Information Warfare Directorate (I2WD) of the Communications-Electronic Research, Development and Engineering Center (CERDEC) is responsible for research and development of both offensive cyber operations and electronic warfare. While the Army has several advantages in being a proving ground for CO and EW effects convergence, it must leverage the knowledge and capabilities of the Air Force and Navy EW communities to tap into their wealth of experience. Lessons learned and successful pilot programs from the Army's efforts on CO and EW effects convergence can then be introduced to Air Force and Navy CO and EW communities to accelerate the introduction of new techniques and operating concepts.

Additionally each Service should embrace the Marine Corps approach towards integrating CO and EW effects. The Marine Corps approach for integrating CO and EW effects focuses on the creation of a Cyber Electronic Warfare Coordination Center (CEWCC). The CEWCC is placed within a Marine Air-Ground Task Force (MAGTF) to synchronize Spectrum Warfare (SW) with a "combined arms concept for the integration of cyberspace operations, electronic warfare (EW), signals intelligence (SIGINT), spectrum management operations, and technical Information operations with conventional fires and maneuver". The CEWCC is a distributed organization, which will include members and liaisons from the fields of information operations, electronic warfare, cyberspace operations and spectrum management. While still in development, the Marine Corps is aggressively developing the CEWCC concept with an interim publication and ongoing proof of concept within the 13th Marine Expeditionary Unit. The concept of SW, which focuses on the relationships within cyberspace and the electromagnetic spectrum, provides a good framework for the integration of cyberspace operations and electronic warfare.

Counterargument

Convergence of CO and EW effects will reduce the ability of commanders to employ offensive EW capabilities given national level approval is required to conduct OCO. In contrast, employment of offensive EW, or EA capabilities typically requires approval only at the operational or tactical level. Commanders with EA assets are able to rapidly impact an adversary's radio communications network through jamming of the links or use of directed energy weapons to destroy the transmitters. The use of OCO to produce the same effect of denying the enemy use of the radio communications network would require "careful planning, in-depth intelligence support, and interagency coordination" in addition to national level approval. Convergence of OCO and EA has the potential of denying commanders the use of an effective, rapidly employable capability by tying a capability that requires only tactical or operational level approval to one that requires national level approval.

Convergence of CO and EW effects will further limit the resources available for EW given the near insatiable demand for resources to develop OCO capabilities, conduct DCO and operate the DODIN. EW capabilities are employed primarily during Phase 2: Seize the Initiative of the continuum of military operations. Conversely CO are employed during all phases of the continuum of military operations, which helps account for the high level of resourcing invested in CO capabilities.

Given the Army's nascent CO and EW capabilities and experience, it is a poor choice to serve as a proving ground for CO and EW effects convergence. Even successful CO and EW effects convergence pilot programs in the Army will be difficult to transition to the Air Force and Navy with fundamentally different requirements for the employment of employment and desired effects of CO and EW effects. Additionally, given the current budget constrained environment and heightened threat level, resources should be focused on enhancing current capabilities instead of investing in unproven concepts.

4

Technology in Network-Centric Warfare

The technology supporting NCW is inherently complex, but not significantly moreso than the technology used to digitise and network the civilian world. It must however be more resilient physically, thermally, electrically and be better resistent to hostile penetration, and in wireless systems, hostile jamming.

The prerequisite for an NCW capability is the digitisation of combat platforms. A combat aircraft with a digital weapon system can be seamlessly integrated in an NCW environment by providing digital wireless connections to other platforms. Without the digital weapon system, and its internal computers, NCW is not implementable. The growing gap between the US military and the EU military largely reflects the Europeans' reluctance to heavily invest in digitising their combat platforms.

Provision of digital wireless connectivity between combat platforms is a major technical challenge which cannot be understated. While civilian networking of computers can largely rely on cabled links, be they copper or optical fibres, with wireless connectivity as an adjunct, in a military environment centred in moving platforms and field deployed basing, wireless connectivity is the central means of carrying information.

The problems faced in providing military networking are generally well understood, but often push the boundaries of available technology. Key issues can be summarised thus:

1. Security of transmission. Since everybody does their best to eavesdrop, digital links have to be difficult to eavesdrop, and robustly encrypted to defeat any eavesdropping which might succeed. Even if a signal cannot be successfully decrypted, its detection provides an opponent with valuable information on the presence, position and often activity of the platform or unit in question.
2. Robustness of transmission. In the face of transmission impairments such as solar flares, bad weather and hostile jamming, networks must continue to function. If a signal cannot penetrate a rainshower or is blotted out by an opponent's barrage jammer, the link is broken and the NCW model also breaks.
3. Transmission capacity. How fast data can be transmitted is vital, especially where digitised imagery must be sent. If a 10 Megabyte recce image must be sent, or a 2 Megabit/sec digitised video feed observed, a 9600 bit/sec channel will be nearly useless. A popular misconception is that digital data compression solves this problem - the reality of Shannon's communication theory is very much at odds with this popular (in some Canberra circles) fantasy. Robustness against jamming and the overheads of encryption both function at the expense of transmission channel capacity for a given radio communications link - the robust the link, the more capacity is soaked up with overheads to protect it.
4. Message and signal routing. Platforms must be able to specifically address and access other platforms or systems in an NCW environment. Just as email on a civilian network must have an address, so must a military messaging scheme. Such addressing must be able to cope with a fluid network topology, as platforms entre and leave an area of operations.
5. Signal format and communications protocol compatibility. It is essential that dissimilar platforms

and systems can communicate in an NCW environment. This problem extends not only to the use of disparate signal modulations and digital protocols, but to the use of partially incompatible implementations of what is ostensibly the same signal modulation or communications protocol. The mutual incompatibility headaches we see in commercial computing are often more traumatic in the challenging military environment.

At the time of writing nearly all military datalinks used in NCW operate at speeds which would be considered intolerable in the civilian/commercial world, reflecting the realities of wireless communications.

Moreover, the military world lives with a veritable Tower of Babel in both signal modulations, operating frequencies and digital communications protocols, and variations of nominally standard protocols.

To contextualise this, Western armed forces currently deploy systems using a wide range of current and legacy signal formats and protocols, examples being:

1. Link 1 at 1200/2400 bits per second used for air defence systems, devised in the 1950s.
2. TADIL A / Link-11/11B at 1364 bits per second used for naval links and ground based SAM systems, using original CLEW DQPSK modulation, or newer FTBCB convolutional coding at 1800 bits per second. It is 1960s technology.
3. TADIL C / Link-4 at 5,000 bits per second in the UHF band, used for naval aviation, AEW&C to fighter links, and fighter to fighter links on the F-14 series. It is also 1960s technology.
4. Link-14 used for HF transmission between naval combatants at low data rates.
5. TADIL J / MIDS/JTIDS / Link-16 which is a jam resistant L-band time division Spread Spectrum Multiple Access (SSMA)system based on 1970s technology. While its time slot model permits some allocation of capacity, in

practical terms it is limited to kilobits/sec data rates, over distances of about 250 nautical miles. JTIDS is multi-platform and multi-service and widely used for transmitting tactical position data, directives, advisories, and for defacto Identification Friend Foe. Its limitation is that it is ill suited to sending reconnaissance imagery and inherently tied to master stations which generate its timebase - reflecting its origins of three decades ago. Satellite link and higher data rate derivatives exist but retain the basic limitations of its time division technique.

6. CDL/TCDL/HIDL/ABIT which are US high speed datalinks design primarily for satellite and UAV transmission of imagery. CDL family links are typically assymetric, using a 200 kilobit/s uplink for control and management, and a 10.71, 45, 137 or 234 Megabit/s high speed uplink, and a specialised for the control of satellite/UAVs and receipt of gathered data. ABIT is a development of CDL operating at 548 Megabits/s with low probability of intercept capabilities.
7. Improved Data Modem (IDM) is used over Have Quick II spread spectrum radios to provide low data rate but secure transmission of targeting coordinates and imagery. It has been used widely for transmission of targeting data to F-15E/F-16C strike fighters and F-16CJ Wild Weasels. It is essentially an analogue to commercial voiceband modems.
8. Army Tactical Data Link 1 - ATDL 1 used for US Army Hawk and Patriot SAM batteries.
9. PATRIOT Digital Information Link - PADIL used by Patriot SAM batteries.
10. Tactical Information Broadcast System - TIBS used for theatre missile defence systems.
11. PLRS/EPLRS/SADL are a family of US Army/Marine Corps datalinks used for tracking ground force units, and providing defacto Identification Friend Foe of ground units. EPRLs is also used for data transmission between ground units.

12. TCP/IP (Internet) protocol implementations running over other channels, to provide connectivity between platforms and remote ground facilities.
13. Joint Tactical Radio System (JTRS), intended to supplant most legacy protocols with networking equipment which can communicate both in legacy prototols and modulations, and its own JTRS protocols and modulations. The JTRS Wideband Netwroking Waveform (WNW) is to provide multi-Megabit/s throughput.

This veritable menagerie of datalink modulations/protocols is by no means exhaustive, but reflects the realities observed in the computer industry in the decades predating the Internet.

New protocols like the Joint Tactical Radio System (JTRS) are in part intended to incorporate mechanisms for translating such legacy protocols into formats which can be sent over a common channel. Separate from these multi-platform protocols and modulations are the type specific datalinks, such as the intra- and interflight datalinks used on the F/A-22A and later the JSF.

As yet there has been little effort to capitalise on the new technology of ad hoc network protocols, designed for self organising networks of mobile platforms, although the JTRS WNW effort looks promising. The DARPA GLOMO program in the late 1980s saw considerable seed money invested, but did not yield any publicised dramatic breakthroughs. Ad hoc networking remains a yet to be fully explored frontier in the networking domain, one which is apt to provide a decisive technology breakthrough for NCW.

The technological issues in NCW often dominate the debate at the expense of the deeper philosophical and functional issues which is unfortunate, since both domains matter and getting either wrong results in an equally disfunctional end result.

NCW and Australia

In Australia networking has been very much in the limelight of the defence debate. Sadly, it has also been used to justify a great many dubious decisions, all predicated on premises which do not hold.

Like most intellectually demanding and complex systems problems, NCW must be properly understood before it can be used as a basis for strategic planning decisions. Clearly this has not been the case in many key areas of the DoD, resulting in public statements which would be comical were not the circumstances so dire. Perhaps the best exposition of this problem lies in the package of submissions presented earlier this year to the JSCFADT committee of Federal Parliament, especially the Air Combat Capability paper.

In this document we learn that networking can substitute for combat fleet numbers, despite the contrary experience in Afghanistan and Iraq, where aircraft size became the pivotal issue. We also learn that the combat effect of the system should exceed the sum of its parts despite the contrary mathematics underpinning this problem. Limitations in the F/A-18A and JSF we learn do not matter, since Australia will evidently have an asymmetric advantage in networking and AEW&C, despite regional buys of Russian/Israeli A-50 AWACS, and Russian marketing of TKS-2 digital datalinks on Su-30 fighters. We also learn in this document that AEW&C aircraft and networks will not be challenged, as evidently Russian R-172, Kh-31 and R-37 missiles, or high power jammers, will never be used in the region - regional buys notwithstanding. No differently, Australia need not invest in high power jamming aircraft since other nations will never use their AEW&C and networking systems. We also learn that five A330-200 tankers will improve the RAAF's combat persistence, since evidently the fuel carried in F-111s need not be counted. No less surprisingly we also discover that the mere AU$20M to 30M required to put networking into the F-111s is unusually expensive and not worth doing - evidently it is better to kill off the aircraft than invest into networking it.

The ugly reality is that networking has become a cure all panacea in the DoD bureacratic machine, one which can magically offset all force structure limitations, and one which magically only Australia can possess and use properly in the Pacrim.

The analytical perspective is very different, however. Most regional nations are now operating, deploying or shopping for AEW&C aircraft. Russia is actively marketing digital datalinks, like the TKS-2 and older APD-518, and marketing counter-ISR weapons like the Novator R-172 (KS-172) or Kh-31 series missiles. Russia is also marketing high power jamming equipment, especially pods using Digital RF Memory (DRFM) technology, and there is a good prospect of a Growler-ski based on the Su-32 materialising before the end of the decade.

In practical terms, by 2010-2015 regional opponents without AEW&C, long range counter-ISR missiles and jamming pods are likely to be the obliging exception to the rule. US thinking is not surprisingly centred in using F/A-22As to sanitise airspace permitting unhindered use of ISR platforms and networks, and the program to replace the lost capabilities of the EF-111A Raven with the B-52J or EB-52, equipped with high power stand-off jamming equipment to disrupt opposing networks and ISR sensors. The reality we observe regionally and globally is, like the physics and mathematics which apply to the network problem, very different to the interpretation of these issues which we observe in the confines of Russell Offices. The Departmental leadership have effectively committed Australia to major strategic decisions, like the JSF program and F-111 retirement, on the basis of beliefs which are simply not supportable by fact. That a major fraction of virtually every public document dealing with the JSF and F-111 issues is dedicated to extolling the virtues of NCW is evidence in its own right.

The sad conclusion is that this emotive rather than rational approach to NCW amounts to little more than a doctrinal and strategic heresy, one which will no doubt vanish into oblivion no differently than the enthusiasm for the 'Revolution in Military Affairs' did some years ago. Until that much awaited day comes, damage will continue to be done to Australia's basic capabilities.

NETWORK CENTRIC WARFARE

The Army is intent on enhancing its awareness of a more complex contemporary battlefield environment by expanding the amount of information available to commanders, staffs and soldiers. To significantly enhance the ability to truly "see" the battle the Army must transform its orientation from Platform Centric Warfare to Network Centric Warfare. In other words, the Army must shift from having the best technology and information needed to fight as an aggregate of separate, individual combat entities, working on their own with the big picture seen only by the senior commanders and move to fighting as a highly networked and integrated system, where each combat element shares information with all other combat systems.

Platform Centric Warfare has historically been the manner in which warfare has been conducted over the last 80 years. The US military has fought each armed conflict since WWII using this concept. It is known as the classic American Way of War, leading to a battle of attrition. This method of warfare employs stand-alone components to provide overwhelming fire power and superior maneuver to seizing the initiative, while fixing, closing and ultimately destroying the enemy.

Warfare of this type is heavily dependant on weaponry platforms to win frontal attrition-style wars. Platform centric warfare depends on a decisive battle, or series of decision battles, of a force-on-force type scenario. The tank, armored personnel carrier, helicopter, and artillery piece are all examples of conventional platforms that support platform centric warfare. Although this type warfare may employ limited digitalization, it is far from the sophistication expected in the network centric environment.

"In contrast, Network Centric Warfare is an information superiority-enabled concept of operations that generates increased combat power by networking sensors, decision makers, and shooters to achieve shared awareness, increased speed of command, higher tempo of operations, greater lethality, increased survivability, and a degree of self-synchronization. In essence, Network Centric Warfare translates information superiority to combat power by effectively linking knowledgeable entities in the battlespace." The basic definition of Network Centric Warfare is the introduction of new technologies and the exploration of a concept of effects-based warfare is the search for greater combat efficiency. The underlying intent of this form of warfare is to reduce the amount of military power needed to complete the mission. The "bright spot" in Network Centric Warfare is the potential to generate to improved combat efficiency.

The Army today is committed to transforming itself while winning the Global War on Terrorism as it is currently being waged —- in both symmetric and asymmetric environments.

For an era in which there are few conventional threats facing the country, the challenge of fighting enemies in asymmetric warfare demands new ways of thinking. Preparing for the future will require the U.S. military to rethink and develop the kind of forces and capabilities that can adapt quickly to new challenges and circumstances. The most combat engagements are being fought largely against groups of individuals. This is evident as the U.S. continues to takes down the Taliban and rolls up the Al Qaida network.

The world is changing and so are our adversaries. They respect the superior combat power of the U.S. military forces and have changed their modus operandi. Current and possible future enemies appear to be fanatically committed to their political and religious ideologies.

They will employ strategies to destroy U.S. resolve by attacking our homeland, killing innocent civilians, and conducting prolonged operations. Our adversaries will immerse themselves in our culture and attack at a time and place of their choosing to create maximum fear in Americans and coalition partners.

This paper will address the Army's expected dependence on Network Centric Warfare to defeat the perpetrators of asymmetric warfare. This paper will also analyze network centric warfare as the replacement for platform centric warfare. Further, it will examine factors associated with sensors, bandwidth, cyberterrorist and Electro-Magnetic Pulse (EMP).

Moving the Army from Platform Centric Warfare to Network Centric Warfare is a major tenet of the Army's Transformation process. In fact, the centerpiece of the Army's Transformation is the change to Network Centric Warfare. It is important to briefly examine platform centric warfare in greater detail to set the stage for a more in-depth discussion of network centric warfare and it's potential.

Platform Centric Warfare

The US Army has the most feared, sophisticated, and lethal armored vehicles in the world. The Abrams Tank and Bradley Fighting Vehicle moving at high rates of speed across the desert, brings fear to the US adversaries. The implementation of these platforms have been so successful, the enemies do not get themselves into a position where they are forced to engage US armored vehicles in the open desert. Although the Army has successfully used Platform Centric Warfare for many years, there are several problems with relying on them in future military operations. It is difficult to rapidly deploy these traditionally large platforms. The US Army has not successfully automated the platform utilizing modern technology across the entire force. Stovepiping of information presents information sharing between systems. Finally, bandwidth constraints have limited information sharing using existing technologies. These four key issues will be examined as they reveal limitations in the current Platform Centric Warfare approach and the need to pursue an alternative conceptual framework.

Deployability

Present platforms are difficult to deploy quickly due to size, weight, and the sheer numbers required to accomplish most missions. Peter Drucker, a strategic management and leadership guru has observed that, "We have tried to substitute mass of purpose. We have tried to regain military potency of defence by making it gigantic, unwieldy, and complex. It never works". Warfare of this type is heavily dependant on weaponry platforms to win frontal attrition- style wars. The Abrams M-1 tank weighs 70 tons and the M-2 Bradley Fighting Vehicle (armor personnel carrier) weighs 32 tons, which make both platforms difficult to move rapidly in a crisis situation. The logistical requirements for the two platforms like fuel, ammunition, and repair parts are massive. "All our combat power is useless if we cannot get it to the theater in time or maneuver it tactically," Major General James Dubik, the head of the experimental force at Fort Lewis, pointed out. "Right now our heavy forces have limited strategic deployability and our light forces have limited tactical utility. Transformation will take care of that disconnect." It requires up to 650 sorties of C-5s and C-17s to move one light division. Former Chief of Staff of the Army General Shinseki said, "there is general recognition that the US Army is too heavy and will arrive too late to affect the difference." The system designer's challenge is to develop systems that have similar killing power and survivability with a quarter of the weight.

DEFINITION OF NETWORK CENTRIC WARFARE

NCW is the embodiment of an "Information Age" transformation of the United States Department of Defence and all the elements that support it. NCW represents a set of war fighting concepts and associated military capabilities that allow warfighters to take full advantage of all available information and bring all available assets to bear in a rapid and flexible manner. NCW is based on the following tenets:

- A robustly networked force improves information sharing,
- Information sharing enhances the quality of information and shared situational awareness,
- Shared situational awareness enables collaboration and self-synchronization, and enhances sustainability and speed of command,

Interoperability Frameworks

NCOIC streamlines systems for the elimination of interoperability issues to reduce operating costs for more effective direction of organizational resources.

Key deliverables

Systems, Capabilities, Operations, Programs, & Enterprises (SCOPE) Model

- The SCOPE interoperability assessment model is designed to characterize interoperability-relevant aspects or capabilities of a system or set of systems over a network in terms of a set of dimensions and values along those dimensions.

NCOIC Interoperability Framework (NIF)

- The NIF is a development framework that helps system architects and system engineers to embed interoperability elements throughout the life cycle of programs, beginning with requirements. Whenever possible, those resources are based upon standards.

Net Centric Patterns

- NCOIC Net Centric Patterns contain prescriptive recommendations on approaches and standards in specific interoperability domains.

Network Centric Analysis Tool (NCAT)

- NCAT is a collaborative, web-enabled questionnaire-based tool developed to assist NCOIC teams and member companies to enhance the likelihood and reduce the time and effort of member companies developing interoperable systems consistent with customers' policies and guidelines, reference models and architectures. It is also available in an excel format.

NCOIC Lexicon

- The Lexicon defines terms and expressions that are relevant to texts published by the NCOIC. This material is offered for dynamic debate, discussion and additional submissions in this online wiki. NCOIC Lexicon Custodian Working Group periodically reviews the wiki, and publishes updates of the consensed catalogue, including comments for entries that have been deleted.

NCOIC internal structure

Functional teams

Functional Teams (FTs) implement the technical roadmap of the Consortium by focusing on specific technical elements that lead to netcentricity. The teams and their associated working groups are coordinated through a Technical Council, composed of the leaders of each Functional Team.

NIF Architecture Concepts FT

- Manages the development of the NCOIC's Interoperability Framework (NIF) and champions its use within the consortium. The NIF provides the framework through which the NCOIC will publish its prescribed use of standards and patterns in specific domains and describes the relationships between the individual Specialized Frameworks.

Specialized Frameworks FT

- Hosts and encourages the development, approval, and publication of specialized Frameworks and Patterns that contain guidelines and standards recommendations for the broad range of domains that are of interest to NCOIC members and their customers.

Building Blocks FT

- Provides a catalog of products for use by government and commercial systems engineers, which meet NCOIC criteria for the support of network centric operations requirements, network centric environments and industry standards.

Netcentric Assessment FT

- Defines, identifies, establishes and assembles the necessary criteria for measuring and assessing network centricity and network enablement in all the relevant forms.

System Engineering & Integration FT

- Helps to integrate the efforts and promote the deliverables of NCOIC Functional Teams for the accomplishment of NCOIC goals.

Integrated Project Teams

Integrated Project Teams (IPTs) serve as domain specific customer teams, who work with global NCO stakeholders in solving their interoperability problems.

The IPTs harness the expertise of the Technical Functional Teams in utilizing NCOIC tools and best practices to provide customers with the appropriate guidance to achieve their netcentric missions.

The IPTs thereby validate and refine NCOIC approaches in collaboration with customers.

Net Enabled Emergency Response IPT (NEER)

- The NEER IPT will recommend net-enabled solutions needed to bridge the gaps among the diverse organizations that need to come together to provide emergency response for day-to-day emergencies as well as for complex humanitarian disasters (CHD).

C3 Interoperability IPT

- Facilitates inter-operation and overarching coordination of the military, civil-military and civil C2-environment", promoting interoperability to achieve Situational Awareness and effective decision-making based on standards and best practices.

Sense & Respond Logistics IPT

- Provides a forum for defence and commercial stakeholders of Logistics Communities of Interest (COIs) to identify and coordinate solutions to obstacles to achieving net-centric interoperability by leveraging NCOIC solutions.

Aviation IPT

- Advocates global aviation transformation through net-centric solutions. The IPT supports this mission through industry best practices and tools to advise the use of existing and emerging standards and their patterns in support of global aviation needs.

Maritime Awareness IPT

- Establishes shared understanding of the net-centric aspects of Maritime Awareness. Advocates the enhancement of Maritime Awareness through application of net-centric concepts and technologies.

TRADITIONAL METHODS OF WARFARE

The main instruments initially used by these agencies were the printed pamphlets, the radio and books. The CIA set up two radio stations in Munich, called Radio Free Europe and Radio Liberty, to broadcast to the communist countries. The Voice of America, which is controlled by the State Department and not by the CIA, worked in concert with the CIA stations of Munich. The MI6 continued to rely on the BBC. Another technique widely used during the Cold War was the co-opting of journalists, authors and publishing houses to help the intelligence agencies.

One would recall the large number of baseless reports regarding India granting base facilities to the Soviet Navy in Vizag and in the Andaman & Nicobar disseminated by the US and UK news agencies and newspapers during the prime ministership of Mrs.Indira Gandhi. Another baseless report disseminated by Western journalists was that experts of the KGB, the intelligence agency of the erstwhile USSR, were attached as advisers to the late Gen.Sunderji during Operation Blue Star of 1984. These reports stopped circulating as mysteriously as they had started after her assassination in 1984.

Following disclosures in the media, the John Major Government of the UK admitted in 1995 that a number of

British authors, whose anti-communist books had become best-sellers during the Cold War, had been co-operating with the External Publicity Division of the British Foreign Office. Their co-operation was, in fact, with the MI6. How did their books become best-sellers? The MI6 encouraged publishing houses under its influence to publish their books, persuaded book reviewers to review their books favourably, bought thousands of copies of these books and had them smuggled into the communist countries and gave them free of cost to book-sellers of Third World countries co-operating with the MI6.

This period also saw the mushrooming, with funds allegedly provided by the CIA, of a large number of private radio stations in South-East Asia. Many of these radio stations, which were run by Christian organisations, were anti-communist and anti-socialist in the contents of their programmes. Another technique, perfected during the Cold War and still used, was the co-opting of policy and decision makers as well as academics and other sections of the elite of the Third World countries by arranging invitations for travel to West Europe and the US, either for research or for participation in seminars, helping individuals in these countries to float think-tanks and non-governmental organisations (NGOs) and arranging funds for them.

The funds were arranged through cut-outs of Western universities, academics and NGOs. The indirect funding of the so-called Track 2 diplomacy gatherings is another psywar technique of recent origin. Amongst well-known NGOs, which in the past had allegedly been in receipt of funds from intelligence agencies, were the Amnesty International of the UK and the International Commission of Jurists (ICJ) of Geneva. The Amnesty International was allegedly in receipt of funds from the Harold Wilson Government in return for its playing down allegations of human rights violations by the British Security forces in Aden and Rhodesia (now Zimbabwe) and the ICJ was allegedly in receipt of funds from private lawyers' organisations in the US, whose contributions to the ICJ were re-imbursed to them by the CIA. Following disclosures to the British media by a secretary of the Amnesty, the Wilson

Government had admitted its links with the organisation and the CIA's alleged contributions to the ICJ through private lawyers' organisations came to notice during the post-Watergate enquiries into the functioning of the CIA and the FBI.

Use of The TV

The TV came on its own as an instrument of perception-management in the 1960s. The role played by the visuals from Vietnam disseminated by the anti-war groups in the West in turning public opinion against the war brought home to the Western agencies the importance of manipulating this medium. TV Marti, the TV station of the CIA, started telecasting programmes to the Cuban people and the CIA helped a number of private businessmen to start TV stations for telecasting programmes to the communist countries from places such as West Berlin and Hong Kong.

Instruments such as printed pamphlets, books, radio broadcasts, the telephone and the fax, the E-mail and the Internet are good for the hard aspects of psywar for alienating the people from their state and for discrediting the state in the eyes of its people and the world, but have only limited use for the soft aspect of projecting the power or group behind the psywar in an attractive light and creating a desire to emulate its culture, ways of life etc. It is here that the value of the TV as a medium comes. Through a sophisticated production and projection of programmes, one can create in the minds of the targeted audience, particularly the urban-based elite and youth, an uncritical admiration of the Western societies, soften their prejudices towards the West and evoke a desire to imitate them. Sections of the targeted audience lose faith in their own society and culture.

Writing in the "Washington Quarterly" of summer 1995, Gerald Segal, Senior Fellow, the International Institute For Strategic Studies, London, said: " It is only when Hong Kong-based consortia began satellite broadcasting of foreign and Chinese soap operas and international sports that the satellite broadcasts were watched by many millions of people on a regular basis. The fact that the BBC World Service TV was carried on the commercial satellite gave it greater penetration of the market, but persistent anecdotal evidence is clear that the viewers (in Asia) were picking up Western values mainly from the entertainment and only in passing from "talking heads" (talk shows) discussing human rights. It was "Baywatch", "Dallas", "Beavis and Butt-Head" or "Kung-Fu" episodes that were watched by most people and precisely because they were so much more attractive than more cerebral television, such programmes were more effective in undermining state retention of authority and control over values." He further said: " When Rupert Murdoch, well-known for his outspoken criticism of Asian and especially communist authoritarians, dropped BBCWSTV from his Hong Kong-based STAR TV because China warned that its presence put at risk the entire venture, many saw the move as an uncharacteristic pre-emptive kowtow to communists. But, by removing the overtly political message and continuing to provide soap operas about conspicuous consumption and loose morals, STAR was actually beginning to do far more damage to the authority of the Chinese Communist Party."

Writing of the CNN and the BBCWSTV, Segal further said: " CNN and, for a time, BBCWSTV added subversive images to the subversive voices that came from the likes of the Voice of America and a wide range of European shortwave broadcasters." As examples of such images, he cited the coverage of the demolition of the Berlin Wall, the popular uprising in Romania in 1989-90 and the student riots in Bangkok in 1992.

India has bitter memories of how doctored TV images and stories were used to incite the Kashmiris against the Government of India. In 1989-90, before the advent of the satellite TV to the South Asian region, Pakistan TV bought large quantities of video clips of the Romanian uprising from Western TV companies and telecast them to the Valley, inciting the local people to emulate the Romanians and rise against their government. Concerned over this, the then V.P.Singh Government set up a special committee to counter the subversion of the Kashmiris through the TV. In October 1993, when the Kashmiri extremists occupied the Hazratbal shrine, the BBC telecast a report alleging that the Indian army had launched an operation Blue Star type raid of the shrine as a result of which it had caught fire. It never corrected this blatantly false report.

In May 1995, after the burning-down of the Charar-e-Sharif holy shrine in Kashmir by the extremists, the BBC, while telecasting the news, showed visuals of Russian-made tanks, apparently to create an impression in the minds of the Muslim viewers that the shrine probably caught fire because of the use of the tanks by the Indian army. When the Government of India protested and pointed out that the same visuals had some days earlier been shown while telecasting the fighting between Russian troops and Muslim extremists in Chechnya, the BBC telecast a correction only in its Asian service and not to the rest of the world. It admitted that the visuals were from Chechnya and not Kashmir and attributed the mistake to a technical mix-up. Digitalisation and Direct-To-Home (DTH) TV have added to the concerns of security experts. The Strategic Assessment for 1995 brought out by the Institute For National Strategic Studies of Washington, which functions under the National Defence University of the Pentagon, said: " Tomorrow's antennas can increasingly be blended into walls and other background, thus frustrating bans on their possession. Electronic focussing can frustrate terrestrial jamming. Video compression, which multiplies the number of channels that any satellite can host, enhances the economics of narrowcasting. A billion dollar investment can yield well over a hundred digital stations, which, in turn, could be profitably leased for perhaps US $ two million a year. At that price, any of several aggrieved national or political groups—Kurds, radical Shiites, Sikhs, Burmese mountain tribes—could afford to broadcast propaganda 24 hours a day to wide swaths of territory."

The DTHTV provides extremist elements, having large funds earned from narcotics, and foreign intelligence agencies with the opportunity of leasing channels under front companies from a DTH operator and using the channels to disseminate doctored images such as those of a Muslim killing Hindus or Christians or vice versa and rumours to the drawing rooms of individual viewers, thereby adding to social and communal tensions. Writing in the "Foreign Policy" (Fall 1997), John Deutch, Director of the CIA during Clinton's first term, referred to the dangers of morphed images and messages being introduced into a country's radio and TV systems, spreading lies and inciting people to violence.

Till recently, in the US, foreigners were not permitted to operate telephone and DTH services. Murdoch had to take up US nationality and permanent residence there before he could apply for a DTH licence. However, he has since abandoned his DTH project because of opposition from local cable operators. Now because of the stipulation of the World Trade Organisation on the opening-up of the telephone services to foreigners, the US Congress has been considering conditions under which foreigners would be issued a licence. One of the conditions seeks to lay down that a licence can be refused in public interest, that is, on grounds of national security. Similar conditions are expected to be imposed in respect of DTH services by foreigners too.

In South-East and East Asia, only Japan allows foreigners to have 25 per cent equity participation in companies offering DTH services. In other countries, including China, there is a ban on foreign participation in DTH services. Writing jointly in the "Foreign Affairs" journal of the US (March-April,1996), Joseph S.Nye, former Chairman of the US National Intelligence Council and former Assistant Secretary of Defence for International Affairs in the Clinton Administration, and Admiral William A.Owens, former Vice-Chairman of the Joint Chiefs of Staff in the Clinton Administration, said as follows: "Soft power is the ability to achieve desired outcomes in international affairs through attraction rather than coercion. It works by convincing others to follow, or getting them to agree to, norms and institutions that produce the desired behaviour. Soft power can rest on the appeal of one's ideas or the ability to set the agenda in ways that shape the preference of others. If a state can make its power legitimate in the perception of others and establish international institutions that encourage them to channel or limit their activities, it may not need to expend as many of its costly traditional economic or military resources." They also added: " The Voice of America has in the last few years become the primary news source for 60 per cent of the educated Chinese. America's increasing technical ability to communicate with the public in foreign countries literally over the heads of their rulers via satellite (TV), provides a great opportunity to foster democracy."

After the collapse of the communist regimes of Europe, the direction of the US psywar machine has turned to Asia. The set-up of Radio Free Europe has reportedly been shifted from Munich to Prague to broadcast anti-Saddam Hussein programmes to Iraq. Since September 1996, a new radio station called Radio Free Asia, ostensibly privately run, but funded by the Congress, has been broadcasting programmes in Chinese, Tibetan, Burmese, Vietnamese and Korean languages. China started jamming these broadcasts in Septembert, 1997.

ANATOMY OF NETWORK-CENTRIC WARFARE

Ubiquitous Connectivity may have Hidden Consequences

As momentum grows for network centricity in military operations, architects of the plans may find themselves closely examining sciences such as sociology or biology to preview where network-centric activity can lead. When command, control, communications, computers and intelligence systems become more highly networked, the need for sophistication in the products and platforms that sit at the edges diminishes. In some cases, too much capability at the edge may actually inhibit self-organizing behaviour and negatively impact the mission of the networked whole.

The term network-centric is an oxymoron. Networks themselves are inherently centerless—it is all about the edges.

The promise of networks is in the dynamic interactions of the nodes at the edges. When these nodes become highly connected, interesting things start to happen.

The fundamental principle that underlies today's thinking about network-centric warfare is Metcalfe's Law, named after Robert Metcalfe, the inventor of Ethernet and founder of 3Com Corporation. It was a phenomenon first observed in commercial communications as Metcalfe sought to address the problem of creating larger networks out of many smaller ones. The law contends that the power of a network increases with the square of the number of nodes connected to the network. Network-centric warfare advocates build on this law by asserting that maximizing the number of nodes increases the chances of realizing the promise of networks through ubiquitous connectivity and interoperability.

Pursuit of ubiquitous connectivity may have hidden consequences, however. Carried to its logical conclusion, such connectivity may give rise to an environment that becomes increasingly "biological" over time and begins to exhibit behaviour similar to that of living systems. However, living pathways represent everything that the traditional business of defence is not. The implications of biological constructs in defence are both surprising and scary.

Albert-László Barabási and Eric Bonabeau outlined recent discoveries regarding highly networked systems in an article in *Scientific American* magazine. Chief among these discoveries is the existence of power laws that underlie networks such as the World Wide Web or the relationships between people in society. The power law behind these networks means that they are inherently scale-free—there is no typical node and no peak in the distribution curve. In networks of this type, the vast majority of nodes have a small number of links but are juxtaposed with a tiny number of nodes that have an extraordinarily large number of connections. The latter are known as hubs.

Hubs are evident in everyday life. In society, a few people operate in a huge circle of acquaintances amidst a world where only a limited number of relationships are nurtured. This also is evident in the disproportional popularity of certain Web sites such as Amazon or Yahoo when compared with nearly every other Web page. Interestingly, these hubs also are present in the command and control (C^2) hierarchy and constructs that are currently employed in the business of defence.

Complex networks operate through the dynamic interaction of nodes and hubs that resemble an unfolding drama more than an engineered system. Perhaps the most conspicuous characteristic of these networks is that they continuously grow. In the push toward connectivity growth in network-centric warfare, the U.S. military may be unwittingly marching down a path that conforms to the logic of scale-free networks. The question is whether this is good or bad.

Barabási and Bonabeau ominously warn that while scale-free networks are quite survivable against random failure, they also are highly vulnerable to a focused attack because of the critical role of hubs in the network.

Their research has shown that up to 80 percent of the nodes in a scale-free network can be randomly removed without compromising the functionality of the networked whole. However, a coordinated attack that disables 5 percent to 15 percent of the hubs simultaneously is all that is needed to mortally wound such a system.

Ubiquitous connectivity of a scale-free variety encourages a dangerous centrality of interaction focused on C^2 hubs. Dynamic tension exists between hierarchical C^2 models and the push for maximizing the number of nodes. While maintaining a hierarchical C^2 model, maximizing the number of nodes is a risky proposition because it amplifies the network's vulnerabilities. However, if maximizing the number of nodes is the overarching imperative, then new models of C^2 may emerge. These frameworks may be more efficacious in monitoring, pre-empting and combating threats of an asymmetric and fluid nature.

But these new C^2 models will likely have to dispense with traditional notions of control and efficiency to accentuate flexibility and adaptability. When networked information flow is nonexistent, hierarchy rules.

When it is abundant and dynamic, the traditional C^2 pyramid gets flipped upside down and the edges become primary. Command intent gradually diminishes in importance in comparison to emergent intent that arises spontaneously through the interaction of autonomous agents at the edge.

A scale-free philosophy also implies nodal expendability—by design. Small failures are bred into the system so that fatal breakdowns are avoided. In today's ethos of casualty avoidance, how does this notion get initiated in battle planning wherein up to 80 percent of the nodes are potentially expendable without mission degradation? When such odds are possible, creation of operational concepts that leverage such odds in favor of overall mission accomplishment will naturally emerge to the benefit of hubs and to the potential detriment of most nodes. From an operational perspective, the needs of the few outweigh the needs of the many if the overarching good of all is to be achieved. The likely consequence of such a construct is the increasing substitution of machines for humans at the nodes. Machines are expendable. Humans are not. This trade-off is already starting to occur in earnest.

The interaction of highly networked systems is not governed by mechanisms that traditional systems engineering techniques can necessarily discern or manage. Their nonlinear characteristics can frustrate the drive for precision, optimization and predictability—the hallmarks of military products, platforms and systems. The messy redundancy of networks has a recursive nature that manifests itself in curious ways.

Author Kevin Kelly, co-founder of *Wired* magazine, talks about simulations that illustrate the dynamics of networked interaction. They reveal a fragile balance between nodal intelligence and range of capability versus networked outcomes. In one simulation, the autonomous, self-organizing actions of thousands at a computer conference enable them to fly and land an airplane effectively without any direction from a coordinator. The key to mission accomplishment, however, was the limited range of behaviour accorded to each participant in the form of a joystick that enabled only up/down and left/right movement.

A follow-on simulation that took place several years later involved a submarine in search of targets. This time, the results were not initially successful. The primary difference was that participants were accorded a much higher level of sophistication and control. The increased range of behaviour resulted in chaos as individuals and groups of individuals nullified each other's actions in the exercise of their autonomy. Success was achieved only after the simulation director stepped up to the microphone and provided some explicit directions to the entire group, which then enabled swarm behaviour to be unleashed effectively. That direction was the visible hand of command and control.

The lessons of these simulations are interesting. For example, a highly networked environment provides the means for less capable legacy assets to be reborn with new purpose and meaning. Kelly has quipped that "dumb parts properly connected can yield smart results." Under certain conditions, ever increasing quantities of "dumber" nodes linked to the network are likely to enhance mission effectiveness as much if not more than adding more sophisticated ones.

However, achieving synergy among intelligence, quantity and control is a tricky proposition. In a network-centric warfare environment, C^2 becomes more of a coaxing and tweaking phenomenon. C^2 will gradually look more like the Federal Reserve chairman's attempts to influence the economy through soft levers like interest rate adjustments rather than through concrete orders and actions.

Biological constructs, much like world economies, however, sometimes give rise to wild-card factors that are not anticipated. The emergent characteristics are often rooted in the profusion of organic systems exerting influence laterally. These systems operate in a peering arrangement involving hundreds of thousands and even millions or billions of nodes. Where is the cross-over point in which unexpected effects begin to appear as the world of big numbers and horizontal causation unfolds? As military operations begin to make greater use of swarm systems in the form of networked microsensors, robots and unmanned vehicles in concert with humans, an understanding of thresholds separating discrete control versus unpredictability is critical.

NETWORK-CENTRIC WARFARE IN ASIA

The USA pioneered network-centric warfare (NCW) doctrine, or network-centric operations, in the 1990s. But first we must define NCW, as it can be a nebulous thing. Indeed, it is a theory of war rather than a collection of hardware.

A US Department of Defence release in 2005, entitled 'The Implementation of Network- Centric Warfare', defined NCW as "the combination of emerging tactics, techniques and procedures that a fully or even partially networked force can employ to create a decisive war-fighting advantage." The document highlighted three characteristics:

- NCW is first of all about human behaviour as opposed to information technology. The focus is on the verb 'to network' rather than on the noun 'network', which is just an enabler;
- NCW is a concept that, at the highest level, constitutes the military's response to the information age;
- NCW is an emerging theory of war because it identifies new sources of power (information sharing, information access, speed), how those sources relate to each other, how they are brought to bear to achieve the desired outcome, and how they link to political objectives.

The term 'network-centric warfare' first appeared in the US Department of Navy publication 'Copernicus: C4ISR for the 21st Century' in 1997. NCW is essentially 'team warfare', where all military services integrate and synchronise to achieve joint warfare. It has four major tenets:

1. A robustly networked force improves information sharing.

2. Information sharing provides a common tactical picture and enhances the quality of information and shared situational awareness.
3. Shared situational awareness enables collaboration and self-synchronisation, and enhances sustainability and speed of command.
4. These, in turn, dramatically increase overall mission effectiveness.

The USA is the world's undisputed proponent of NCW, turning its vast information-gathering apparatus into a competitive advantage through robust networking of interconnected forces across the globe. This article offers a quick précis of NCW developments in the Asia-Pacific region. NCW involves three domains: (1) Physical domain where events occur and reality is perceived by sensors and individuals; (2) Information domain where collected data is transmitted; and (3) Cognitive domain that receives information so it can be assessed and acted upon. Because NCW encompasses many intangibles that are difficult to gauge, much of the following content focuses on new hardware being employed. In theory, such acquisitions should reflect more deep-seated NCW changes occurring within militaries.

Singapore has made the most progress regionally as it transforms into a 'Third-Generation Force' thanks to high levels of investment and an advanced technological base. The Singapore Army's newest vehicles such as the Terrex carry a battlefield management system (BMS) from ST Electronics. Vehicles possess two BMS terminals, while the Command, Control and Information System (CCIS) synchronises dismounted infantrymen fitted with the Advanced Combat Man System (ACM) to higher headquarters. The CCIS interacts with other ground-based systems and aerial platforms too. Another element aboard the Terrex is a Blue Force Tracking and Red Force Marking (BFT/RFM) system.

Singapore's network-enabled force is the region's most advanced user of unmanned aerial vehicles (UAV) like the Heron 1 and Hermes 450. The Republic of Singapore Air Force

(RSAF) has four Gulfstream G550 airborne early warning and control (AEW&C) aircraft fitted with an Elta EL/W-2085 Phalcon radar, and data from such platforms feed into Singapore's tactical picture.

In Malaysia, Sapura has commenced Phase 1A of the nation's Network-Centric Operations (NCO) contract. The two-year programme is due for completion in early 2014 and aims to integrate existing command, control, communications, computers and intelligence (C4I) systems and to study future capabilities. Phase 1B will be more comprehensive, probably adding capabilities like a BMS and integrating the Soldier Advanced Kombat Technology Integrated (SAKTI) programme. Thales, based on existing cooperation with Sapura, seems a likely foreign partner. Thales is also involved in fitting the Open Information Communication System (OICS) onto the AV8 armoured vehicle to allow internal/external information exchange and serve as a BMS platform.

In 2010, Northrop Grumman UK won a contract to create a Joint Operations Centre (JOC) in Brunei. Its heart is the company's International-Joint Operational Command and Control System. The contract provides both a static headquarters and deployable JOC. Common core software allows interoperability with regional partners. Phase 2 is believed to be under way, and it should implement tactical components such as a BMS. The network encompasses Harris Corporation Falcon II radios, but wideband networking radios and high-capacity line-of-sight (HCLOS) radios are an obvious future purchase.

In Thailand the Directorate of Signals is in charge of NCW technical aspects. Thailand employs commercial off-the-shelf (COTS) solutions alongside military-specific C4I systems as this proves more economical. In recent times the Royal Thai Air Force (RTAF) has made significant gains owing to a package of Saab JAS 39 Gripen fighters and Saab S100B Argus AEW&C aircraft. An integral part of the Swedish deal was installation of the StriC network, whose data-links connect Gripen and AEW&C aircraft into a complete air defence system. StriC, which greatly enhances the RTAF's networkcentricity was delivered in March 2011. Saab was subsequently requested to expand Thailand's air defence C2 system with a contract running from 2011-13.

Since 2001, Taiwan has invested heavily in its Lockheed Martin-derived Po Sheng ('Broad Victory') C4ISR system. The high-level Po Sheng system can quickly plug into the Joint Tactical Information Distribution System (JTIDS) of the USA's Pacific Command (PACOM). In the worst case of Chinese espionage in 50 years, authorities conceded Taiwan's C4ISR platform may have been compromised by Major General Lo Hsien-che before his arrest in 2011. The military has been hardening its communication system that is primarily based on a fibre-optic cable backbone connecting bases. There is now a need to extend it into an agile tactical network, and to add ISR capabilities. Furthermore, work is required to integrate Taiwan's Surveillance Radar Programme (SRP), a mountain-top missile early-warning radar, with Patriot PAC-3 and Po Sheng networks. Cyber-warfare is a threat to NCW, with Taiwan's National Security Bureau (NSB) revealing that, in the first half of 2012, hackers launched more than one million attacks on the NSB.

Over the years the author has observed increasing digitisation in China's People's Liberation Army (PLA), primarily through equipment being fielded in the elite Hong Kong Garrison. New assets include the Z-9ZH helicopter, a C2 platform with forward-looking infrared (FLIR) system and cabin command console. In addition, the garrison received the Type 07 6x6 Armoured Command Vehicle accommodating the latest radio equipment that can transmit/receive real-time data.

These platforms illustrate PLA advances in its drive towards NCW. 'Informationisation' is a fundamental goal, and in one sense, because the PLA was a late starter, it can take advantage of leapfrog technologies. C4ISR is crucial to China's blue-water naval presence, anti-access/area denial and missile capability. China has procured both KJ-2000 and KJ-200 AEW&C aircraft. China still has much to learn about gaining maximum benefit from them, plus their practicality is stymied by the fact that older fighters do not have digital data-links.

South Korea is rolling out its Tactical Information Communication Network (TICN) to replace its SPIDER communications system.

The USD3.8 billion TICN deal involving Samsung Thales, Huneed and LIG Nex1 has five subsystems such as High-Capacity Trunk Radio, Tactical Multiband and Multirole Radio, and Network Management System. Other important C4ISR projects include: (1) Korea Joint Command and Control System (KJCCS) to connect the Joint Chiefs of Staff to each service; (2) Military Information Management System (MIMS) to enable tactical-level cross-service interoperability; and (3) Joint Tactical Data Link System (JTDLS) to allow dissemination of digitised tactical information between all services.

South Korea knows it needs to improve C4ISR capabilities before it takes over wartime operational control (OPCON) of military forces on the peninsula in December 2015. Four Boeing 737 "Peace Eye" AEW&C aircraft have been inducted, plus it is contemplating RQ-4 Global Hawk UAVs, despite blanching at the USD1.2 billion price last year. The government has delayed any decision by at least a year, and is investigating cheaper alternatives. Since 2006, South Korea has been developing its Korea Air and Missile Defence (KAMD) system due for completion in 2015. Key components include Aegis-equipped KDX-III destroyers, EL/M-2080 Super Green Pine early-warning radars and Patriot missiles.

Japan is greatly concerned at North Korea's missile arsenal, as well as maritime territorial disputes with China. The Japan Air Self-Defence Force (JASDF) operates four Boeing E-767 AEW&C aircraft with JTIDS and 13 E-2C Hawkeyes. Missile defence incorporates four FPS-5 and seven FPS-4 radar installations, six Aegis-equipped destroyers, plus a series of communications and imagery satellites. Money is being invested in a new X-band satellite network. Initiated in 2009, the USD935 million Japan Aerospace Defence Ground Environment (JADGE) system, centralised at Yokota, brings a wider upgrade to conventional air defence and ballistic-missile defence systems. JADGE is closely interlinked to US systems. A JSDF C4 Systems Command was established in 2008, while a far-reaching mobile communication network is promoting information sharing. However, the 2011 tsunami revealed communication capability gaps, leading to funding for the Next-Generation Field Communication System. The government stated the system "will enable the rapid creation of high-speed and wide-area communication networks and also be useful for disaster response."

Moving to a different continent, two years ago the author witnessed Elbit Systems' Battle Group and Below Command, Control and Communications (BGC3) system being trialled by Australia's 7th Brigade. This forms part of the $300 million LAND 75/125 programme awarded in 2010, with full operational capacity scheduled for late 2013. The Israeli system has two core software components: TORC2H and Tactical Intranet Geographic Dissemination in Real-time (TIGER). BGC3 was first installed on Bushmaster vehicles and used a layer of Harris radios. Australia has performed a lot of engineering to make it work with non-Israeli applications such as Raytheon's Advanced Field Artillery Tactical Data System (AFATDS) and Northrop Grumman's Force XXI Battle Command Brigade and Below (FBCB2) system aboard Abrams tanks.

The Royal Australian Air Force (RAAF) has six Boeing E-7A "Wedgetail" aircraft, and initial operational capability was declared last November. The RAAF instituted the Project Vigilare Network- Centric Command and Control System (NC3S) under AIR 5333, with new installations at RAAF Bases Tindal and Williamtown. Boeing helped develop NC3S along with an Air Defence System communications network integrating data from 45 different land, sea, air and space interfaces. It commenced operations on 2 September 2010.

Across the Tasman Sea, New Zealand is acquiring a Defence Command and Control System (DC2S) to support high-level decision-making as well as joint operations. Delivery is expected in 2015-16. The Network Enabled Army programme will deliver most of the tactical C4I capability from 2013-33, though it needs a new communications network and strategic links via the Strategic Bearer Network Project. India has high hopes for its Tactical Communications Systems (TCS) though, as usual, movement has bogged down. Two local companies – Bharat Electronics Limited (BEL), and an L&T, Tata Power and HCL Infosys consortium – were shortlisted. An important step is a BMS for the Indian Army, but its delivery to a combat group is unlikely before 2015. Phase 2 should offer wider fielding of BMS from 2017-21, and the third phase would see upgrades in 2022-26. Total cost will be at least INR2.3 billion. It will also align with the Futuristic Infantry Soldier As a System (F-INSAS) programme.

The Combined Information & Decision Support System (CIDSS) has been stymied by the failed appearance of TCS as its key bearer. Last May the military ordered an investigation into the substandard CIDSS programme, though BEL is still working on it. CIDSS is one element of the army's Tac C3I system, with other elements being the Battlefield Surveillance System (BSS), Artillery Combat Command and Control System (ACCCS), and Air Defence Control and Reporting System (ADC&RS). India is essentially pursuing a bottom-up approach because of a lack of tri-service cooperation.

Cisco Systems helped the Indian Air Force inaugurate its fibre optic-based Air Force Network (AFNet) in September 2010. Riding on its backbone is the Integrated Air Command and Control System (IACCS) that provides connectivity and real-time transfer of voice, data and images between aircraft, satellites, UAVs, aerostats and ground bases. It also offers a ballistic-missile defence capacity. The Israel-launched RISAT-2 satellite is crucial to India's NCW capabilities, and the first element of the seven-satellite Indian Regional Navigational Satellite System (IRNSS) was launched in July.

Conclusion

Independent business analyst Vision gain calculated that the international C4ISR market amounted to some US $70.3

billion in 2011, or 5% of global defence spending. NCW is still undergoing growing pains around Asia-Pacific, with service interoperability one of the greatest challenges. This is complicated by the spectre of combined operations with allied nations that will require harmonisation of international technical standards. Architectural difficulties exist because various communication systems must be integrated into a unified whole, which is especially difficult where new equipment must be tightly integrated with legacy platforms. Regional nations are taking steps in the NCW direction, though few could be described as making great strides.

NETWORK-CENTRIC ORGANIZATION

A network-centric organization is a network governance pattern emerging in many progressive 21st century enterprises. This implies new ways of working, with consequences for the enterprise's infrastructure, processes, people and culture.

Overview

With a network-centric configuration, knowledge workers are able to create and leverage information to increase competitive advantage through the collaboration of small and agile self-directed teams. For this, the organizational culture needs to change from one solely determined by a single form of organizing (e.g., hierarchy) to an adaptive hybrid enabling multiple forms of organizing within the same organization. The nature of the work, in an area, determines best the way its conduct is organized and the networked mediation of work activities affords interoperability among differentially-organized areas of work.

A network-centric organization is both a sensible response to a complex environment and an enactor of sensibility on that environment. The business climate of the new millennium is characterized by profound and continuous changes due to globalization, exponential leaps in technological capabilities, and other market forces. Rapid developments of ICT are driving and supporting the change from the industrial to the information age. In this world of rapid change and uncertainty, organizations need to continually renew, reinvent and reinvigorate themselves in order to respond creatively. The network-centric approach aims to tap into the hidden resources of knowledge workers supported and enabled by ICT, in particular the social technologies associated with Web 2.0 and Enterprise 2.0. Essentially though, a network-centric organization is more about people and culture than technology. A useful survey of network organization theory appears in Van Alstyne (1997)

Network-centric organization topics

Knowledge Work

There is a synthesis of thinking, learning and doing at the core of creative human activity that underpins the concept of knowledge work. Knowledge workers collaborate on tasks that are cognitively demanding, involving complex technical judgements, a high degree of professional and individual expertise and experience.

The knowledge worker is astutely aware, not only of the means and purpose of their work, but also its political and social dimensions. Much of this knowledge is tacit and shared among the work group becoming embedded in its culture.

There is a broad expanse of uncharted territory between the real knowledge work that occurs in an organization and the formal organizational structure and espoused practices. The concentration on formal organizational programs aimed at the individual workers ignored the real nature of work practices that reside in a space between the organization and individual perspectives. This space often remain hidden from the organizational landscape, unappreciated and undervalued. Revealing the nature of this hidden space holds the key to understanding knowledge work and is critical to successful organizational outcomes and learning.

Hybrid enterprises

Many enterprises are hybrids of hierarchical bureaucracies, heterarchic work groups distributed across organizational and spatial boundaries, and responsibly autonomous individuals where competition and cooperation coexist due to a strict division of work activities. Network-centric organizations locate the partitioning of work activities in the self-direction of individuals and work groups, rather than in the hierarchy.

Enterprises which have complex hybrid structures consisting of hierarchies and networks are more like organic eco-systems than machines.

The latter are likely to be exploitative and bureaucratic while the former can be networked and innovative. This reflects the tension between the natural tendency for disorder to increase while humans strive to impose order by developing ever more complex rigid structures and systems. It is quite a natural state of affairs that organizations can be part mechanistic and part organic with continual transformations among these forms. Network-centric organizations enact governance systems that manage these ongoing transformations.

Sensible organization

A complex environment presents an enterprise with too large a range and diversity of inputs to comprehend logically so the sensible response is not to try.

Attempts to deal with complexity are unsuccessful if they aim to either simplify or assert control over complex situations. It makes more sense to maintain and support the natural creative energies of complex environments, encouraging the emergence of innovative new forms of working.

Sensible enterprises will become agile, flexible and adaptable by incorporating more creativity and diversity into their structures, processes and human resources. The informality, interactivity and adaptability of small teams of people retains a space for what we traditionally call 'common sense' for both understanding and action amid the accountability and constraints of the formal enterprise. Sensible managers will relinquish some of their traditional control to knowledge workers in small self-directed teams. A network-centric organization will also have an increased need and reliance on data sensing, analysis, and closed-loop action driven by repeated application of "sense-and-respond" cycle.

Social technologies

At the current time, a new civil digital culture has taken hold, in which so-called 'social' and/or 'conversational' technologies or social software are providing unprecedented opportunities for everyday user activities. The term Web 2.0 has entered the vocabulary to reflect the ongoing transition of the World Wide Web from a collection of websites to a full-fledged computing platform serving social web applications such as email, discussion forums, chatrooms, Weblogs and Wikis to end users. Constructivist learning theorists explained that the process of expressing knowledge aids its creation and conversations benefits the refinement of knowledge. Cheung et al. (2005) maintains that conversational knowledge management fulfils this purpose because conversations, e.g. questions and answers, become the source of relevant knowledge.

Social technologies facilitate processes where knowledge creation and storage is carried out through a discussion forum where participants contribute to the discussion with questions and answers, or through a Weblog which is typified by a process of storytelling or through a Wiki using collaborative writing (Hasan and Pfaff 2006). In the corporate setting, the term Enterprise 2.0 is emerging to reflect the use of freeform social software within companies to support work units and the individual knowledge worker. Gordon and Ganesan (2005) advocates a different vision for knowledge management systems to one that is specifically targeted to the capture and use of the stories told in communities and organizations in the context of normal, spoken conversations.

Conversation and other types of human-human communication must be exploited in today's knowledge management systems so as harness the value of conversation in packaging and transmitting tacit knowledge. The attraction of these social technologies is their low cost, intuitive functionality and connectivity. Social technologies support new forms of network-centric interaction and activity between people, allowing and enhancing informal access to create and distribute information. These technologies empower ordinary people to have a global presence for business, political and social purposes. The new social technologies at the focus of this project are tools of a rising digital democracy.

One of the newest approaches on the horizon is worknetting. A worknet is a form of organization where stakeholders, individuals or institutions or both, can come together around a shared purpose. Whereas a network centres around the relationships between partners, a worknet centres around each partner's relationship with the shared purpose. In this way, the unique strengths and contributions of each partner can be optimized and enhanced, as they are situated in the context of the worknets common interest.

Power shift in traditional organizations

Traditional organizations that favor a rigid hierarchical structure and ego-centric methods still employ the outmoded concept where the decision-making authority lies solely in the domain of its corporate headquarters. Changes resulting from developments in ICT and the growth of the Internet, have made it increasingly difficult to provide a platform for effective and efficient management and operations. As observed by De Vulpian (2005), "we are in the process of moving from a pyramidal, hierarchical society to a single-story society whereheterarchical relationships dominate".

There is a tension between ego-centric thinking and network-centric thinking – the tension between the institutional power that emanates from an organization and the transactional power that inheres in its members' daily interactions. Progressive organizations are tending to refocus on supporting teams in community-style networks. There is a growing realization that if "decisions are allowed to move out of the corporate headquarters to individual business units, business units will in turn distribute power and decision-making to self-managed teams and profit centers (Allee 2003)." This is the basis of the concept of knowledge work where workers have control over their own activities through knowledge acquired in the course of both training and experience.

Links to Network Centric Warfare

Network-centric warfare is a simple concept that involves the linkage of engagement systems to sensors through networks and the sharing of information between force elements. The early development of the concept evolved by connecting information systems and creating software applications that allow people to use the available data. McKenna, Moon, Davis and Warne (2006) emphasise on the human dimension of NCW which is based on the idea that information is only useful if it allows people to act more effectively.

NETWORK CENTRIC OPERATIONS TO DEFENCE

As global defence agencies face new threats to security and stability, maintaining a high level of effectiveness and preparedness is more critical than ever. Forces are relying more heavily on stealth and precision weaponry, and must operate more efficiently with reduced staff. Improved communications and collaboration are increasingly important for geographically dispersed personnel, joint forces, and coalition partners.

To meet these new priorities, defence agencies are redefining themselves by investing in IT to create a closely integrated, tightly synchronized force. By putting timely, accurate information in the hands of the right people in the right location, a force can gain a significant strategic and tactical advantage over a threat. This type of mission-critical information plays an even more crucial role today, as defence establishments look to new technology to extend the power of information to every aspect of their organizations.

According to a report prepared by the U.S. Department of Defence entitled Network-Centric Warfare, "The challenge for DoD is to harness the power of information technologies to develop concepts of operation and command and control approaches that will be information-driven rather than uncertainty-driven."

To develop the mission-critical information they require, defence agencies are investing in network-centric operations (NCO) initiatives that create an integrated, tightly synchronized force. NCO is a real-time operation model designed to securely deliver mission-critical information throughout the chain of command—anytime, anywhere—to achieve an advantage over an adversary. Its goal is to use relevant information to achieve the desired results of a military operation with minimal casualties, and at minimal cost. NCO affects all levels of military activity, from the tactical to the strategic. At the operational level, it gives commanders the capability to perform precisely, at an efficient operational tempo.

In its "Network-Centric Warfare" report, the U.S. Department of Defence states, "Network-centric capabilities allow the force to attain an improved information position that can partially 'lift the fog of war' and enable commanders to improve their decision making and fight in ways that were not previously possible."

In the future, NCO will play a vital role in creating environments that empower the military to take proactive measures such as minimizing the impact of a natural disaster, or dissuading a potential adversary from taking a threatening course of action. Forces will be able to access information quickly enough to anticipate the impact of a situation and positively influence the outcome.

THE COMPUTER TECHNOLOGY AND CYBERNETIC WARFARE

The Cold War and the constant threat of nuclear annihilation required ever greater levels of automation and centralization of the war machine; and cybernetics, with its promise of stability in the face of perturbation, appeared best suited to the containment and management of a conflict of potentially apocalyptic proportions.

Vast command and control architectures were established to organize the global projection of armed force and the rapid mobilization of military systems within the shrinking windows of opportunity afforded by nuclear weaponry. Scientific methodology was applied to warfare more systematically than ever, with operations research and systems analysis applied comprehensively to both tactical and strategic questions. The first two decades of the postwar era saw the rise of the defence intellectuals and their analytical tools in the United States, culminating in the nomination of Robert McNamara as Secretary of Defence.

In its most pristine form, cybernetic warfare fuelled wild yet enduring fantasies of omniscience and omnipotence on the battlefield. In 1969 General William Westmoreland, commander-in-chief of US forces in Vietnam, formulated his vision of the military's future, encapsulating this cybernetic ideal:

> On the battlefield of the future, enemy forces will be located, tracked, and targeted almost instantaneously through the use of data links, computer assisted intelligence evaluation, and automated fire control. With first round kill probabilities approaching certainty, and with surveillance devices that can continually track the enemy, the need for large forces to fix the opponent becomes less important.

The Dawn of Chaoplexic Warfare

Cybernetic warfare experienced its first serious reversal with the Vietnam War, where its analytical techniques and military systems foundered in the conditions of a low-intensity conflict. James Gibson has written persuasively about the failure in the jungles of South-East Asia of 'technowar', an approach to military conflict in which war was viewed as 'a production system that can be rationally managed and warfare as a kind of activity that can be scientifically determined by constructing computer models'.

The conduct of the war was blighted by the attempts of the military and political hierarchy to micro-manage the conflict and by an obsession with statistical evaluation and information-gathering which frequently created assessments of the war that were completely at variance with the reality on the ground.

Despite the deployment of an unprecedented telecommunications network in the field of operations, command and control technologies failed to perform as expected, with saturation and bottlenecks preventing information on Vietcong positions and movements from arriving in time to be actionable.

Perhaps most seriously, a misguided faith in the powers of technoscience to grant military omnipotence led policy-makers to embrace armed force more willingly as the means to solve complex strategic problems. Such hubris was perfectly encapsulated by Henry Kissinger's claim in 1968 that 'a scientific revolution has, for all practical purposes, removed technical limits from the exercise of power in foreign policy'.

The debacle in Vietnam provoked some soul-searching among strategists and military men but did not result in an immediate abandonment of the central principles of cybernetic warfare, which continued to dominate military thinking through the 1980s. All the early contributions to the debate on the revolution in military affairs were premised on the idea that computers, telecommunication links and precision-guided munitions would finally deliver the frictionless, automated battlefield promised by Westmoreland. However, new thinking drawing on the emerging non-linear sciences did begin to penetrate military theory, at first espoused only by isolated individuals but entering the mainstream at the turn of the century.

The late US air force colonel John Boyd is perhaps the most prominent pioneer of chaoplexic warfare, and increasingly is considered to be one of the most important military thinkers of recent times. Boyd is best known for his formulation of the OODA loop (observe–orient–decide–act), describing the decision-making process of the warfighter engaged in combat. Although this is at first sight reminiscent of a typical cybernetic feedback loop, whereby a system adjusts its behaviour to incoming information from its environment in order to meet a desired objective, Boyd was insistent on the need for the analytical frameworks used during the orientation phase to be continually challenged and reinvented through a perpetual process of 'destruction and creation'.

No predetermined automated response can prevail for long in a world that is 'uncertain, everchanging, unpredictable'. Boyd went on to contribute to US Marine Corps doctrine, which displays clear signs of the influence of chaoplexity in asserting that 'the best we can hope for is to impose a general framework of order on the disorder, to prescribe the general flow of action rather than to try to control each event', and that 'like a living organism, a military organization is never in a state of stable equilibrium but is instead in a continuous state of flux—continuously adjusting to its surroundings'.

If the earlier proclamations of an imminent revolution in military affairs remained firmly tributary to cybernetic conceptions, the ascent of network-centric warfare (NCW) marked the onset of a shift towards chaoplexic notions on the centre ground of debates over military doctrine. With its ideas couched in the language and concepts of the non-linear sciences, NCW first appeared on the scene within the US navy in the late 1990s before rapidly rising to become the new official Pentagon gospel under the agenda of 'Transformation' with the founding of the Office of Force Transformation in 2001 under the stewardship of its original formulator Vice Admiral Arthur Cebrowski.

According to Cebrowski, networkcentric warfare views war as a 'complex, adaptive system where non-linear variables continuously interact'. Since 'coordination from the top down inevitably results in delays and errors in force dispositions', the military should seek to acquire 'the ability of a well-informed force to organize and coordinate complex warfare activities from the bottom up'. For Cebrowski, what is being proposed is nothing less than a 'new theory of war'.

Such a new theory can emerge only by breaking with the command and control principles that governed cybernetic warfare during the Cold War, as suggested by Alberts and Hayes:

Control Theory requires both prediction and the existence of an adequate set of levers of control ... [But] having effective, centrally managed levers that can control or even predictably influence a complex, adaptive system is far from guaranteed ... In the Information Age, control needs to be thought about and approached differently.

Control is not something that can be imposed on a complex adaptive system, particularly when there are many independent actors. Control, that is, ensuring that behavior stays within or moving to within acceptable bounds, can only be achieved indirectly.

The most promising approach involves establishing, to the extent possible, a set of initial conditions that will *result* in the desired behavior. In other words, control is not achieved by imposing a parallel process, but rather emerges from influencing the behaviors of independent agents. NCW theorists claim that through the distribution of information across the battlefield and the constitution of a common operational picture via an overarching 'Global Information Grid', command and control will be decentralized and individual troops will be freed to act on their own initiative, leading to self-synchronization, a clear nod to the chaoplexic notion of self-organization.

New tactical schemes denied to their hierarchical counterparts are seen as the emergent properties that will be unlocked by fully networked self-synchronizing forces. Drawing further from the writings of complexity theorists and deploying biological metaphors, military theorists appeal to the 'swarm', the networks of distributed intelligence that enable bees, ants and termites to evolve complex forms of collective behaviour on the basis of the simple rules of interaction of their individual members.

Of particular interest are the resilience and flexibility of these swarms as amorphous ensembles whose continued existence and successful operation is not critically dependent on any single individual. Military swarms promise not only more adaptable and survivable forces but also new offensive and defensive tactics better suited to the contemporary battlespace. According to Alberts and Hayes, decentralization and information-sharing will permit military platforms to 'evolve from being networked entities to being nodes in the network, to organizing efforts resembling "packs" and "swarms"'. The ensembles of different entities making up fighting forces, whether human or robotic, will 'ultimately become dynamically reconfigurable packs, swarms, or other organizations of highly specialized components that work together like the cells of our bodies' and will be 'less mechanical and more organic, less engineered and more "grown"'.

Beyond the flexibility and evolutionary capability that are attributed to military swarms, it is also claimed that they will be able to bring force to bear in a new manner.

Rather than throwing themselves onto the enemy in 'waves', forces will be able to converge on their target from all directions in offensive bursts, thereby maximizing the shock effect.

For Arquilla and Ronfeldt, the full effects of swarming are achieved when the dispersed nodes of a network of small (and also perhaps some large) forces can converge on an enemy from multiple directions, through either fire or maneuver. The overall aim should be *sustainable pulsing*—swarm networks must be able to coalesce rapidly and stealthily on a target, then dissever and redisperse, immediately ready to recombine for a new pulse. A swarm network should have little to no mass as a rule (except perhaps during a pulse), but it should have a high energy potential—like a swarm of bees that can fell a mighty beast, or a network of antibodies that can attack a spreading virus.

Troops that can disperse swiftly after an attack or 'pulse' also have the advantage of being less vulnerable to enemy attacks, particularly in the context of the high lethality and precision characteristic of contemporary and future battlefields. The promises of network-centric warfare are bold and, for all its deployment of chaoplexic language, the doctrine suffers from a number of potentially critical weaknesses. In several respects it has not significantly broken with cybernetic warfare and therefore may not in fact implement all the features of a truly chaoplexic way of warfare. While 'decentralization' is the order-word of the day, the networking of troops may in fact provide the technological infrastructure for greater micro-management than ever by a military brass which will have access to data feeds from anywhere in the battlespace.

Second, dependence on a unified 'Global Information Grid' could both create a critical vulnerability likely to be targeted by competent adversaries and deprive troops of the skills required to respond creatively to situations in which only limited local information is available (as most of the complex adaptive systems studied are found to do).

Furthermore, NCW advocates fall back all too often on impoverished conceptions of Boyd's OODA loop which substitute speed of execution of predetermined responses for creative thinking and adaptability to the unforeseen.

Finally, there persists a tendency to see information technology as the panacea which will permanently lift the friction and fog of war which has plagued all past militaries, when in fact chaoplexity points to the irreducible contingency and unpredictability of war and the need to organize so as to tolerate and even take advantage of this uncertainty.

Ultimately chaoplexic warfare will depend more on doctrinal and organizational commitments than on any particular information technologies, which are liable to be employed to quite contrary purposes.

The full arrival of chaoplexic warfare may therefore still lie ahead; but the debates around network-centric warfare clearly show an impetus towards greater decentralization and the use of the network form of organization within armed forces. NCW now has its counterparts in most major western militaries, including Network Enabled Capabilities (NEC) in the United Kingdom, NATO Network Enabled Capabilities (NNEC), and Network Enabled Operations (NEOps) in Canada.

Where such militaries have encountered recent setbacks, for example in Iraq, Afghanistan or Lebanon, it has been against opponents that have employed decentralized networks to good effect against better-equipped forces, thereby further stimulating discussion about their merits and underlining the limitations of established modes of operation.

Just as the ideas of mechanism, thermodynamics and cybernetics inspired past military thought and practice in association with their respective paradigmatic technologies, a new set of scientific theories are now occupying a central role within the doctrinal and organizational changes of the armies of the early twenty-first century. Our network age is therefore also that of chaoplexity.

5

Information Warfare: Defence Technology in Cyberspace

Over 35 years ago, computer scientists of the United States Department of Defense, and four western-state universities were constructing the precursor to the Internet. Named ARPANET, for Advanced Research Projects Agency Network, one of the projects goals was to study how communications could be maintained in the event of an all-out nuclear attack, as this was the middle of the Cold War.

After realizing that ARPANET would not be immune to a nuclear assault, the computer scientists using it recognized that assisting human communication was the most fundamental advance that the ARPANET made possible. Today, the Internet provides incredible opportunities for the hundreds of millions of users around the world. Globalization is due, in part, to the connections nations and corporations have been able to establish on behalf of the Internet. Previously, most computerized information was stored on disks or hard drives, but the Internet has allowed for easier access of data by storing information on networks so that it may be accessed from, and sent to any connected location.

Expanding at a phenomenal rate, 200 million Americans used the Internet in 2000, and the number of websites doubles every 37 days, according to the Federal Bureau of Investigation. The convenience and ease of transmitting information around the globe in seconds makes the Internet priceless for business, government agencies and anyone else who can go on-line. The Internet is now one of several regions that create the ever-growing entity known as Cyberspace. Governments, corporations, and educational institutions the world over became conscious of the potential of cyberspace, in which they could communicate, conduct business, and share information in ways previously unavailable. The benefits of this new medium were appealing not only to those using computers for productive means, but for those who sought to unlawfully use information in order to cause damage in a variety of ways. And thus, the unethical use of computers helped create Information Warfare.

According to the Institute for The Advanced Study of Information Warfare, "Information warfare is the offensive and defensive use of information and information systems to deny, exploit, corrupt, or destroy, an adversary's information, information-based processes, information systems, and computer-based networks while protecting one's own. Such actions are designed to achieve advantages over military or business adversaries."

Although a global menace, a focus on the causes and effects of Information Warfare threatening Canada, and mainly the United States will demonstrate the extent to which this phenomenon may reach. Granted, militaries and governments rely on computers for day-to-day operations, this essay will focus more on the aspect of computers that are used and depended on by the general public.

Although virtually every nation in the world could be the victim or purveyor of an Information attack, the most likely target is the United States. The US military is arguably the most powerful in the world and most enemies cannot match their arsenal and power. Rather than try to build an equivalent military, a more efficient alternative of attack would be through computers, with Information Warfare, i.e. cyber terrorism and cyber warfare.

The most severely threatening and destructive forma of Information Warfare are indeed the most difficult to defend against, says the Canadian Security Intelligence Service (CSIS).

Terrorist groups and criminal hackers are often far more educated in the area of computers than law enforcement agents, and they have the knowledge and equipment to stay ahead of advances in protective security. Targets could include governments of all levels, military and police forces, political groups and prominent individuals; basically anyone with a computer hooked up to a modem. Using the Internet for terrorist activity reduces the chances of detection or capture. Terrorists can cause disruptions and economic damage to their target by attacking computer systems, rather than using weapons that inflict physical damage. Industrialized nations that are heavily reliant on computer systems are vulnerable to Information Warfare attacks.

A 1999 report by the Center for Strategic and International Studies, "Cybercrime...Cyberterrorism...Cyberwarfare" warned of the severe risk to the critical infrastructures in the United States. Current defenses are inadequate to protect against an attack as the Pentagon estimates that a coordinated attack by fewer than 20 strategically placed computer experts, with a budget of $10 million, could cripple the United States. Within a matter of seconds, a cyber attack could cripple a nation's government and economy, not to mention its society. It is interesting to note that the Internet was created by the US military and now they must protect themselves and their country from others who want to attack the US by means of computers and the Internet.

All industrialized nations, especially those of the Group of Eight Industrialized Nations, G8, are becoming increasingly dependent on their critical infrastructures, which virtually keep nations running. Critical infrastructures, of the government and private sector, are essential to the routine operations of the economy and government, and are both physical and cyber based. Technological advances have linked many infrastructures, such as telecommunications, energy, banking and finance, transportation, water, sewage and emergency systems, and these systems are becoming progressively automated. The reliance and importance of infrastructures have created potential targets for physical and cyber attacks.

The vulnerability of critical infrastructures, and the unique risks associated with networked computing have been recognized by the U.S. for some time, but not until 1998 was this issue applied the urgent status it deserves. The Presidential Decision Directive 63 was approved by Bill Clinton, and a national infrastructure protection policy was developed. The National Infrastructure Protection Center (NIPC), run by the FBI, and the Critical Infrastructure Assurance Office (CIAO), run by the Department of Commerce were created in order to protect and examine infrastructure vulnerabilities. Both the NIPC and CIAO are an administrative types of protection, whereas major cyber-terrorist attacks or network sabotages are handled by the Federal Computer Emergency Response Team (Fed Cert), which is likened to a SWAT team. By creating these agencies, and addressing the threats they face, the US government has made cyberspace security and Information Warfare a top priority. None of these agencies mention the moral and ethical implications of Information Warfare, as this aspect is not evident to be a military or law enforcement concern.

The Canadian Security Intelligence Service is concerned with foreign governments, terrorist groups and politically motivated extremists who may now use Information Warfare instead of traditional method of attack. Terrorism and industrial espionage, among many other malicious acts, are unethical regardless if committed with the aid of computers or not. However, using a computer, the Internet or other forms of IT to facilitate Information Warfare can be considered even more unethical than traditional methods of terrorism and related offences. Compared to the U.S., Canada is less economically and politically influential on the rest of the world, and is fortunately not an enemy to as many foreign states. However, this does not give Canada immunity from transnational Information Warfare. Director of the FBI, Louis J. Freeh, characterized Canada as a "hacker haven" as a result of our "sophisticated information technology system and our open society."

John Deutch, Director of Central Intelligence, testified before an American congressional committee and warned that, "an electronic Pearl Harbour was now a real threat" because, "criminal hackers were offering their services to so-called rogue states with various schemes to undo vital US interests through computer intrusions."Previously, terrorist groups used to take credit for their actions so their objectives would be well known, but a new trend is to avoid responsibility, which is quite easy with cyber attacks, so tracking such organizations is becoming increasingly difficult.

Information Warfare has international implications and virtually any one with access to a particular district of cyberspace is at risk. Several of the many features that make the Internet so unique, such as the speed at which information can be transferred, the ability to remain anonymous, and the ease of accessibility, attract many people, including the criminally minded. The broad range of crimes committed on the Internet, or with the aid of computers, poses new challenges for governments and law enforcement agencies around the world.

Transnational computer crimes, such as cyber terrorism and cyber warfare, are pertinent global matters that must be prevented if cyberspace is to prosper in the future. The future of cyberspace depends on the prevention of the most destructive types of crimes. Therefore, governments, aided by law enforcement agencies and private corporations must address and prevent the most severe threats to cyberspace. Again, ethical implications are not considered.

Not only must industry continue to develop security policies and safeguards for their networks and systems, but it should also continue its efforts to identify security flaws that threaten the Internet. These massive companies, such as Microsoft, Cisco, and Oracle have the knowledge, resources and personnel to create effective solutions. The technology to monitor vast areas of cyberspace, in real time, are available, as well as methods to detect network intrusions. These companies have the ability to inform governments of potential attacks, if and where there is a gap in an infrastructures security system, and they can block against many types of attacks and intrusions.

These abilities could be extremely beneficial for cyberspace as a whole by protecting governments, infrastructures and economies. As well these types of technologies could be incorporated into combating smaller scale crimes. The reason these measures are not commonplace is the initial costs incurred. As well, many companies do not want their vulnerabilities to be known for fear of further violations and loss of consumer confidence. Countless businesses, e-business and real space as well, rely on IT corporations for their products and innovations. Perhaps even more importantly, these corporations provide the global market with the hardware and software needed to access and effectively use cyberspace, and subsequently make the economy even more computer dependent.

These companies made and continue to manufacture the products now in use by terrorists and others who engage in Information Warfare. Although their products intended use is not for such malevolent activities, American and Canadian made products can be used by terrorists to carry out their attacks on the American economy and government networks. These major corporations have a moral obligation to research and fund protective measures that can prevent and shield infrastructures, themselves, governments, not to mention cyberspace as a whole.

The private sector cannot depend on law enforcement agencies for protection. Raymond Kendall, Secretary General of Interpol, (International Criminal Police Organization, consisting of 178 nations) told senior executives of large and growing companies, "The private sector must shoulder the responsibility for its own defense because government agencies do not have the technology necessary to do the job."

Military and law enforcement agencies are the protectors of society, but this may not be the case for cyberspace. They do not have the expertise, time, or resources to effectively deal with the concepts of Information Warfare, as the major firms of the IT industry do. Both government and private sector must put more effort and consideration into the threat of an Information attack, as they both could be the targets. As well, existing computer ethics should be stricter and enforced if the unethical and immoral use of computers is to be significantly reduced. Perhaps the makers of ARPANET should have included ethical guidelines into their creation, as the future of Cyberspace is in jeopardy as the threat of Information Warfare looms.

INFORMATION WARFARE

The history of the Second World War offers great examples of the military and civilian leadership manipulating information, even in a very crude fashion, to achieve rather spectacular results. In those days, as we thought about dominating the information spectrum, we turned to the cryptographers who were on the leading edge of these efforts, the so-called "code breakers." These specialized folks focused intently upon breaking the Japanese and German codes. In Europe, the ULTRA project -- "ULTRA" for the "ULTRA secret" -- produced spectacular results. Our code breakers literally worked miracles.

After the Normandy invasion, the German 7th Army attempted a counterattack to drive the Allied forces from the rather tenuous beachhead that they held. But with the help of ULTRA's ability to read the German mail and message traffic, we knew precisely what they were doing as they began to gather their forces to make this attack. We were able to put the British Second Tactical Air Force and the United States Ninth Tactical Air Force immediately upon these armor formations just as they massed. ULTRA gave us the critical information that allowed us to defeat the German forces before they ever came in contact with our ground forces.

By comparison, if you think to December of 1944 and the Battle of the Bulge, we see an example of where the Germans were able to catch us by surprise. They used an alternative communications network, and the Allies did not realize that the Germans had made this switch. It was our lack of information that really fueled the initial German success in the Battle of the Bulge. We had come to rely on ULTRA and had developed a little bit of self-delusion -- and the Germans took advantage of it very effectively.

Our ability to monitor the enemy's communications and use that information as an integral part of our operations is really nothing new. There is another example we should not forget. That's how we control the information that we allow the enemy to receive. Again, I am going back to the Second World War and talking about disinformation, particularly the disinformation campaign that centered on General Patton before and during the D-Day landings. At that time, the Allies understood the other guy's ability to intercept our open signals, so we devised a rather elaborate plan that played to this emerging capability on the part of the Germans. The Allies set up a fake Army headquarters and generated false communications transmissions in England. As a result, the Nazis ended up with a significant number of troops placed in the wrong positions.

Even as they started to pick up indications that there was this great Allied armada that was going to invade Normandy, the Germans refused to believe that there could actually be an Allied invasion of Europe led by anyone but Patton. We played on that expectation in a way that kept Patton associated with his fake headquarters. Even as the Germans began to get higher and higher fidelity intelligence that indicated a real attack at Normandy, their leaders were frozen in indecision and, as a result, tied down considerable forces in France across from the shortest invasion route from England.

For instance, the aircraft we will fly over this time frame are fundamentally the same kinds of aircraft we are flying today. Some will have more advanced avionics, more advanced stealth characteristics or other features; but in the main, aircraft will remain fundamentally aircraft as we know them today. Ships will remain fundamentally ships as we know them today. The same holds true for tanks and armored personnel carriers.

Information warfare is not the exclusive domain of the Air Force, or any other service. I think information warfare has different meanings to a soldier, sailor, Marine, or airman. For instance, the soldier's focus may be on what happens at the corps level and below. The sailor's and Marine's focus is on the maritime and littoral regions. At the same time, an airman's focus is theatre-wide, from the front lines to the adversary's capital. You begin to see how IW covers the entire battlefield. But, because of these divergent views and unique needs, I think it's critical that all services come to grips with and develop capabilities for their respective mediums of operations -- that is land, sea, and air. Then, it falls to the joint force commander, or the regional commander-in-chief, to integrate these capabilities to accomplish the mission.

The Air Force has put considerable effort into developing our concepts. In fact, over the past four months, we have had a team travel to every commander-in-chief (CINC) of a U.S. unified command and brief them on our efforts to incorporate IW into our doctrine and to integrate these concepts into our force employment. Most importantly, we want to be sure that what we are doing and how we approach the subject as an institution will be consistent with the way the CINCs intend to fight. And we want to make sure that what we are doing will meet their needs.

As a practitioner of the profession of arms, I view information technology advances with a single-minded interest. I am motivated by the fact that throughout history, soldiers, sailors, Marines, and airmen have learned one extremely valuable lesson relative to engagement with an opposing force. That is, if you can analyze, act, and assess faster than your opponent, you will win.

The information explosion discussed here today is going to make dramatic changes in how this nation fights wars in the future. Such technology will allow a commander's vision and view of the battlefield to be shared at the lowest level -- to the flight for the airman, to the company on the ground, and to the ship's bridge. Simultaneously, soldiers, Marines, sailors, and airmen on the front lines will be able to see and exploit opportunities as they occur.

What this means is our joint forces may enjoy what some are calling "dominant battlefield awareness." We have some of this kind of capability today. We've made significant enhancements to our ability to leverage our forces with faster command and control and intelligence networks. Among other capabilities, these networks are dramatically reducing the time required to detect and destroy a target.

This process starts with how we gather data. Our intelligence, surveillance, and reconnaissance efforts have been significantly and dramatically improved since Desert Storm. If you are familiar with our TALON programs, you will appreciate what we are doing to reduce the sensor-to-shooter loop -- that is injecting what is detected by our space-based assets directly into the cockpit or a flight deck. We are making similar advances with the systems that operate within the earth's atmosphere. For example, our AWACS early warning aircraft have been greatly improved. Their current radar upgrade allows us to detect cruise missiles at twice the range that we could previously. The AWACS is being fitted with the Joint Tactical Information Distribution Systems, or JTIDS. We will start the initial JTIDS operational test this August. Expect that we will reach full operational capability before the end of the decade. JTIDS alone will give us some pretty significant capabilities. It is not restricted just to AWACS. It also gives our warfighters a secure and jam-resistant data link between Air Force, Navy, Army, and Marine units and future coalition partners -- on land, at sea, and in the air. What that really means is all the players will have a real-time picture and awareness of both what is happening on the ground and what is going on in the air above those forces. JTIDS will give us a tremendous capability to know, at a much higher fidelity, the location of both the enemy and our own forces.

We are also making similar improvements in how we plan and control air operations. Today, we are fielding CTAPS -- the Contingency Theatre Automated Planning System. CTAPS will connect our command and control from the joint forces air component commander (JFACC) to the air wings and the base-level planning cells. It will allow us to generate, disseminate, and monitor the progress of the daily air tasking order much faster than we ever have been able to do before. CTAPS also will tie in with the Combat Intelligence System which will provide us the enemy's order of battle through imagery and integrated threat data.

What does this really mean to us? During Desert Storm, it took us about 48 hours to plan and disseminate the ATO. That doesn't mean that it took 48 hours to execute a request from the field. But, it means that the deliberative process that planners went through to service targets was a 36- to 48-hour process. And you had to have someone manually intervene with an immediate air request to get inside those planning cycles. What the CTAPS system will do for us is take this 48-hour cycle and compress it to 12 hours. This really isn't some pie-in-the-sky system that we're dreaming about or visualizing. This is something that is in full use in exercises today and will be operational across the force next year. We have a similar planning tool that has been operational with our global air mobility forces for about three years.

These are a couple of examples of the kinds of tools we are putting in place. They are going to do more than replace the grease pencil and butcher block paper that (retired Air Force General) Chuck Horner and his staff had to use to run the air war during Desert Storm. These systems are going to help us dominate the information spectrum. I am convinced that this capability will be critical the next time our forces are employed in combat.

If you recall, I described information warfare in terms of how we deny, corrupt, or destroy our adversary's information base while we protect our own. Much of this activity has a very offensive element to it. I think we have been doing this for some time, but perhaps we didn't use that term. For example, during Desert Storm, we targeted many of the Iraqi communications nodes and physically destroyed Saddam Hussein's ability to talk to his troops through normal channels. We forced him into sub-optimum modes of communicating.

In the future, we will approach this objective by viewing our adversary's information activities as a system, and we will engage that system in a variety of ways. In fact, rather than put a precision guided munition into the central telephone exchange in Baghdad and destroy it next time, we may elect to leave it standing so we can better exploit it through our advances in information warfare. So, there will be trade-offs between lethal and non-lethal dimensions in the IW arena.

In the same manner, we have been doing some things along the way that we could properly classify as offensive information operations. There are ways that we corrupt information available to the enemy to deceive him. They include using psychological operations and our electronic warfare assets, like the Compass Call aircraft. I think that these kinds of measures that are designed to corrupt information the enemy has are really critical tools that we provide to the CINCs today. They open the envelope for the potential of further operations tomorrow. Again, if you think back to what we did on D-Day with disinformation, and you consider the tremendous advances in technology since 1944, you begin to appreciate the tremendous potential that exists in this area.

If we recognize an adversary's information network as a lucrative target, an adversary will view our data banks and weapon systems the same way. Information security -- the classic OPSEC, COMSEC, and the more recently stressed computer security -- takes on a whole new level of urgency. As a result, the Air Force is taking some rather significant measures to safeguard our assets. This year, we are spending more than $80 million on defensive measures alone, including establishing a base network control center to protect access to computers and communications. This same center will permit us to see if someone has tried to gain access to our system and, hopefully, will allow us to track down who tried to intrude on the system. These initiatives are important because we run a tremendous risk if we look at information warfare as something that is unique to America. It is not, and by the same token, the U.S. military is not alone in this vulnerability.

Our commercial sector, other elements of the government, and our industrial sectors rely on information systems just as much, if not more, than the military. If you've read Tom Clancy's recent thriller, Debt of Honor, you're familiar with what may be plausible. In this fictional tale, Clancy describes the problems caused when someone infects the stock exchange's computers with a virus, literally bringing the stock market to a standstill. To me, Clancy's work reinforces how the information threat is more than just a unique military concern.

As I look at information warfare and how it relates to the services, I'm reminded of a story about a football team. It seems that during one of the games, the local team had to put in a back-up quarterback late in the fourth quarter. They were ahead, and they were just trying to hang on. So, they put this relatively untested young man into the game, and all he had to do was avoid making a mistake and the team would win. So, the coach grabbed the guy as he was about to go on the field and said, "OK, here's what I want you to do. Run the ball three times, and then punt." So, the kid understood that and goes out onto the field.

His first run gains 20 yards -- great. On the second play, he gains 30 yards. Now, this is going a lot better than he ever expected. On the third play, he gains 30 more yards. Now they are down on the 10-yard line, the fans are going crazy, and it appears they're going to wrap this thing up. All he has to do is score, and he'll seal the victory for sure. So, the center snaps the ball to him and he punts. Everyone is stunned by this. His coach pulls him over to the sidelines and asks him what he was thinking. And the quarterback replied, "I was thinking that since you didn't change that play, I must have the dumbest coach around."

It is not enough to make a game plan and go with it. You must act and react to what is happening around you. What we're doing today with information warfare is a little bit like that football game -- IW gives us the ability to plan faster with better information so that we can call the optimum play. It may allow us to know what defensive stunt the other team is going to use. It may allow us to give our opponent false information on what play we're about to use. And, most importantly, it may allow us to call an audible and adjust to a fluid situation.

But unlike the game that I just described, when America sends her military forces into action, we don't want a close, exciting game, and we don't want an inexperienced quarterback. This nation has come to expect in our military operations nothing but blow-outs -- 100 to nothing is a good score. And, I believe that exploiting this new and emerging information technology is going to be the key to making this happen. As we approach tomorrow, we need to do more as a service and with the other services. Let me touch just briefly on what we are doing in terms of changing the way we organize, train, and equip our forces.

First, in terms of organizing, in September 1993, the United States Air Force stood up the Air Force Information Warfare Center in San Antonio. This center has more than 1,000 men and women chartered to support IW planning, intelligence gathering, weapon system analysis, and related activities. This group will be a source of IW support teams to go out and assist the CINCs and JFACCs during crises or exercises. They will help build information warfare into the air campaign planning and execution. The Air Force is not alone in this. The Army has an Information Warfare Center at Fort Belvoir, Virginia, and the Navy has created a center at Fort Meade, Maryland.

Additionally, the Air Force is adjusting our training and education programs to include IW concepts. We have had a course for our major air command and numbered air force staffs to give them basic understanding of the issues. We are incorporating IW into our doctrine, so that airmen everywhere will share a common foundation and a common terminology. We're adjusting our mid- and senior-level professional military education schools at Maxwell Air Force Base, Alabama. You see part of this effort here today. We have four Air Force officers attending the inaugural class of the National Defense University's School for Information Warfare.

Finally, and most significantly, we are beginning to procure weapon systems with a mindset that places high priority on maximizing their performance as an information warfare platform. One example of that is the United States' new air superiority fighter, the F-22. This aircraft is the first platform to be built around information technologies. This was an established objective when we started the program, not something added after the fact. A lot of people have heard about the F-22's stealth. You've heard about its supercruise capability -- that is the ability to cruise faster than the speed of sound in military power. And possibly you've heard about the fact that it has tremendous agility in the air-to-air arena. But, you cannot begin to appreciate its potential until you sit in the concept demonstrator and see how the F-22's integrated avionics work. The quality of the composite picture that's compiled from a variety of sources will literally water your eyes, particularly if you're an old-time fighter pilot. For the first time, you'll be able to sit with those flat glass displays and have tremendous situational awareness readily available to you. That is something we've needed for years, and we're finally in the process of getting it. It will allow our pilots to act and assess faster even when outnumbered. And I tell you it isn't just a concept -- it's being put into production today! The F-22 is just one of many Air Force programs that we're continuing to push forward. You see the same thought processes in the space-based infrared system, in our Joint STARS, and in our precision munitions program. As we move forward, we are establishing an additional requirement for our weapon systems -- that is security against the information threat -- that's being written into the requirements documents.

This new mindset is found throughout our acquisition strategy. We are changing how we view our modernization needs. We're taking another look at IW capabilities, like those associated with command and control, and we're treating them more like force structure than support structure. It's part of how we must change the way we do business to incorporate the fundamentals of information warfare.

This broad approach means that we must get the lawyers involved. When I first heard about bringing in the lawyers, I thought we had really slipped off the deep end one more time. I apologize if I offend any lawyers out there -- I always have held lawyers in fairly high esteem. The more I thought about bringing the lawyers into the equation, the more I realized we need their expertise. Because exploiting the information spectrum will readily cross international borders, we must be cognizant of what the law allows and will not allow.

When do you begin information warfare in the spin up to a conflict? When do you begin to go out there and intrude in somebody's banking system? When do you begin to get into somebody's telecommunications system? These are all very difficult questions. Clearly, information warfare is not something that is focused solely on the confines of a constrained battle area. While we will fight in a theatre, information warfare will force us to be engaged worldwide. Thus, we must have some good advice as we pursue this capability.

I appreciate this opportunity to share with you what the Air Force is doing to try and keep up with the information technology explosion. The American way of war has very strong roots in understanding the value of exploiting information to deny information to our adversary, to corrupt what data he has, and to exploit what we know.

World War II was filled with many examples of information warfare. Perhaps Winston Churchill offered the best summary of its importance. At the Tehran conference, when discussing the Allied plans to manipulate information before D-Day, many of these same ethical questions came up. When do we do it? How do we do it? Who are the innocent victims of this thing? And Churchill, addressing the other Allied leaders said, "In wartime, truth is so precious that she should always be attended by a bodyguard of lies" (Anthony Cave Brown, Bodyguard of Lies (New York: Harper and Row, 1975), p. 10). Something to think about. Later, there was a book written with that title by Anthony Brown. If you read his thick volume, it is rather chilling to see what was possible in that era, and then think about how much more is possible today with the technology that's available. Today and in the future, information warfare is, in fact, going to be this nation's bodyguard. It is essential for the success of our joint forces. To succeed, we are going to need help from a lot of people, including all the very interested people in this room. You understand the far-reaching implications of systems like LANDSAT or SATCOM which are readily available and widely employed at relatively low cost. You appreciate the potential for information technology to allow an adversary to build small, capable, autonomous, operating systems that can threaten U.S. forces on land, sea, or in the air. Such devices might operate relatively unseen and unobserved until they unleash their destructive power.

INNATE FEATURES OF INFORMATION WARFARE

While information warfare in the true sense has not yet arrived in the battlefield arena, the repeated live-troop maneuvers and simulated drills of the armies of Western nations such as the United States, as well as the Gulf War, have enabled us to determine certain innate features of information warfare:

- Battlefield transparency. While "battlefield fog" used to be a major problem troubling battlefield commanders, with digitized units, the battlefield is transparent. All belligerent troops will have the battlefield situation at their fingertips both day and night, and be able to see clearly on computer terminal display screens both their own and the enemy's positions, postures, concentrations, and movements. Sullivan says that the transparency of coming wars will be "a quantitative step higher than in the Gulf War."
- Battlefield transparency will be the result of digitized technology. Digitized technology can transmit battlefield intelligence to commanders quickly and accurately in a noiseless and graphics-plus-words form. Digitized cameras on reconnaissance planes can send, in 30 seconds, a 24-power photo that was shot in the morning to an operational command center as far as 315 km away. Frontline troops using digitized infrared sights can detect maneuvers by over 100 enemy tanks, immediately reporting them to their superiors with

digitized information equipment. Digital compression technology can determine enemy detection distance, raising information processing capability, and transmitting intelligence in real time to all units (subunits), even to individual soldiers, for joint information sharing.

- Overall coordination. Overall coordination is another feature of information warfare. The building of the battlefield information superhighway will mean that all operational systems such as combat forces, combat support units, and combat logistics support units, as well as all operational functions such as battlefield intelligence, command, control, communications, and assaults, will be linked into an organic whole. Coordinated actions by all units of this whole can raise combat effectiveness. For instance, coordinated firepower can raise fire assault effectiveness. Air and land sensors detect enemy target activity, which is immediately displayed on screens at the support arm operational center, with the target positioning system accurately converting enemy target coordinates; the target assignment system then assigns suitable targets to the weapons-launching platforms (such as cannons, helicopters, and tanks) that are most suited to attack.
- Operations in real time. Real time is defined as the time of dealing with a certain event being almost the same as the real time of the occurrence of the event. Real-time operations mean immediate responses to all events that occur on the battlefield between ourselves and the enemy and involves the taking of countermeasures such as timely target detection, timely command, timely mobility, real-time strikes, and real-time support. The advantage of this is that missions that used to be hours or even longer can now be completed in minutes or even seconds, making decisionmaking and the course of battle nearly simultaneous.
- Precision strike. Long-range precision strikes without collateral damage will become the essential fire-assault

form of future information warfare, making carpet bombing and area fire part of history. Future warfare will be as accurate, clean, and neat as a scalpel cutting out a brain tumor, because future wars will use smart weapons on a large scale. Such weapons include guided bombs, guided shells, guided shrapnel, cruise missiles, no-tip guided missiles, and antiradiation missiles. Their sensors will be capable of capturing all useable direct or indirect target information, such as sound waves, electric waves, visible light, infrared waves, lasers, and even odors and gasses, which information computers will be able to differentiate and analyze. Such smart ammunition not only can hit targets 100 percent of the time, but can also hit predetermined target positions. To conduct and win information warfare, two major supports will be needed.

A Digitized Battlefield

A digitized battlefield is a composite network system covering the whole operational space. It is made up of a communications system, a command and control system, an intelligence transmission system, a computerized battlefield database, and user terminals, all of which can provide users with large amounts of operation-related information in real time or nearly real time. This network system's function is to use information technology to acquire, exchange, and use digitized information in real time, promptly meeting the information demand of commanders, combat personnel, and combat support personnel, so that they can clearly and accurately grasp all battlefield conditions needed to draw up and apply operational plans. This system can transmit information such as voice, graphics, text, and data, and can also provide users with a battlefield image portrayed by a common database and the supreme battlefield command knowledge-base (including substance such as one's own posture, the enemy's posture, combat readiness, logistics conditions, and operating environment).

This picture is dynamic, changing with the movements of both combatants and changes in terrain and weather. A digitized battlefield is a prerequisite for information warfare. The establishment of a digitized battlefield has many advantages. For instance, information sharing clarifies the position of the enemy and one's own units, sharply lowering accidental injuries; it enables battlefield commanders to amass key units at crucial sites at critical times; it can effectively coordinate short-distance, in-depth, and rear operations, providing intelligence support for all-out, in-depth, simultaneous offensive operations. As all come to know the battlefield conditions, subordinate commanders can bring their initiative into play, acting promptly at their own discretion in line with their superiors' intentions; it makes logistics support "very accurate," for such activities as material provision variety and quantity "accuracy," logistics support provision-time "accuracy," and wounded treatment "timely accuracy."

The establishment of a digitized battlefield is a sort of systems engineering. Many U.S. military specialists claim that this project is more challenging than the Manhattan Project. To carry out this project, the United States is taking many steps.

In line with Clinton's Presidential Order #29 issued in September 1994, the U.S. Defense Department has set up the National Security Policy Commission and the National Information System Security Commission. The former is charged with formulating military security policy and digitized battlefield establishment principles, while the latter is responsible for controlling the security and secrecy of classified and sensitive information on the military information superhighway and the digitized battlefield. The U.S. Army set up in January 1994 the Army Digitized Special Taskforce under the direct leadership of the Army's first deputy chief of staff. In June 1994, that taskforce was expanded into the Army Digitized Office, and charged with the design and establishment of the digitized army battlefield. In July 1994, the U.S. Navy set up the Theatre of Operations Information Warfare Center; in January 1995, it established the Fleet Information Warfare Center. Their joint responsibilities are to study and design the technology and software needed for the digitized naval battlefield. The U.S. Air Force Information Warfare Center was set up in October 1993, and charged with establishing a digitized air battlefield.

To build a digitized land, sea, and air battlefield, the computer system structures, operating programs, program design languages, software applications, database languages, and communications rules of all information systems must be standardized and interchangeable throughout all branches of the military. Thus the U.S. military is now pursuing two information resource standardization plans: 1) the all-service command, control, communications, computer, and intelligence system standardization plan, which will set up a global military information database and a global joint network system, thus deploying throughout the world global information sharing for the U.S. military; and 2) the defense information control standardization plan, which is aimed at upgrading the interchangeable software technology of all Defense Department information systems, to eventually make information control and usage standardized and interchangeable.

To achieve battlefield digitization for all arms of the service, the U.S. military is now pursuing a diversified C&C digitized joint-network plan. For instance, the U.S. Army has seven plans:

- The "composite unit C&C, a high-tech demonstration" plan aimed at improving and developing the computer assisted C&C system
- The "joint ground station" plan to provide rapid operational intelligence information to brigade commanders
- The "global network grid" plan to bring many combat units into a single working network
- The "survival adaptation system demonstration" plan that uses multi-media technology to transmit information such as voice, graphics, and data to combat troops

- The "21st century ground warrior" plan to achieve a free battlefield dialogue between man and machine
- The "brigade and below unit (subunit) C&C plan" to provide battlefield information to units (subunits) at the brigade level and below
- The "battlefield combat friend and foe recognition demonstration" plan.

An Informationized Military

The second major support for information warfare [IW] is an informationized military. While many developed Western nations are now considering the establishment of technology-intensive informationized armies, the United States is the only one that has drawn up and started to implement plans for an informationized military establishment.

An informationized army is a brand-new "information-based" military category, with its combat theory, system establishment, personnel quality, and weaponry being completely suited to IW needs. The U.S. informationized military establishment plans are in two stages, which are estimated to be completed by the mid-21st century.

In the first stage, the U.S. Army will first be digitized. While digitized units will be essentially the same in authorized strength and structure as units with ordinary equipment, they will be units with digitized communications technology; integrated command, control, communications, and intelligence; smart weaponry; and networking of all operating systems. The major signs that a unit is digitized will be that its main outfits will be equipped with digitized communications equipment, second-generation forward-looking radar, identification friend-and-foe [IFF] equipment, and the global positioning system [GPS]. Such equipment will include M1A2 tanks, M2A2 fire support vehicles, M2A3 fighting vehicles, Black Eagle command helicopters, Apache attack choppers, Kiowa Brave reconnaissance choppers, M109A6 Warrior self-propelled guns, and M106A2 mortars. The U.S. Army now has a digitized battalion and will have established a digitized army by 1999, with all Army units digitized by 2010. To test the combat capability of digitized units, the U.S.

Army has conducted repeated simulated tests and live-troop confrontation exercises between digitized task forces and nondigitized units. The simulated tests show that digitized technology can shorten the time of choppers going into action from 26 minutes to 18 minutes, while raising the hit rate of antitank missiles from 55 percent to 90 percent.

The live-troop exercises show that using conventional communications means to send on-site reports to battalion headquarters takes 9 minutes, while digitized communications means takes only 5 minutes; that the repetition rate is 30 percent for (telegram) text sent by conventional means, but only 4 percent for that sent by digitized means; and that the completion rate of on-site reports is only 22 percent by phone, but as high as 98 percent by digitized means. Through repeated demonstrations the U.S. Army has reached the initial conclusion that "digitized units have enormous combat potential," with their combat effectiveness being "about three times that of ordinary units."

In the second stage, the U.S. Army will grow more informationized on that digitized foundation, as well as build the entire U.S. military, including the Navy and Air Force, into a fully informationized force. After 2010, the U.S. Army will probably be the first to draw up "IW theory," as well as act in line with that theory to reform its system establishment, carry out military training, and develop weaponry, to informationize its units. For two reasons this will probably take about three decades, with completion by 2040:

- The shortage of money for military expenditures dictates that, only once its key combat equipment is digitized, can its related combat support and combat logistics support equipment be gradually digitized. Also, it will have to develop a batch of new smart weapons. So projected from an arms development cycle of about 15 years, it is estimated that its equipment will be completely informationized by 2030.

- The conversion of a military establishment from one structure to another that can operate effectively will take roughly two decades. The U.S. military that can begin to adjust its troop structure after 2010 will still need around two decades to establish the mechanisms suited to fight an information war. Also, as weaponry informationization and military establishment reform cannot be completely synchronous, with an approximate time lag of at least a decade, it is projected that the U.S. Army will be fully informationized only by 2040. The U.S. Navy and Air Force are now also informationizing. By about 2040, once all services are informationized, it will still take more than a decade to get the entire military into a digitized joint network. So it is obvious that by mid-century, the United States probably will have built the world's first completely smart military.

While IW has not yet occurred or at most has only started to show up, as it is an exceptional and new form of warfare with milestone significance, it will have an enormous impact on all aspects of the military arena.

The IW Impact on Combat Concepts

The IW proposition will have an impact on many aspects of combat concepts:

- It will make the rivalry over "information dominance" particularly intense. Certain experts note, "information dominance can be defined most easily and accurately as knowing all enemy information, while keeping the enemy from learning one's own." In future wars, most participating troops in most situations will be dealing not with material, but rather with information. The formation and development of troop combat effectiveness will rely mainly on information collection, processing, transmission, control, and usage. A superior force that loses "information dominance" will be passive, beaten, and in trouble, while an inferior one that seizes the information advantage will be able to win the battlefield initiative. As future combat actions will all be dependent and focused on information, the struggle to wrest information dominance will permeate everything and will be exceptionally fierce and intense.

- It will expand the implications of warfare. This will be manifested mainly in two areas. 1) It will make it harder to win wars. In the agricultural age, it was necessary only to exterminate the enemy's armed forces to win the war. In the industrial age, in addition to wiping out the enemy country's military, it has also been necessary to destroy its military-industrial base. However, in the information age, it will be necessary not only to eliminate the enemy country's war making "material base," but also to control and destroy the enemy's information systems, which will be the primary assault targets. 2) It will expand the limits of war into outer space. That is because the key IW systems space monitoring, positioning, guidance, and communications systems will all be deployed there.
- It will shorten the time of battle. The institution of IW will shorten future wars for two reasons: 1) On one hand, attack means will be highly precise, with the strike targets also being key enemy military positions such as "brain centers," which can be forced to submit very quickly. 2) On the other, in the information age as compared to the industrial age, the combat objectives pursued by both belligerents will be more limited, not total surrender or extermination of the other side, but rather limited political objectives.
- It will make combat more integrated. As information will flow more quickly and not be subject to service branch or time-space limitations, future wars are going to be unprecedentedly integrated.

Land, sea, air, and space warfare will be highly integrated, which will be the case not only in large-scale wars, but also in small-scale armed conflicts. - The combat lines among service arms will be hard to distinguish. For instance, the weapons that destroy enemy tanks may not be one's own [friendly] tanks, but rather smart missiles fired from friendly naval submarines.

War zone combat operations will be integrated. As information-age units will have real-time information for rapid mobility both day and night, "the decentralized campaigns developed in the industrial age will no longer exist, being replaced by integrated combat operations in the entire theatre of operations."

The lines among the strategic, campaign, and tactical levels will be blurred. As smart weapons will provide effective means of meeting combat objectives, it will be possible at times to meet strategic and campaign objectives without losing large units.

- It will change the substance of force concentrations. As the use of precision-strike and stealth weapons will make it possible for force concentrations to meet campaign and even strategic objectives, the force-concentration priority will change from the tactical to the campaign and strategic level. A concentration of mostly personnel will change to a concentration of mainly firepower and information, and a concentration of mostly troop and weapons quantity will change to mainly quality. Force concentrations will occur faster, more precisely, and more often during operations.

CYBER-DEFENSE

It is clear to those who have studied the problem that the United States (and other technologically advanced nations) faces a dangerous, sustained, and increasingly effective attack on its critical information infrastructure. This paper differs from many others in presenting a strategic approach to boosting the inherent security of the Internet and related infrastructure, rather than a series of tactical responses to known weaknesses and threats.

The Internet is the Great Facilitator. The coupling of data communication and high-speed computers unifies things which were formerly disparate. The Internet unifies geography, extending our reach instantly around the world. And it unifies information, allowing data formerly scattered in numerous sources to be easily combined. The Internet aids communication, collaboration and exchange. While generally beneficial, new risks arise when these increased capabilities are used by our attackers.

We have often likened the Internet to a highway. Another analogy is to compare the Internet to the oceans. Prior to the development of modern roads, water transport was even more important than it is today. Much as the Internet today is a medium for attacking us, the oceans made the British Isles a constant and pleasing target for invaders. Britain, having a long and easily reached coastline, was the target of numerous invasions in historical times from the Romans through the Normans, and no doubt extending back indefinitely through prehistory.

Something quite different, however, has happened in the last one thousand years. Britain holds the unique distinction among major powers of not having been successfully invaded since the year 1066. The reason is largely the development of the British navy. The British navy had the effect of converting the oceans from a highway for invaders into a powerful defensive moat. In essence, the British found a strategic solution to a structural problem.

It is worth noting some of the things which the British did not do (or which were not effective), as they have some bearing on the discussion of Internet security today. British security did not rely primarily on tracking all possible invasion plans; on intercepting all suspicious communication; on a system of rapid response to landings; on massive retaliation; on seizure of suspicious Scandinavian fishing boats; or on keeping a low international profile to avoid threats. Nor is it likely that any of these approaches, by themselves, would have been effective, regardless of how Draconian they were in implementation. Instead, the British simply held control of the seas, which stopped all potential invasions, known or otherwise.

The approach taken here is similarly based on a strategic solution to the structural weaknesses of the Internet. In the short-term, it complements tactical responses such as surveillance and expanded enforcement. In the long-term, it renders tactical response less necessary, and thus acts to further secure our civil liberties. The advantage of a strategic approach is that it increases our actual security, while reducing our need to develop a fortress mentality.

The Extent of the Threat

There is no serious question that the United States currently has an extremely dangerous vulnerability to attacks on its information infrastructure. This vulnerability has been extencively documented elsewhere: see, for instance, *Critical Foundations: Protecting America's Infrastructure.* Numerous specific instances have also been reported in the popular press. It is worth, however, briefly summarizing the nature and extent of the threat as a basis for the discussion in subsequent sections.

Cyber-attacks based on viruses (embedded code fragments) and worms (standalone programs) have already cost us well into the tens of billions of dollars in quantifiable damage and lost productivity. Lloyds of London, which has an institutional interest in accurate cost estimates, puts the worldwide cost of the LoveBug virus alone at over $15 billion (mostly uninsured). A separate estimate by the firm Computer Economics puts the worldwide cost of virus and worm attacks on information systems at $10.7 billion for 2001 through August; $17.1 billion for all of 2000; and $12.1 billion in 1999.

Quantifiable damage, however, is only part of the problem. For instance, the Sircam worm, which infects all versions of Microsoft Windows, was discovered on July 17th of this year. Aside from sometimes filling all unused memory or deleting all files, Sircam e-mails out files from an infected computer's hard disk. To the extent that this compromises medical, financial or trade-secret information, the cost can not be quantified.

Besides Sircam, recent months have seen several potent new worms, including Code Red, Code Red II, and Nimda, all of which exploit vulnerabilities in Microsoft's IIS server software. Nimda, for instance, infects computers running Microsoft

Windows 95, 98, ME, NT and 2000; uses multiple infections routes, including e-mail, browsers, open network shares and vulnerabilities left behind by other viruses; and has the effect of leaving infected computers open to intruders. In addition to direct damage to infected computers themselves, once an intruder has control of your computer it can be used as a base to infect other computers, or to launch "denial-of-service" (DoS) attacks against major sites. In one kind of a DoS attack, the target site is bombarded with spurious information requests which prevent its normal operation. The most famous such attacks occurred during February of 2000, when major sites such as Amazon.com, Buy.com, CNN and eBay were disrupted.

As another example, on July 19th, 2001 the White House was the target of a DoS attack made possible by the Code Red worm. Current trends suggest that things are getting worse, rather than better. It is expected that over 2,000 new software vulnerabilities will be discovered this year. This is about twice the 1,090 from last year, which in turn is more than twice the number from the year before. At the same time, the sophistication and damage caused by computer worms is also rapidly increasing. Nimda propagates with unprecedented speed. Some researchers predict new classes of "flash worms" which could spread in minutes or seconds, leaving little time to react.

We should also note that criminal groups have been moving aggressively online. The FBI estimates that electronic crime costs about $10 billion per year, and that organized crime groups based in Eastern Europe have stolen over 1 million credit card numbers from web sites in the U.S., making use of vulnerabilities in Microsoft Windows NT. An estimate by the Director of the Privacy Rights Clearinghouse puts the cost from the fraudulent use of credit cards at $4 billion per year. Aside from the substantial disturbance to the lives of those directly victimized, the cost of credit card fraud is passed on to businesses and consumers in the form of higher credit card fees and interest rates, and to law enforcement in terms of a higher case load.

Theft of credit card information is one example of the more general problem of identity theft, in which one person uses the identifying information of another. Identify theft is useful to criminals both as a means to misappropriate the assets of the victim, and as a way to camouflage the origin of criminal activity. Identity theft is also of use to terrorists. Testimony before the U.S. Senate Judiciary Subcommittee on Technology, Terrorism, and Government Information estimated 500,000 to 700,000 victims of identity theft in the year 2000.

Victims are often unaware that their identity has been stolen until years afterwards, when they discover damage to their credit rating or criminal charges on their record, affecting their purchase or employment opportunities and possibly landing them in jail. Clearing the record is difficult and time-consuming, and by one victim's estimate can easily generate costs of $10,000-$15,000. Consider, too, the hidden cost on the legal system of dealing with this volume of crime. Identity theft is facilitated by the existence of personal information on poorly-secured web sites (although more traditional means of obtaining personal information are of course also widely used, such as retrieving discarded, unsolicited credit card offers). The range of sites which have been shown to be vulnerable to computer intruders is quite comprehensive. Some examples:

- Almost all of the Fortune 500 corporations have been successfully penetrated.
- One pre-approved test attack in 1996 demonstrated the ability to completely take over the information systems of a major metropolitan police force, including the ability to monitor and alter dispatches and court records. While that particular police force has since taken substantial steps to improve its security, there is little doubt that vulnerabilities remain both there and across the country.
- Public statements in November, 1997 by the U.S. Senate Judiciary Subcommittee on Technology, Terrorism and Government Information concerning the "Eligible Receiver" exercises include the following findings: 62-65% of all Federal Computer Systems have known

security holes which can be exploited; between 250 and 600 DoD systems were broken into in 1996; and more than 120 countries or foreign organizations have or are developing formal programs that can be used to attack and disrupt critical Information Systems Technology (IST) used by the U.S. "While much of the [Eligible Receiver] exercise remains classified, I believe it is fair to say that it revealed some serious vulnerabilities in government information systems that must be corrected."

- According to an April 16th, 1998 report in the Washington Times on the Eligible Receiver exercise, "Using software obtained easily from hacker sites on the Internet, a group of National Security Agency officials could have shut down the U.S. electric-power grid within days and rendered impotent the command-and-control elements of the U.S. Pacific Command, said officials familiar with the war game."
- An actual penetration of a computer system controlling the California power grid, undetected for 17 days, occurred this year. (Different views are given concerning how close the attackers came to being able to affect the power supply.)
- The FBI recently issued a list of the top 20 Internet vulnerabilities, stating that "the Internet wouldn't be able to withstand a major attack."
- Comments by senior Bush advisor Karl Rove to the New York Times shortly after the September 11th tragedies suggest that the attackers had access to White House codes. According to one report, those responsible for the September 11th, 2001 attack on the World Trade Center were in possession of the top-secret White House code words; of the code groups of the NSA; and of all or part of the codes used by the Drug Enforcement Administration, the National Reconnaissance Office, Air Force Intelligence, Army Intelligence, Naval Intelligence, Marine Corps Intelligence and the intelligence offices of the State Department and Department of Energy.

They had also allegedly penetrated the NSA's electronic surveillance system.

- "Information warfare specialists at the Pentagon estimate that a properly prepared and well-coordinated attack by fewer than 30 computer virtuosos strategically located around the world, with a budget of less than $10 million, could bring the United States to its knees."

The Cisco routers which direct the vast majority of traffic on the Internet are also known to have vulnerabilities.

Based on prior experience, we can expect an increase in cyber-attacks in the wake of the September 11th tragedies. It may or may not be coincidental that the dangerous Nimda worm was first detected exactly one week after the World Trade Center attack.

The consensus of the information security community appears to be that our systems are becoming less secure, rather than more secure, over time. For one report on the current state of cyber-security, see the recent Congressional testimony by Jeff Carpenter, Manager of the CERT/CC. For a discussion of current weaknesses in governmental cyber-security, see the September 26th, 2001 Washington Post article "Key U.S. computer systems called vulnerable to attack".

It is not clear that it is currently possible, with the tools in common use, to guarantee the protection of sensitive information which is accessible via the Internet.

Why is our information infrastructure sustaining such large (and growing) damage? The structural weaknesses of the Internet, and the means to strengthen it, will be discussed below. Put simply, however, the Internet was built out of straw. And the world is full of wolves.

THE ROOTS OF THE INTERNET SECURITY PROBLEM

"For Zeus, who guided men to think, has laid it down That wisdom comes alone through suffering." — Aeschylus, Agamemnon

There are technical approaches to securing the Internet which will be discussed below. However, these technical approaches are secondary. They can only be effective to the extent that we first reduce a bias against strong Internet security. The poor state of Internet security (as documented above) is an extreme case of a general pattern. We invent technologies to provide convenience.

However, any powerful tool may also create new problems, which it may take years to fully understand and control. This delayed response between embracing the convenience of a new technology, and responding to its safety concerns, might be termed "the convenience overshoot". For instance, the modern automobile industry can be dated to the introduction of the Ford Model T in 1909, or to its moving assembly line production in 1913. However, it was only in the 1930's that some physicians began self-installing lap belts, and not until 1956 that Ford introduced lap belts as an option for some models.

Similarly, while the first steam powered locomotive was operating in 1804, it was not until the 1870's that a safe and effective braking system came into use, based on the ideas of George Westinghouse. One interpretation of the convenience overshoot is that it results simply from the time to grasp the safety issues for a new technology, followed by the time to overcome inertia sufficiently to address them. A somewhat a deeper analysis may be useful, however.

There is a fundamental trade-off between convenience and safety. Safety does not come for free. Putting a lock on a door, for instance, increases safety while increasing the price of the door and making it slightly more time-consuming for authorized people to enter. The convenience of successful technologies is readily apparent and easily marketed. A constituency for safety develops only over time, and requires a concerted effort by customers, manufacturers, and perhaps government to carry the day.

For the Internet, the convenience vs. safety trade-off occurs at three layers.

Layer 1: *Data communication* between different sites on the Internet.

Layer 2: *Operating systems* controlling computers.

Layer 3: *Software applications* running on top of operating systems.

In all three cases, there has existed a strong bias in favor of convenience, rather than security, to the detriment of both individual and collective safety. Let us first outline the form of this bias for each layer, followed by more general discussion.

At Layer 1, the underlying data communication protocol standard for most of the Internet is Internet Protocol Version 4, or IPv4, whose origins trace back to the mid-1970's. Descended from a time when the precursor of the Internet was a relatively small, closed network of trusted sites, IPv4 established a simple, open protocol lacking built-in security against malicious uses such as IP spoofing, in which one site masquerades as another for purposes of intrusion or data theft. Despite the radical change in the character of the Internet over the last 25 years, we are only now making the transition from IPv4 to a more secure (and robust) IPv6 data communication protocol.

At Layer 2, one form that the convenience bias takes is the presence of a high number of (at least theoretically) useful operating system features. Any powerful feature is potentially a weapon which can be used by intruders. By default, operating systems tend to ship with a multitude of features turned on. It is then up to end-users, many of them with insufficient computer training, to figure out how to turn off potentially insecure features. In a recent FBI list of the top 20 Internet security flaws, this practice of shipping software with all features turned on is listed first.

At Layer 3, we again have the problem of a bias towards convenient but dangerous features. An additional risk at the application level is poor integration between the application and the operating system, or between different applications. Poor integration may lead to "chinks in the armor", creating vulnerabilities.

While the Internet convenience overshoot outlined above is typical in form to other new technologies, the magnitude of the problem has now risen to constitute a national security threat. This level of severity is due to three factors. The first factor is the incredible power of software, to both help and threaten. Software is limited primarily by ideas, not by the properties of materials. It is thus the closest that engineering has come to magic. Networking extends this power immensely, and the misuse of its capabilities makes cyber-attacks possible.

The second factor is the speed with which the Internet has developed. We have had very little time, by historical standards, to respond to the Internet convenience overshoot. The Internet, as a platform for commerce and use by the general public, is less than 10 years old and continues to grow exponentially. We do not have 40 years to wait for the Internet equivalent of a seat belt to reach the market, nor 70 years for the equivalent of the locomotive pneumatic brake. The third factor is that software security problems are invisible to the naked eye. We do not see software vulnerabilities with the same ease that we notice an unlocked door. Even security experts may not be aware of security flaws in new software until well after it has been released and installed on millions of computers.

As yet, market pressures have not worked strongly in the direction of producing secure software. For the above reasons, customers have had difficulty evaluating their risk, and making a corresponding vote in the market place. Software manufacturers have therefore lacked strong pressure from their customers to produce secure software. A further factor is that software manufacturers in general do not bear the costs associated with security flaws in their products.

Because security costs are not yet accurately reflected in purchase decisions, competitive pressures make it difficult for software manufacturers to provide a high level of security. Any "good Samaritan" company which does aim for high security is placed at a competitive disadvantage. Its products will be slower to market; may have less features; and will have higher development costs. This analysis may help to explain why the number of new software security vulnerabilities discovered has doubled in each of the last two years. According to the CERT/CC (a major reporting center for Internet security problems):

"There is little evidence of improvement in the security of most products; developers are not devoting sufficient effort to applying lessons learned about the sources of vulnerabilities. The CERT/CC routinely receives reports of new vulnerabilities.

We continue to see the same types of vulnerabilities in newer versions of products that we saw in earlier versions. Technology evolves so rapidly that vendors concentrate on time to market, often minimizing that time by placing a low priority on the security of their products. Until customers demand products that are more secure or there are legal or liability changes, the situation is unlikely to change."

Yet a further impediment to Internet security is the distributed nature of the problem. A cup that leaks in one spot leaks in its entirety.

While subnets can be and are protected separately, the presence of vulnerable computers on the Internet poses some degree of threat to everyone else on the Internet. For example, in a denial-of-service (DoS) attack, huge numbers of infected computers may be used to bombard a major site. Owners of computers contributing to the attack are often unaware of their role, or even that their computer has been infected.

The protection of the private data which forms the basis for identity theft is similarly a distributed problem. Our private data is held in the databases of myriad institutions, in many cases without our knowledge. Penetration of any one of these databases as the result of a cyber-attack is just as damaging as penetrating all of them. The chain hangs by its weakest link.

Specific Recommendations

"For a successful technology, reality must take precedence over public relations, for nature can not be fooled." — Richard Feynman, Physics Nobel Laureate, in his report on the Challenger Space Shuttle disaster.

This section provides specific recommendations to secure the Internet. The essence of the approach is not to focus primarily on the tactics of fixing specific security problems (although that is necessary as well), but rather to correct the structural deficiencies which have consistently produced these problems for many years. A two-level hierarchy of actions is required. The first, and most important, is to correct the Internet convenience overshoot: that is, to speed up the natural process whereby the market place will increasingly reflect true safety costs. The second level has to do with software development and usage.

Level 1: Correcting the Internet Convenience Overshoot

As discussed earlier, there is a fundamental trade-off between convenience and safety. Early in a technology's history, there is a tendency to focus on the conveniences which it can provide. Over time, we become wiser and make safety adjustments where necessary. The Internet is currently in the midst of this transition. We have created a tool of great convenience. Unfortunately, it has left us unsafe from acts of malice. In the natural unfolding of events, Internet security will be enhanced.

However, we do not have time for this natural process to pursue its stately trajectory. The degree to which the Internet is now vulnerable constitutes a national security threat. It is encumbant on users of the Internet; on manufacturers; and on government to act in such a way as to reduce this threat.

The first requirement is one of education, so that the market place will better reflect true security costs. We need to make generally known the extent of the threat, both individual and collective; the dangers of specific products, as well as the degree to which they have been tested by independent third parties; and the steps which can be taken to reduce security threats, as outlined below.

The second requirement is organization. Organization in terms of both people and standards. Groups provide a forum to identify problems, disseminate possible solutions, and agitate for change. Standards are a organized means by which to judge the practical world. One security standard, Common Criteria certification, is described below.

The third requirement (the necessity of which one hopes will be eliminated or reduced by the first two) is regulation. We do not allow convenience vs. safety issues for new medical drugs to be arbitrated in the market place. We require that new medical drugs be proven safe before they are made available to the public. This limitation to free markets is justified by the extreme danger of acting otherwise. If less drastic measures are unsuccessful, the same may be judged true of Internet products.

Level 2: Software Development and Usage

The Level 1 discussion above was concerned with reducing the bias against Internet security. Level 2 is concerned with implementation steps to strengthen Internet security as rapidly as possible.

Recommendation: Ship Software with Most Features Turned Off

In October, 2001, the FBI and the SANS Institute jointly released the "Twenty Most Critical Internet Security Vulnerabilities." In their opinion, the majority of successful attacks via the Internet can be traced to these twenty problems. Number one on the list, affecting all systems, is that most software manufacturers by default enable too many functions, some with security holes.

"The vendor philosophy is that it is better to enable functions that are not needed, than to make the user install additional functions when they are needed. This approach, although convenient for the user, creates many of the most dangerous security vulnerabilities because users do not actively maintain and patch software components they don't use. Furthermore, many users fail to realize what is actually installed, leaving dangerous samples on a system simply because users do not know they are there."

The software necessary to perform common end-user tasks such as browsing the web, sending e-mail and word processing is not inherently more complex than a Volvo. There is no reason why it should not be similarly robust and secure.

Consumers have a reasonable expectation that a software product, installed straight out of the box in accordance with the manufacturer's directions, is safe to use. Currently, this is far from being the case.

PromoteTrusted Operating Systems

Current Internet practice notwithstanding, it is in fact possible to create highly secure operating systems. And they do in fact exist. For instance, in January, 2001 a $50,000 prize was offered to any hacker able to break into a test ecommerce site protected by the Argus Pitbull software product. Despite more than 5 million attacks from an estimated 100,000 to 200,000 would-be intruders, the prize went unclaimed. Similarly, Pitbull stood up to all attacks at a recent hackers' convention in Las Vegas.

Pitbull makes use of "trusted operating system" techniques. The essential idea behind trusted operating systems, which goes back to the 1980's, is compartmentalization. Users and processes are limited to the specific information and capabilities needed to carry out their tasks.

The various approaches to operating system security can be understood by analogy to the problem of designing ships that are less likely to sink. Software firewalls are roughly equivalent to wrapping a strong hull around a leaky ship. This approach can work reasonably well but is prone to catastrophic failure.

A single puncture in the hull, either through an accident or deliberate malice by an insider, will sink the ship. The common software practice of opening ports through the firewall (to support, for instance, e-mail, web services, or Internet chats) is roughly equivalent to deliberately dynamiting a doorway in a ship's hull in order to facilitate loading and unloading goods. It works well until such time as the ship sinks.

Trusted operating system techniques are equivalent to creating separate, watertight compartments in a ship, so that even if one (or more) compartment develops a leak the ship will stay afloat. Why, despite a history dating back to the early 1980's, are trusted operating systems not in widespread use?

The answer goes back to the discussion in Section 3 of the bias towards convenience over safety. Just as watertight compartments in a ship add to design and development costs, as well as reducing ease-of-motion for passengers and crew, similar inconveniences affect trusted operating systems. Trusted operating systems cost more to develop and administer, as well as reducing ease-of-use.

Never-the-less, trusted operating systems should be promoted, perhaps legislatively, for the same safety reasons that we promote compartmentalized ship design. Perhaps more so: a sinking ship is an isolated event; an operating system that is taken over by an intruder is a platform for attacking other sites. A trend towards trusted operating systems will occur naturally as Internet security problems begin to be addressed.

However, the need to secure our information infrastructure is sufficiently compelling that additional steps should be considered. These steps might include requiring trusted operating systems for critical government (and possibly commercial) sites at some point in the future; taxing sites based on the security level of their operating system; or supporting research and training in the use of trusted operating systems.

In view of the cost of identity theft, securing private data about individuals is a long-term goal of considerable importance. One possible approach is to require that institutions holding private data either protect it behind a trusted operating system or else keep it unconnected to the Internet.

Promote Open-Source Software

Traditionally, commercial software products have been distributed as "machine code" (readable by computers), but without the "source code", which is the human-readable version. Source code is something like the blueprint for a building. You can learn a lot by examining a completed skyscraper. But you can learn a lot more (such as how to upgrade the wiring or whether the plumbing was set up correctly) if you also have the blueprint.

"Open source" software products comes with source code available, and generally (although not necessarily for this discussion) with rights to redistribution. The emergence of open source software is interesting economically and socially. However, it is also important from a security perspective.

One's first instinct might be that having software source code widely available decreases security. After all, if the source code is available, does this not make it easier to plan an attack? Somewhat surprisingly, the truth is quite the opposite. Hiding the source code can only improve "accidental" security: security which arises simply because a particular vulnerability has not yet been discovered. Accidental security is a disaster waiting to happen. What we want instead is "intrinsic" security: software products which can stand up to any possible attack. Intrinsic security is enhanced by having as many people as possible examine the source code. Insurance premiums are beginning to support this argument.

Having source code available reduces the security risk associated with poor software engineering. Open source code also reduces the risk of deliberately inserted backdoors for intruders. The European Parliament recognized this point in a resolution favoring open source software passed in September, 2001. Under the Clinton Administration, the President's Information Technology Advisory Committee (PITAC) endorsed open-source software as the new model for high-end computing needs.

It is in our security interests that the software defending our online sites have been read and tested by as many people as possible. For this reason, government procurement policy should favor the acquisition of products which use open source software.

Open source need not imply the absence of a commercial organization supporting the software. It does, however tend towards a service model (in which a company contracts to support certain capabilities using an available body of open source software) rather than towards a manufacturing model (in which a company sells software as a finished good).

Upgrade the Internet Data Communication Protocol to IPv6

The dominant Internet protocol for data communications is still IPv4, with a design that is over 20 years old. IPv4 is vulnerable to "IP spoofing", in which one site pretends to be another for purposes of intrusion. IPv4 also.lacks a built-in way to protect the confidentially of data at the level of individual information packets sent across the Internet.

The transition to the more secure IPv6 protocol is under way. This transistion should be encouraged. The European Union has called for the rapid adoption of IPv6 as a data security measure.

Encourage Diverse Software Platforms

Widespread standardization on the same software tools reduces development, purchase, maintenance, training and usage costs. It also magnifies the destruction if a weakness is found in these tools. "Government systems are often bought in bulk and installed to the same recipe. Finding a flaw and taking over one allows you to take over others easily."

Similarly, the speed with which Internet worms can travel, and the systematic damage which they can cause, is related to the fact that a small number of weaknesses will get them into a very large number of computers. Such systematic software vulnerabilities are akin to the weakness of monocultures in biology. It is known that plant disease epidemics tend to move more rapidly through a "monoculture" (population of one species) than a mixed population. An efficiency is gained by only growing the most productive grains available; but the entire crop can be lost if a pest specific to that particular plant arises.

The convenience of standardization comes at the risk of epidemic. It is hard to know what advice to give on this knowledge; except to be aware that standardization is not an unmitigated good. A diverse software environment may tend to arise naturally as Internet security problems are taken more seriously. For instance, banks and other institutions may have the incentive to create special-purpose software tools for their customer's online transactions.

These tools will provide limited functionality specific to that institution, highly tested for security. More inconvenient than current practice?

Most certainly. But that is the cost of safety. The Internet was created with a decentralized design in order to prevent a single hardware point-of-failure from bringing the entire system down. However, using the same software everywhere, with the same vulnerabilities, comes close to creating a single software point-of-failure. The degree to which it holds a software monoculture goes some way towards explaining why the Internet is now much more vulnerable to attacks on its software than on its hardware.

Promote Use of the Common Criteria Framework

The Common Criteria (CC) for Information Technology Security Evaluation is a framework for tackling information security problems.68 It provides concepts and principles of IT security. It also provides constructs for expressing IT security objectives; for selecting and defining IT security requirements; and for writing high-level specifications for products and systems.

The CC is an international standard aimed at a wide audience. It is intended to provide a shared security language for consumers, developers, vendors, evaluators, certifiers, validators, overseers, accreditors and approvers. Product developers can seek CC certification from independent evaluation facilities as an indication of the product's level of security. The CC is also useful for organizations developing their own internal security policies.

The most important thing about the CC is simply to know that it exists, what it means, and that it holds the respect of security professionals. Over time, checking CC certification should be a part of the decision-making process in acquiring new products.

Promote Internet Immune Response

When a new security weakness is found, the health of the Internet depends on how quickly defensive patches propagate, compared to the speed with which new attacks appear. If a new attack exploiting a weakness appears before computers on the Internet have been patched, the result is an epidemic of invaded computers. The Internet footrace between the defense and the attackers is currently being won easily by the attackers. For instance, as of March, 2001 computer criminals were still making use of vulnerabilities in Microsoft Windows NT for which free security patches were available in 1998. Even if security patches have been downloaded, steps may not have been taken to remove the effects of previous infections. It is estimated that 430,000 Microsoft servers currently have back-door programs installed which allow sensitive data (such as credit card numbers) to be stolen.

Unless the supply of new Internet vulnerabilities drops considerably, the health of the Internet will essentially depend on the relative speed with which the defense and attackers respond to newly-discovered weaknesses. As discussed above, Internet security is a distributed problem: all computers on the Internet, even those properly secured, are threatened by infected computers. It should therefore be a matter of policy to try to speed up the Internet "immune response": the speed with which all computers on the Internet are protected against newly discovered weaknesses.

Methods for doing so include:

1. Supporting and publicizing services to check computers for the currentness of their security patches, and for installed back-door programs.
2. Refusing to accept communication from computers which are not up-to-date on their security patches, instead refering them to the appropriate site to improve their security.

Promote the Use of Integrity Filters

Many "data" files sent around the Internet contain powerful "macros" (software fragments) to execute certain functions. XML and Microsoft Word, for instance, support this capability. The convenience which these macros may provide comes with the risk that their power will be used maliciously. One does not want to ban such macros, as they are often useful. One would, however, like to know whether they are present and make an informed decision about one's level of risk.

A possibility is to systematically develop the use of "integrity filters". The idea would be that files could be developed using integrity filters which monitor the use of macros. Using cryptographic techniques, the integrity filter could certify that the file was created using the filter, and report on the level to which macros are present in the file.

Anyone receiving the file could then use automated tools to check the macro report from the integrity filter, and make an informed decision about whether to accept the file.

Note that the use of integrity filters need not be in any sense mandatory. They would provide an optional added level of security to those who wanted it.

Promote Gradations of Software Capabilities

The discussion indicated that small number of people using easily available software have the capability to cause enormous damage on an international scale. From this viewpoint, a modern personal computer connected to the Internet comes reasonably under the definition of a munition. It is both futile and undesirable to attempt to limit the availability of powerful software on personal computers connected to the Internet. However, making available computer operating systems with different levels of capability would be of assistance to the defense. Currently, it is standard practice to ship operating systems to all customers which have the full feature set needed by the most sophisticated users. Refering back to the discussion of convenience vs. safety, this means that all operating systems shipped are maximally dangerous.

A safer approach might be to provide most users with stripped down operating systems supporting only the most common functionality. These operating systems would contain less code, would change less often, and would be heavily tested for security problems. State-of-the-art operating systems would be aimed only at the most sophisticated users with a need for their capabilities. There would be nothing to prevent any user from acquiring a high-end, state-of the art operating system. However, sites might chose to reduce their security risk by not accepting communication from high-end operating systems; or only accepting communication if the owners of such systems are technically certified as being able to operate them safely.

One might see the Internet as evolving into an environment in which most endusers have relatively simple operating systems which lack dangerous features and have been carefully tested for security problems. Those with technical sophistication would continue to use current operating systems. And sensitive government or e-commerce sites would use trusted operating systems, which are more expensive and time-consuming to maintain, but which provide both a high degree of functionality and a high degree of security.

INTELLIGENCE FOR CYBER-SPACE

Although many of the intelligence methodologies and principles remain the same, new ways of thinking appropriate to the cyber-domain are essential. The lack of borders in cyber-space is a critical difference from the more familiar domains of intelligence. Indeed, geography and political borders often aided traditional military intelligence analysis-it is a simple thing to develop threat scenarios if the potential enemy can only use certain terrain or sea lines of communication and then, only at certain times of the year-while simple factors of physics such as time and distance also provided opportunities for warning. Within the Internet, however, these limiting factors are absent, (although other limiting factors, such as geometry of network connectivity, might exist in a form useful to be incorporated into intelligence analysis), contributing to what can appear to be "instantaneous threats". Assessment of cyber-space threats requires not only a merger of old methodologies and new modes of thinking but also analysts willing and able to approach the art of threat assessment and warning from new perspectives. Only with a distinctive blend of the traditional and the new will it be possible to obtain real understanding of threats and vulnerabilities, to differentiate among types of intrusions and to forecast or anticipate specific incidents or clusters of incidents in ways that lengthen warning time. Enhancing the ability to identify perpetrators is also highly desirable: removing the cloak of anonymity would make perpetrators more concerned about the potential costs and risks of their actions and could have an important deterrent effect. In short, there are several fundamental questions at the heart of the intelligence process. They consist of variations on the who, what, when, where, why and how questions that are familiar parts of most research and analysis.

Security Challenging

Efforts to identify intruders are critical both to the assessment of the challenge and the nature of the response. Potential intruders run the gamut from young hobbyists engaged in the equivalent of joy riding to terrorist organizations and nations that are intent on maximizing damage to the target. The problem of identification is particularly difficult in a domain where maintaining anonymity is easy and there are sometimes time lapses between the intruder action, the intrusion itself, and the actual disruptive effects. Moreover, the consequences are not always commensurate with the objectives, in some cases falling short of what the intruders hoped to achieve, and in others going well beyond what they had envisaged.

There is a broad spectrum of potential intruders on the Internet and an almost equal number of motives for intrusions against organizations. Not surprisingly, this includes perpetrators conducting operations against other perpetrators. As enticing as this prospect is, it does not mitigate the effects of such internecine rivalry. New and more sophisticated tools are often the result of such interplay. This sort of jousting can also provide valuable insights to analysts once it is recognized, but does not simplify the analytic task and puts an incredible strain on limited analytic/warning resources. With the continuing proliferation of sophisticated computer technologies into the mainstream population, attribution for an intrusion becomes more difficult by the day.

The dynamism of the intruder population is itself a problem. On the one hand, success breeds imitation and the sophistication of readily available tools means that even those with limited skills can become intruders.

On the one hand, there is a certain degree of attrition in the intruder community. Indeed, there are many reasons why intruders might cease their activity, including increased maturity, a need to find gainful employment, and a perception of the rewards of working to increase network security rather than attack it. The implication, of course, is that the mix of agents threatening network security is changing as the nature of the Internet changes.

The vast majority of the intrusions are probably being conducted by nuisance hackers or "ankle-biters" who have limited objectives and are usually satisfied with the actual penetration of the system or conduct relatively harmless cyber-vandalism such as the defacement or alteration of web-sites. While aggravating to the target, no significant or lasting damage occurs. The more serious problem occurs when an intrusion is carried out by a more sophisticated intruder (either an individual or a group) whose objective is better defined and involves malicious intent. Motives for these sorts of intrusions are also as varied as the persons carrying them out. They range from greed to defined military strategy and doctrine, and all that falls in between.

Four of the more dangerous, and less well defined categories of intruder are governments conducting operations against other sovereign states, the organized terrorist group, insurgency or revolutionary groups, and organized crime. All these entities are beginning to appreciate the potential power, anonymity, and effectiveness of the Internet. There are myriad examples of governments instituting programmes for Computer Network Warfare. In the case of Russia, policy-makers consider the security of their information infrastructure so critical that–rhetorically at least-they equate an attack against it with a strategic nuclear strike (and have promised an appropriate response). As a result of the realization of the criticality of information infrastructures, computer warfare is now a part of the formal Russian Military Strategy and Doctrine. The same is true of organized terrorist groups. In fact, "most of the 30 top terrorist organizations identified by the U.S. government have web pages and use e-mail, and are ``fairly well developed" at using the Internet."[Casciano] In many cases, dependence on technology is viewed as an Achilles Heel to be exploited by terrorist organizations.

Within the U.S., many of the more militant indigenous groups have discovered the power of the Internet and have well designed and effective Web sites. Indeed, militia and supremacist groups have had significant increases in membership since developing their Web pages. It is a natural progression from using the Internet for propaganda and recruiting to exploiting its potential as a weapon. There is also growing evidence that some of the active insurgency groups around the world are discovering the potential of the computer. It is just a matter of time until they discover the effect of a computer-generated attack against the infrastructure of the government they are fighting. Once that realization is made, cyber-attacks will likely become a weapon of choice for organizations intent on overthrowing an existing government. Disturbingly, Aum Shinrikyo, the group responsible for the Sarin gas attack on the Japanese subway, has increasingly been involved in the Japanese software industry!

Organized crime probably was the first of the sophisticated intruder threats to realize the power and value of the computer. In 1995, it was discovered that the Cali cartel had sophisticated state-of-the-art equipment for electronic eavesdropping, while smaller drug trafficking organizations in Colombia are using the Internet to pressure the Colombian government to change the policy of extraditing traffickers to the United States. Furthermore, the use of computers by organized crime organizations to garner illicit profits is well documented. However, some criminal efforts have gone beyond simple siphoning of funds and money laundering. Extortion of money from financial institutions by threatening to destroy or modify their computer databases is also evident. It is probable that at least some of these extortion operations are conducted by transnational criminal groups. Some of the extortion efforts go wrong–as did the effort to extort Bloomberg. In other cases, however, large payoffs are almost certainly made to the extortionist. It seems likely, therefore, that larger and potentially more dangerous operations should be anticipated.

The obvious challenge is to develop a capacity to identify and track the activities of these potential intruders with the goal of being able to provide predictive analysis and warning of intrusions. Some of the traditional intelligence techniques should apply to these threats, but new methodologies and the ability to contemplate new and complex concepts have to be developed concurrently. This will become even more important (and difficult) as perpetrators of increasing sophistication operate on the Internet. As motivations vary, so will the efforts of the individuals behind malicious operations to either conceal or reveal their responsibility. All of this complicates efforts to track responsible parties determine attribution. Nations and transnational criminal organizations, by their nature, will be diligent in their efforts to maintain anonymity. In some of these cases, identifying the intended victim may give valuable insight into tracking the intruder. Sometimes the target of an intrusion allows the analyst to rule out certain possible perpetrators. A multi-million dollar extortion plot against a major financial institution is probably not the work of a 13-year-old hacker working out of his bedroom. At the same time, however, many victims, especially within government or sensitive industries such as banking or insurance, often complicate the effort to track intruders because of their reluctance to report the incident. In other cases, such as politically motivated attacks, the perpetrators may want their identity known, but not their location. As such operations become more sophisticated, tracking the attack back to its point of origin will be a major challenge to the intelligence analysts involved. What is clear from all of this is that tracking intruders and gaining attribution is much more than just a technical challenge.

One difficulty, of course, is that there are legal constraints on intelligence collection, especially by the military and the national security establishment. Traditionally the focus of intelligence has been on foreign threats, and there are restrictions on intelligence activities directed against individuals or groups that are domestic in nature. Insofar as these groups are the focus of government attention, it is from the law enforcement community. This points to yet another problem: that of coordination and information sharing between the traditional national security agencies and the law enforcement community. Generally law enforcement focuses on individual cases and wants evidence that stands up in court; intelligence agencies in contrast are concerned with protecting the sources of their information so that they can continue to use them. The problem with cyber-threats is that they fall in the gray area where crime and national security merge into one another.

Forms of Intrusion are Occurring

It is tempting to see intrusions in terms of a pyramid that goes from transient vulnerability probing and defacing websites at the base to large scale efforts to undermine the critical missions of an organization or the critical functions of a nation at the top-and to suggest that there is an inverse relationship between frequency and significance, with many trivial incidents and comparatively few of the more serious incidents. There are several difficulties with this however. The first is that probes that appear relatively insignificant could be a harbinger of more serious intrusions. The second is that there is sometimes a gap between intent and consequences–the effects and impact of an incident can either fall far short of what was intended, or far exceed what the perpetrator initially envisaged. This lack of congruence between limited intent and far-reaching consequences stems from the capacity of worms and viruses for infinite replication and multiplication combined with the seamless inter-connectivity of systems. Incidents such as the Love Bug cross the public-private divide and have an indiscriminate impact on corporations, governments, and private individuals irrespective of the initial target. In cases such as this, the consequences have less to do with targeting than with the ubiquity of a particular programme such as Microsoft Outlook that is used as the vector of transmission. In effect, the incident takes on its own momentum.

When the consequences are widespread, of course, the incident becomes very public and is the subject of much media and official commentary. In many other cases, however, there is far greater reticence about the scale, type and targets of attack. The analytic effort must successfully build a trust relationship for the collection of data across a broad variety of organizations. This trust relationship allows for observation of incidents from early probing and experimentation through widespread deployment of automated forms of intrusion. For example, in recent months (June and July 2000) CERTÒ/CC has received reports of intrusions involving a wide variety of automated tools, ranging from simple viruses and system corruption toolkits through complex viruses designed to attack relatively hardened sites with low probability of detection and distributed tools designed to crash network infrastructure. Roughly 10%-25% of the CERT/CC reports involve viruses. Roughly 20%-40% are intrusions where the victim site cannot discern the type of the intrusion from available data. The remaining intrusions are a large number of other forms of intrusion, including compromise of system administration accounts, web defacements, reconnaissance attempts and misuse of computing resources.

Being intruded Upon

Determining who are the victims of intrusions is, in some respects, an enormously significant part of the intelligence process. It is important-at least in those cases where attacks are not indiscriminate-to differentiate between public and private targets, to distinguish infrastructure targets from individual targets, to distinguish between intrusions that focus on targets of convenience and those that are much more precise and calculated.

For example, existing analysis has shown a link between port scanning and certain types of later intrusions, but this needs to be more fully explored to provide for effective warnings. Profiling victims can sometimes play a critical role in determining the nature of the intrusion and the nature of the intruders. For this to be done, understanding is needed of the level of "background noise", probes and intrusion attempts occurring across the Internet. Once understood, it may be possible to isolate this activity from the more significant activity directed at a particular victim.

Victim profiles will be just as important, in terms of strategic intelligence analysis of the Internet, as profiling potential intruders. The more serious the intrusion, the more critical this sort of profiling will be. One of the potential hurdles to this effort, however, will be the natural tendency of the victim, whether private or public, to withhold sensitive or proprietary information.

A few examples of this kind of reticence would be financial institutions withholding information about loses due to intrusions; companies failing to divulge the nature of an intrusion due to proprietary corporate data; or a government agency protecting information that is sensitive or even classified. Beyond simply protecting proprietary or sensitive data, there are also serious legal questions that have not yet been resolved in the courts or in the legislature. These include constitutional guarantees of privacy; contradictory national laws (or lack of laws) as perpetrators use the global network; laws limiting various governmental agency's efforts to track down the source of an intrusion, and the need to determine what is domestic and what is foreign.

If these barriers can be overcome, critical information will become available. Details of the victim's infrastructure, the nature of the intrusion, identity clues left by the intruder, network traffic flow as observed by the victim site, and intrusion tools left as artifacts on the victim hosts can all provide indispensable clues. Without such information, motivation becomes more difficult to define and profiling efforts will be seriously flawed. Some work has already been accomplished in this area by organizations involved in incident monitoring, including the members of the Forum of Incident Response and Security Teams (FIRST) community.

Much more remains to be accomplished, however, as new cooperative agreements are forged and additional analytic efforts and methodologies are developed. Furthermore, while it is true that some of the legal restrictions are avoided by the voluntary nature of the cooperative relationships, they are by no means completely overcome. The keys to success seem to be twofold. First, the analytic organization has to prove itself to be a highly secure confidant, never disclosing victim identities while working to assist victims in recovering from intrusions. Second, it must return information that is of value to the victims, including information that might place the intrusion in a larger context as well as providing assistance in dealing with vendors or other sites. More simply put, the exchange of information must be in both directions. Experience with other organizations has shown that neither trustworthiness nor returned value alone is sufficient, but both appear to be required for effective information gathering with victims.

Beyond their reticence, victim organizations are often unaware of critical parts of their security stance. Available data suggests that victims are often not aware that their networks have been intruded upon. The effectiveness of installed security measures is often overestimated. Levels of trust given to users by computing practices are often unwarranted. All of this hampers both analysis and defence.

One of the reasons that profiling the victims is so critical is that it provides insights in to motivations that can greatly assist analysts in predicting future intrusions under similar circumstances. This insight will need to incorporate identification of circumstances that facilitate or hamper intrusion. For example, K-12 educational institutions might offer a significant opportunity for intruders to stage their attacks, since many such institutions lack knowledgeable system administrators. However, such hosts may be removed from the network during summer break and other times when school is not in session.

During the Year 2000 rollover, conditions for system intrusion were relatively poor not only because of the active presence of a large number of system administrators, carefully monitoring their systems, but also the significant number of alternative activities available to potential intruders. These examples serve to identify that there exist time-varying circumstances; further analysis is required to delineate these factors more fully.

6

The Computer Technology and Cybernetic Warfare

As the intensity and breadth of the battlefield grew along with its logistical requirements, new communication technologies became necessary to achieve the required integration and coordination of increasingly large and intricate military systems.

The harnessing of electromagnetic forces for telecommunication purposes proceeded with telegraphy and telephony, simultaneously stimulating growing scientific interest in the concept of information. Cybernetics emerged from the unprecedented technological and industrial effort of the Second World War, in particular the work on the automation of anti-aircraft defences. The selfproclaimed 'science of communications and control' promised to manage chaos and disruption through self-regulating mechanisms of negative information feedback. By being defined in terms of negative entropy (negentropy), information became conceptualized as the source of all order. The computer, also developed during the war for the purposes of code-breaking and the computation of nuclear physics, emerged as the new dominant technology and abstract model through which the world came to be understood chiefly in terms of information processing.

The drive for complete predictability and centralized control over armed conflict was renewed under cybernetic warfare with the deployment of computers and automated control technologies, and the widespread application of the analytical tools of operations research and systems analysis.

CYBER WAR: FIFTH DOMAIN OF WARFARE

The cyber warfare that this chapter addresses is that which is practised mainly by nation states or their proxies. The potency of this threat has compelled almost every country to develop capabilities in the cyber domain, as is the case for land, air, sea and space. According to Spy Ops, by the end of 2008 nearly 140 countries possessed varying degrees of cyber attack capabilities. In addition, an unknown number of extremist groups and non-state actors have developed or acquired cyber weapons.

Some commercially available products are flexible enough to be classified as dual purpose – security testing tools and weapons of attack. Thus some organisations have or are developing cyber weapons and cloaking them as security testing tools. All this is classified information and each nation works on its own. An assessment of cyber warfare threat matrix by the USA, which covered over 175 countries and organisations, made a watchlist in which the top ten in order of priority were: China; Russian business network; Iran; Russia tied with France; extremist/terrorist groups; Israel; North Korea; Japan; Turkey; and Pakistan. India on its growth path is vulnerable. Located in an unstable region where the larger neighbours possess this capacity, it is logical to assume that the country is under serious threat and constant attack. The impact on national security is thus serious and such that all institutions and organs of the state must jointly work to counter this challenge. In order to understand the challenge, the following issues need to be addressed:

Coordination

It is appreciated that in keeping with current needs, the Defence forces, DRDO (Defence Research and Development Organisation), NTRO (National Technical Research

Organisation), CERT-In (Computer Emergency Response Team India), RAW (Research and Analysis Wing), IB (Intelligence Bureau), C-DAC (Centre for Development of Advanced Computing), Ministries, NIC (National Informatics Centre), NASSCOM (National Association of Software and Services Companies), private industry et al. have to work in concert.

The impact of this on every aspect of electronic media requires a coordinated and integrated approach. Given its all encompassing nature, it also follows that control of all cyber and IW (Information Warfare) activities at the national level must fall under the purview of the NSC and controlled by its Secretariat i.e. the NSCS. Within this lead agencies for executing offensive cyber operations interalia could be the NTRO, CIDS (Chief of Integrated Defence Staff) and the DRDO.

Defining Objectives and Doctrine Application

Defining Objectives and Doctrine Application of such measures must be in accordance with clearly defined objectives that would be in keeping with customary international law and practice.

The primary objective would be to garner knowledge to find how systems are breached and thus provide the ability for defensive measures to be developed and put in place. There is a further argument that it must be visible as an armour of selfdefence so as to deter an attack. While this capability will be ambiguous, subtle signals and clear definition of objectives will lend credibility. Moral arguments stand thin in the face of realities. There is therefore a need to lay down the objectives and include them in the draft NCSP (National Cyber Security Policy) or issue a doctrine in this regard.

Proactive Cyber Defence

This comprises actions taken in anticipation to prevent an attack against computers and NWs. As opposed to the current practice of passive defence, it provides a via media between purely offensive and defensive action: interdicting and disrupting an attack, or an adversary's preparation to attack, either preemptively or in self-defence. Proactive cyber defence will most often require operationalising upstream security mechanisms of the telecommunications or Internet providers. The most compelling reasons for a proactive defence can be couched in terms of cost and choice. Decision-makers will have few choices after an impact, and all of them are costly to start with. Proactive defence is thus the key to mitigating operational risk. The USA had set up a Proactive Pre-emptive Operations Group (P2OG) in 2002. Such actions thus find international acceptability.

Critical Infrastructure

There is a need to prioritise and protect critical infrastructure. In the USA 18 sectors have been identified. In India's case, the sectors of power, water supply, communications, transportation, defence and finance are vital constituents of national security. These need to be defined and suitable protection measures ensured as laid down in the IT Act. Steps to guard against threats, i.e. destructive actions or cyber exploitation will constitute a basis for research on offensive action.

The electric power system merits top priority. While the risk of an attack can be reduced, it would be unrealistic to assume that an attack can be prevented. This leads to the conclusion that containment, isolation, minimising the impact, backup systems and reactivation are areas of capacity building. The debate on which agency will undertake this in India rages and begs immediate resolution. As critical infrastructure spans both the public and private domains, the organisation to ensure its protection has to be in the public realm and, in a manner, accountable.

Legal Provisions

The IT Act of 2008 covers all actions in this domain. Sections 69, 69A and 69B contain provisions for intercepting, monitoring or blocking traffic where, amongst other reasons, there is a threat to national security. Section 70A covers protection of critical infrastructure. There is a need to work within these provisions. LOAC (Laws of Armed Conflict) provide the primary legal framework within which one can analyse constraints for offensive cyber operations. Immunity for actions taken against another nation, institutions, hostile group or individual is possible if taken under LOAC or for selfdefence under Article 51 of the UN Charter. The cyber realm, with scope of non-attributable actions as also ease of deniability, provides immense scope for exploitation. The fact that there are no international cyber laws or treaties at present is also used to advantage. Offensive cyber operations by their very nature have to remain in the grey realm and restricted. Each nation would thus determine the structure best suited to its needs. However, the necessity to clearly enunciate such measures or self-defence actions in a doctrine as also the NCSP is essential for steps in this regard; it also acts as an element for deterrence. The emphasis must remain on protecting NWs, systems and users.

Controversy over terms

There is debate on whether the term "cyberwarfare" is accurate. In October 2011, for instance, the Journal of Strategic Studies, a leading journal in that field, published an article by Thomas Rid, "Cyber War Will Not Take Place." An act of cyber war would have to be potentially lethal, instrumental, and political. Then not one single cyber offense on record constitutes an act of war on its own. Instead, all politically motivated cyber attacks, Rid argued, are merely sophisticated versions of three activities that are as old as warfare itself: sabotage, espionage, and subversion.Howard Schmidt, an American cybersecurity expert, argued in March 2010 that "there is no cyberwar... I think that is a terrible metaphor and I think that is a terrible concept.

There are no winners in that environment." Other experts, however, believe that this type of activity already constitutes a war. The warfare analogy is often seen intended to motivate a militaristic response when that is not necessarily appropriate. Ron Deibert, of Canada's Citizen Lab, has warned of a "militarization of cyberspace." The European cybersecurity expert Sandro Gaycken argued for a middle position. He considers cyberwar from a legal perspective an unlikely scenario, due to the reasons lined out by Rid (and, before him, Sommer), but the situation looks different from a strategic point of view. States have to consider military-led cyber operations an attractive activity, within and without war, as they offer a large variety of cheap and risk-free options to weaken other countries and strengthen their own positions. Considered from a long-term, geostrategic perspective, cyber offensive operations can cripple whole economies, change political views, agitate conflicts within or among states, reduce their military efficiency and equalize the capacities of high-tech nations to that of low-tech nations, and use access to their critical infrastructures to blackmail them.

TOWARDS CHAOPLEXIC WARFARE

Since the mid-1970s, the cybernetic mode of warfare has come under increasing challenge from the military reversal for US forces in Vietnam, geopolitical transformation following the end of the Cold War, and novel scientific developments growing out of the original corpus of cybernetics.

Chaos is seen no longer as simply a threat to order which must be averted at all costs, but as the very condition of possibility of order. The key notions here are those of non-linearity, self-organization and emergence, and the pivotal technological figure is that of the network, the distributed model of information exchange perhaps best embodied by the internet.

The Science of Chaoplexity

Although still firmly set in the informational paradigm, chaos theory and complexity science departed from cybernetics in shifting the focus away from the stabilizing self-regulation (or homeostasis) underlying the persistence of existing systems towards runaway processes of change leading to the emergence of new systems or patterns of behaviour.

Non-linear dynamics and positive feedback processes, whereby small causes can amplify into large effects, are crucial here. Chaos theorists have used computer simulations of non-linear systems to reveal how initially minute variations can ramp up into dramatic changes in the long-term behaviour of the system. The popular image invoked to illustrate this phenomenon is the 'butterfly effect': the notion that a butterfly flapping its wings in (say) Tokyo can cause a tornado in (say) California. While chaos theory has imposed serious limits on the ability to predict the long-term behaviour of systems, it has also provided new insights, uncovering a subtle order and structure to phenomena previously believed to be completely devoid of recognizable patterns, such as the turbulence of fluids or plate tectonics.

Building on the original insights of chaos theory, complexity scientists turned to the interactions of the different component parts of living systems, and particularly to the new properties and behaviours constituted through the networked selforganization of autonomous agents.

Self-organization is the process by which the autonomous interaction of individual entities results in the bottom-up emergence of complex systems, systems composed of many parts which are connected in a non-linear fashion.

The notion of the network is central to describing the patterns of interaction which are constituted by the interplay of entities in a complex system: 'The first and most obvious property of any network is its non-linearity— it goes in all directions. Thus the relationships in a network pattern are non-linear relationships. In particular, an influence, or message, may travel along a cyclical path, which may become a feedback loop. The concept of feedback is intimately connected with the network pattern.'

Of special interest are the 'complex adaptive systems' which display the ability to change and learn from experience. Complexity theorist John Holland defines a complex adaptive system as a dynamic network of many agents acting simultaneously, constantly both acting and reacting to what the other agents are doing. Since the control of a complex adaptive system tends to be highly dispersed and decentralized, any coherent behaviour in the system arises from competition and cooperation among the agents themselves. It is the accumulation of all the individual decisions taken by the multitude of agents which produces the overall behaviour of the system, which can thus be said to be emergent. Complex adaptive systems include living organisms, insect colonies, bird flocks, ecosystems, businesses, stock markets and other forms of social organization; the constituent agents may be cells, species, individuals, firms or nations. From the perspective of chaoplexity, the most successful systems are those that retain flexibility and openness in the interaction and organization of their parts within environments which elude complete predictability.

No longer is order to be sought in a natural tendency towards equilibrium. On the contrary, it is with non-equilibrium that order emerges from chaos, at the point where instability and creative mutation allow for the genesis of new forms and actions. As Ian King puts it, 'networking [is] a way of maintaining a low-level chaotic substrate so that—as in the brain—the chaos will from time to time give birth to an intellectual self-organizing structure'.

Decentralized self-organizing systems are inherently better equipped than centralized systems to deal with limited predictability and contingency. According to the biologist Christopher Langton, 'since it's effectively impossible to cover every conceivable situation, top-down systems are forever running into combinations of events they don't know how to handle. They tend to be touchy and fragile, and they all too often grind to a halt in a dither of indecision.' In contrast, decentralized systems of quasi-autonomous units can operate more effectively and with a greater degree of adaptability on the basis of the local calculations of the networked agents constituting them. For Stuart Kauffman, 'networks in the regime near the edge of chaos—this compromise between order and surprise—appear best able to coordinate complex activities and best able to evolve as well'.

Chaoplexity has challenged some of the most deeply held scientific convictions about the natural world and opened up whole new areas of research. It is now also increasingly weighing on the debates about military organization, heralding a new era in the scientific way of warfare.

NETWORK WARFARE: ARMED FORCES AND NCW

Network centric warfare or NCW is redefining the future battle-space. In the information age, power is increasingly derived from information sharing, information access and speed. The Indian armed forces are moving fast in this direction. The usage of information technology as a force multiplier in warfare stems from the belief that information advantage leads to information superiority eventually enhancing combat effectiveness of platforms.

This is achieved by "networking" of sensors, decision-makers, and shooting platforms, thereby creating shared awareness, speed of command, high-tempo manoeuvre, close coordination and synchronisation during operations resulting in greater lethality, and enhanced combat capabilities. The primary objective of applying modern information technology is to enhance battle-space awareness between operational and command elements.

Within the above concept "Battlefield Management Systems (BMS)" act as force-enablers. It gives combat-advantage to Armed Forces, enabling a state-of-the-art networked theatre in a spit-fire battlefield environment. The recognition of information dominance in future wars is based on the success of information dominated military command and control, in influencing outcome of the battle.

Since the 1980s, Indian defence scientists in general, and specialists at the Centre for Artificial Intelligence and Robotics (CAIR) in particular, have been playing back-room role in enabling the transformation of Indian armed forces. "Third generation war focuses on using speed and surprise to bypass the enemy's lines and collapse their forces. Essentially, this means the end of linear warfare at the tactical level, with units instead of seeking frontal contact attempt to out-manoeuvre each other to gain the greatest battlefield advantage. The impact of C2 capabilities have kept increasing with each generation of warfare and have become an essential ingredient of third generation warfare and beyond. Integrated command and control (C2) capabilities are essential to meet the complexities of third generation warfare and spearheaded the digitisation of the battle space. Hence, the sensors and weapon interfaces, together with the communication infrastructure have migrated to digital technology. These developments have been driven by the adoption of Information and Communication Technologies (ICT) for supporting the C2 chains. The units enabling the above are collectively called Battle Management Systems (BMS) or C4I2SR (command, control, communication, computers, information, intelligence, surveillance and reconnaissance) systems.

The C2 process has been characterized as a series of sequential and interactive steps by a US Air Force strategist Col John Boyd, who termed it the Observe-Orient-Decide-Act (OODA) loop. The central tenet of modern BMS is the OODA loop (see image below). An entity that can process this cycle quickly, by observing and reacting to unfolding events more rapidly than an opponent, can thereby get inside the opponent's decision cycle and gain operational advantage. In the last two decades, armed forces have been investing in the design and development of various C2 systems.

COMPUTER TECHNOLOGY AND BATTLEFIELD INFORMATION NETWORKS

First, we should establish battlefield information networks and battlefield databases for the battlefields in priority strategic directions. By bringing all branches of the military into an information network, information may be shared on the network. Near-real-time communication can be gained in all directions and a better solution can be achieved for the problem of vertical and horizontal coordination in warfare.

Firm Control of Battlefield Information

To achieve victory in information warfare, the central issue is control of information.

Preparation and Defense with Attacking and Fighting

In comparison with the strength of potential enemies, the information technology and information weapons of China's military may all be inferior for quite some time. When China's enemies mainly use their air forces and navies to conduct strategic information warfare, China will be in the strategic position of engaging in defensive warfare along interior lines. The progress and outcome of the war will be determined by the state of China's advance preparations and defensive situation during the war. In defensive warfare, China should still thoroughly implement an active defensive strategy. In addition to hiding and concealing forces, in combat, especially during key phases in key areas, we must engage even more actively in air defense warfare and intercept and attack enemy weapons as they arrive in surprise attack. When conditions permit, we should also engage in counterattacks against the enemy and interfere with or misguide their guided weapons, thus damaging or destroying their equipment. Strategically, we should use preparation and defense, and in combat we should use attacking and fighting to achieve victory.

Organize Offensive and Defensive Information Warfare

Information warfare includes engaging in an active offense of information suppression and attack, as well as in the reactive defense of information counter-reconnaissance, resistance to interference, and defense against destruction. The issue of an information offensive can only be discussed if one has superior technology for information suppression. In a strategic defense situation, sometimes information offensives can be undertaken during warfare actions in limited areas. In that case, information technology suppression superiority must first be achieved in warfare actions in that limited area. Under the conditions of modern high technology, an information offensive is often a prelude to a strategic offensive. Take, for example, the surprise attack on Libya by the United States. Before the attack, 18 electronic-warfare aircraft were sent to Libya to engage in powerful interference.

Fighter aircraft were then sent to launch counterradiation guided missiles to destroy Libya's air defense radar stations, then fighter aircraft were sent to launch precision-guided bombs to attack five important targets. The information offensives in this raid included: 1) information reconnaissance to gain information on targets of the raid and to study the target in detail; 2) electronic interference to paralyze the opponents's communications and blind the opponent's air defense guided missiles; 3) information suppression by using counter radiation guided missiles to destroy air defense radar stations, and 4) information attack by using precision-guided warheads to attack pre-set targets. During the Gulf War, the information offensives of the multilateral forces were even more representative. In addition to the four types listed above at least the following should be added: 1) Computer viruses were used to destroy the computer systems of Iraq's air defense system and thus paralyze it, and 2) stealth aircraft were used to launch precision-guided bombs against the communications building and the command center, thus achieving information suppression.

In situations of information defense, we must strive for an active approach in a reactive situation and use every means possible to destroy the opponent's information superiority and transform our inferior position in information. We must pay attention to:

- Counter reconnaissance to prevent the opponent from obtaining information about the true situation. For example, secret falsification can be used to plant false intelligence and false targets in the place of true intelligence and true targets to confuse the real and the false and muddle the opponent's perceptions and inspire false assessments. When conditions exist, active methods may be used to engage in interference to blind or even destroy the opponent's reconnaissance instruments.
- Resistance to interference to maintain one's own channels of information. By using defense advantages, multiple-communication methods can be used to weaken the impact of the enemy's interference.

- Resist viruses to protect the normal operations of information processing in computer systems.
- Information counterattack. This is an important action to be carried out according to the general strategic plan and in coordination with strategic and combat counterattacks. The specific content and form is the same as that of information offensives.

The information offenses and defenses outlined above, in addition to using information technology extensively, also use information weapons extensively. Thus, during the process of a war, these do not exist alone but accompany strategic offenses and defenses and are consistent with the overall situation of strategic offenses and defenses. Before and after war, information hassling never stops for a moment but usually does not involve the use of information weapons.

Using Strengths to Attack Weaknesses

This is the basic warfare style which Mao Zedong taught us, and it is an excellent tradition of China's military. Strengths and weaknesses are in comparison with those of the enemy. What then will China's strengths be in future wars? What will be China's weaknesses? Politically speaking, China's military has the advantage of justness, which is conducive to gaining international sympathy and support, and it has the support of the people domestically. In terms of warfare space, when China's military engages in war on China's soil, it will have the advantages of topography and position. In air, sea, space, and electronic warfare, however, the enemy will have the advantage. In terms of the choice of timing for warfare, because the enemy will have more advanced night-vision instruments, the advantage will not be China's, especially in air and sea warfare at night. The enemy will have advantages in instrumentation. China will have advantages in familiarity with the topography. Each will have half the advantages. In terms of warfare techniques, China's military has a tradition of flexible fighting methods and is more adapted to nonlinear warfare, but lacks practical battle experience in information warfare with high technology. In terms of weapons and equipment, generally speaking the enemy will have the advantage, but in some areas, such as guided missiles and submarines, China can still shock the enemy to a certain degree. China is strong in close warfare; the enemy is strong in distant warfare.

In wars of the future, China will face the enemy's more complete information technology with incomplete information technology. Because sometimes superior tactics can make up for inferior technology, China will still carry out its traditional warfare method of "you fight your way, I'll fight my way," and use its strengths to attack the enemy's weaknesses and adhere to an active role in warfare. To do this, it appears that we must pay even more attention to:

- Fully utilizing the advantages of national territory and front information facilities to carry out reconnaissance on the enemy's situation and protect ourselves and attack the enemy
- Developing, improving, and utilizing China's information weapons in a concentrated way to carry out raids on enemy operation platforms and bases and damage and foil the enemy's offensive
- Emphasizing mobile war in the context of information warfare
- Conscientiously organizing sabotage operations by the Army, Navy, and Air Force, grasp exploitable opportunities, and make continuous raids to exhaust and wear down the enemy
- Organizing specialized combined special warfare troops and equip these with information technology weapons to carry out powerful special warfare.

In summary, our warfare methods must adapt to the needs of information warfare. We must use all types, forms, and methods of force, and especially make more use of nonlinear warfare and many types of information warfare methods which combine native and Western elements to use our strengths in order to attack the enemy's weaknesses, avoid being reactive, and strive for being active. In this way, it will be entirely possible for China to achieve comprehensive victory over the enemy even under the conditions of inferiority in information technology.

Cultivating Talent

In the final analysis, information warfare is conducted by people. The basic great plan is to cultivate talented people suited to information warfare. One aspect is to cultivate talent in information science and technology. The development and resolution of information warfare can be predicted to a great degree in the laboratory. Information science and technology talent is the forerunners of science and technology talent is the forerunner of science and technology research. The achievements and practical use of their research will play a key role in the development and advancement of society and military construction and warfare. The second aspect is talented people in command and control. They especially need to have the ability to conduct comprehensive analysis and policy-information processing, to understand themselves and the enemy, as well as the battlefield, and also to have a capacity for scientific strategic thinking and a comprehensive point of view. Senior command personnel especially need to have information knowledge and the ability to control information warfare and must be adept at using information technology to organize and command warfare. They must be very knowledgeable, brave, and talented people.

Combat personnel must also be familiar with the technical and strategic aspects of the weapons and equipment in their hands and must be very well versed in the operation of those weapons and equipment. They must be able to understand accurately the combat plan and resolutely and flexibly utilize weapons and equipment to wipe out the enemy. The combat personnel of information warfare are not only the warriors who charge enemy lines for face to face struggles of life or death, but sometimes are the operating technical personnel who sit before computers and instruments. They stand at the first line in electronic warfare and in the resistance against C4I systems and on the front line in information technology conflicts.

Rear support and technical support are very important in information warfare. Information technology relates to a number of high-technology groups of people and touches on new energy, new materials, artificial intelligence, space travel, marine engineering, systems engineering, and other high-technology subjects. The demands for the technical level of support personnel are quite high. They are required to be able to guarantee that weapons and equipment are always kept in excellent condition. While carrying out rear and front-line support, the use of information technology is a support method just like other methods. In information warfare, the support of information technology penetrates the contents of information resistance and is also one method of warfare support.

The main methods of cultivating talent are study and training. In addition to conducting training in politics, ethics, and psychology, there must also be study of high-tech knowledge and the fundamental knowledge of and warfare techniques related to information warfare. If conditions permit, we want to create as much as possible the conditions necessary for implementing simulation training. We can first consider creating stimulated battlefields with information in key areas of the army, navy, air force, and artillery, and, second, conducting rotational training of cadres and key troops. Colleges and universities should also establish curriculae in information warfare. Scientific research institutions should also engage in research on information warfare.

The large-scale importation of information technology deep into the field of warfare will inevitably bring about a military revolution. This revolution has actually already started. Those who perceive it first will swiftly rise to the top and have the advantage of the first opportunities. Those who perceive it late will unavoidably also be caught up in the vortex of this revolution. Every military will receive this baptism. This revolution is first a revolution in concepts, then it is a revolution in science and technology, equipment, troop strength, strategy, and tactics as well as a revolution in training. Thus, the issue of how to adapt to and achieve victory in the information warfare which we will face from now on is an important question which we need to study carefully.

THE FUTURE OF COMMAND AND CONTROL WITH DBK

The Vice Chairman of the Joint Chief of Staff has posed a deceptively simple question: How would we do things differently if we had DBK?

While the explosion of information and communications technologies has profoundly affected the basic structure and operations of some organizations, others, including DOD, have adapted in an incremental fashion. Yet to fully understand the implications that a vastly improved awareness of the situation could have on concepts of our defense posture -- including operations, command structures, forces structures, doctrine, training, weapon systems, and logistics -- we need to consider the possibility of revolutionary change and we need to build a mission-oriented DOD based on the opportunities afforded by technology -- in this instance, the opportunities afforded by achieving DBK. To do this we need to explore one important aspect of this challenge; how we might capitalize on the opportunities made possible by having a vastly improved capability of situation awareness by changing the way we approach command and control (C2).

This paper begins by laying out the terms of reference followed by an analysis of the overall impact that having this capability would have on U.S. Force Structure, Organization, and Doctrine and the role that C2 plays in determining these attributes of our defense posture. The historic role of C2 in warfare is then sketched in terms of how it contributes to the achievement of the fundamental principles of warfare. The C2 capabilities necessary to leverage fully these opportunities are then identified. Finally, the changes that need to be made to current approaches to command concepts, organizations, doctrine, and systems in order to exploit our improved knowledge of the situation are explored. The paper concludes that the potential benefits of achieving DBK are well worth pursuing and identifies a number of issues and action items to address and realize these benefits.

Terms of Reference and Assumptions

The impact that any improvement in our capabilities will have is a function of the particular mission and scenario at hand. As a baseline for the analysis, from which excursions in the form of sensitivity analyses can be taken, a Major Regional Contingency (MRC) with a regional power is considered. The horizon for the analysis is the year 2008. This is far enough out to achieve significant advances in capability as well to provide the time needed to adjust our doctrine and organization to take advantage of those advances.

The baseline case does not consider coalition warfare, which could significantly complicate C2. In addition, this analysis initially focuses on a combat mission unencumbered by tight political constraints of the type that have limited our ability to act in Bosnia.

Situation awareness has many different dimensions, and while given the time horizon and the nature of the resources likely to be available, "total" or perfect situation awareness is beyond our reach. Nevertheless, improvements in our capabilities well short of achieving total or perfect situation awareness could provide quantum improvements in our effectiveness. By 2008 we could achieve considerable improvements in our current ability to see and understand the battlefield. Our adversary, a regional power, will also be able to take advantage of some of the available technology, albeit not to the extent we will. Thus, the United States will continue to have "information dominance" in a notional 200 nm- square battlefield, maintaining or even increasing the edge we have over others. Information dominance would be of only academic interest, if we could not turn this information dominance into battlefield dominance.

The ability to approach total situation awareness and prevent our adversaries from achieving it, and our capability to exploit our relative advantage in information result in a situation in which we have achieved DBK. Achieving DBK without being able to respond militarily to an adversary's moves is a nonstarter, so this paper analyzes a situation in which the united States can strike at virtually any target or a kill-at-will capability and establish a virtual link between any sensor and any weapon in near real time -- but not necessarily between all sensors and all weapons simultaneously. As with situation assessment, kill-at-will capability comes in varying degrees characterized mainly by Pk, the probability of kill, which in turn is a function of target latency and hardness; travel time or the amount of time it takes to put "ordinance" on target; and the accuracy of the delivery system. While post-kinetic weapons may reduce travel time to virtually zero and increase accuracy dramatically, significant delays associated with targeting and command decision processes associated with combat will remain. Thus, the tradeoffs between the quality of decisions and speed (addressed later) will remain a central issue for C2 for the foreseeable future.

As noted, situation awareness is multidimensional. It includes knowing the current position, classification, identity, condition, and recent history of all items of military significance on the battlefield (in the 200 nm square). It also can be said to include knowledge of the objectives, intentions, and plans of all players. Items of interest include "strategic" targets of both the conventional kind (e.g., factories) as well as the unconventional kind (e.g., financial networks). A baseline assumption for DBK is that we know, in near real time, the positions of all friendly, neutral, and enemy objects of interest; we have more limited information regarding their current conditions and recent histories; and we have somewhat less information about enemy intents and plans. The information associated with DBK is assumed to be "corporate" knowledge -- that is, we collectively have this information. It is not assumed that this information is instantaneously available to everyone. If fact, figuring out how best to distribute elements of available information is a major challenge and will, to a large extent, drive our approach to C2.

Implicit in DBK and kill-at-will assumption is our possession of considerable stand off capability (for example, remotely piloted vehicles); few manned systems would be placed at risk. In fact, in the kind of warfare in which both sides have good situation assessment ability and relatively smart munitions, high value targets become extremely vulnerable unless this vulnerability is reduced by stealth or speed.

Finally, it is assumed that we are resource constrained. That is, weapons, logistics, communications, and computer processing are limited and need to be allocated and scheduled. In fact, in a very real sense, the problem boils down to resource allocation questions and our ability to make these investment decisions in ways that allow us to take full advantage of the opportunities that technology affords to defeat the enemy with minimum casualties, collateral damage, and time and resources expended.

Potential of DBK

A common analytical technique is to make some simplifying assumptions to "bound the problem" in an attempt to establish the feasibility of an approach or concept.

In this case, a gross feel for the potential value of DBK can be derived from looking at the problem of destroying a given number of targets with different levels of C2 capability (figure 1). While the word destroy is used to simplify this discussion, it should be understood that in reality a full range of actions, including exploitation, co-option, disruption, and degradation need to be considered.

The worst case is when one has no C2 and weapons are free to fire on any target. In this case, unintentional, duplicative, and/or overlapping fire will result. Some targets will be "over killed" while others will escape unharmed. Given no C2 or what amounts to random targeting, there is also no ability to prioritize targets, which on the battlefield have widely differing values, values that change as the dynamics of the battle unfold. The values of targets are not limited to positive numbers; there are also numerous situations when targets may actually have negative values and thus need to be avoided rather than hit. Obvious cases include the sort of collateral damage that can be exploited for its propaganda value. Less obvious cases are situations in which killing a particular target sacrifices possible long-term benefits for short-term gains.

Given perfect C2 (which in turn is dependent on perfect information), an optimal allocation of weapons assignments can be made dynamically as a function of ordnance available, weapon capabilities (Pks), and target values.

The result will be that high-value targets are destroyed with high probability; that valuable ordnance is not wasted on low value targets; and that targets with negative values are spared. The result will be that more operationally significant damage will be inflicted along with a more effective use of resources. The leverage of C2 grows as the effective Pks increase. Our current ability to do C2 falls in between these two extremes, and the value of achieving DBK is bounded by the spread between the line that represents our current ability and the line that represents perfect C2. The potential impact of DBK goes well beyond any tactical advantage associated with being able to destroy targets efficiently.

DBK, in providing us with an opportunity to hit the right targets at the right time, offers us an opportunity to change the way we organize, command, and equip our forces. It is the impact associated with these changes that will determine the ultimate value of having DBK.

We be careful to build an organization with significant teeth, and if we choose to embark on a path that makes us heavily reliant on technology, we must also take steps to ensure that the systems that we will come to rely upon to give us DBK and C2 are designed to deliver appropriately high levels of reliability and availability. We will also need to deal with the possibility of technology failures or degraded capability, however rare they are projected to be, to ensure the success of our missions. The safety blanket of having force in depth to hedge against failures in systems may not be a viable approach given current budgetary trends.

Investment Challenge

Determining the role that a vastly improvement situation assessment capability can play in our defense posture is a part of the perennial debate regarding the proper balance between investments in C2 and other elements of our warfighting ability including manpower, readiness, high- and low-technology weapons, training, and education. Despite the growing consensus that additional investments in C2 will pay off handsomely, beyond some point it will be more than offset by reductions in force structure or readiness.

The remainder of this chapter develops a view of future C2 that evolves from the achievement of DBK. DBK represents a quantum leap from even our current level of capability, which is nevertheless formidable by historical standards. Therefore, it would be incorrect to simply extrapolate linearly from today's capability. This approach would also lead to incremental change that will not get us to the point where we could fully exploit the opportunities afforded by DBK. Put in another way, business as usual is not the answer. Incremental changes will not result in speediness or efficiency.

DBK provides an opportunity that can not be fully taken without turning to new command concepts and organizational approaches. Given the assumptions used in this analysis, command control will undergo change in a number of key ways. Commanders will be more focused on strategic issues; the role of staffs will be diminished; and, organizations will be flattened. New concepts of operations will be required to achieve the desired levels of target damage necessary for success and there will need to be associated changes in force structure, the mix of weapons, and the nature of logistics. The reductions needed in response times (decision/execution cycle times) and the number of decisions that needed in high- intensity combat situations, all in a short time span, are beyond human capability. Fortunately, the changes brought about by DBK make automating a large subset of decisions a viable approach.

To follow the reasoning that led to these conclusions, we must start with a review of the objectives of C2 and how, over the years, we have attempted to improve our ability to plan and conduct warfare.

C2 Objectives

C2 exists only to facilitate the accomplishment of a mission. Its has no intrinsic value, rather its value derives from the contribution that it makes to mission success. A brief review of what C2 has traditionally sought to achieve and how it attempts to achieve it will provide a good foundation for understanding what will change with DBK.

C2 provides commanders and their staffs with the tools necessary to successfully operate in an environment clouded by the fog of war and uncertainty. This environment of "fog" and of uncertainty has profoundly influenced military thought and strategy throughout history. The principles of war are rooted in this fundamental characteristic of the battle field. Therefore, it should be of no surprise that the way the military is currently structured results, in large part, from a desire to minimize confusion and misunderstanding and to deal with uncertainty. Unity of command and appropriate span of control involve structural approaches to the problem, while approaches to the development and management of information have been process oriented. While much progress has been made in improving the C2 process, less attention has been focused on the structural or doctrinal aspects of C2. Specifically, C2 and associated organizational structures, military tactics, procedures, and doctrine have sought to:

- Reduce the fog of war
- Exercise control over forces in a way that accommodates the fog of war
- Exploit the fog surrounding the enemy commander and forces
- Increase the fog for the enemy.

Given this way of looking at the objectives of C2, it is clear that what has become known as "information war," or IW, is intimately related to C2. C2 has sometimes been confused with communications or information systems, and IW has sometimes been confused with electronic countermeasures. These misunderstandings are obstacles to progress and need to be addressed, because achieving DBK requires an full understanding of C2 and IW.

Command, control, communications, and intelligence systems (C3I) have been primarily concerned with reducing a commander's fog by attempting to provide a complete and accurate picture of the enemy and the environment, reports on the disposition and capability of friendly forces, and battle damage assessments.

C3I systems have also been used to achieve timely and assured dissemination of information (and orders) and in achieving a common perception of both the situation and commands (missions, objectives, and tasks). With the addition of significant information processing power and decision aids, C3I systems have begun to support a capability for near real-time reassessment of the situation and continuous option development and analysis.

C2 as an Offensive Weapon

While C2 has long been considered an enabler necessary to help attain the goals contained in the often stated Principals of War, it has only been very recently that C2 has been seen as an offensive weapon. The essence of the offensive nature of C2 derives from its contribution to maintaining the offensive in classic terms.

Maintaining the offensive involves the ability to dictate both the time and place of action. The offensive nature of IW has long been understood, for IW both utilizes friendly C3I systems and targets enemy C3I systems. One of the greatest potential benefits of DBK is, in fact, the improved ability it provides to conduct IW. The ability to neutralize, disrupt, subvert, deceive, weaken, or fragment an enemy's offensive or defensive capability by taking actions against enemy commanders, staffs, and systems translates into a powerful offensive capability. When combined with a strategy to achieve option dominance, IW and C2 achieve their greatest synergism.

Option Dominance: Ultimate Offensive Weapon

A key to achieving option dominance is being able to respond faster than one's adversary -- to always be one step ahead. Such an ability will permit us to co-opt enemy plans and actions before they can be effective. In order for us to achieve option dominance, three conditions or prerequisites must be met:

We must recognize what needs to be done. This involves a number of inter-related steps including the development of an understanding of the current situation and its implications, the generation of options to be considered, the analysis of these options, and, a command decision regarding what option will be taken.Having recognized what needs to be done, we need the ability to accomplish all this faster that it takes for the enemy to act (or react). This involves not only all the tasks implicit in recognizing what needs to be done, but also the time it takes to translate an option into understandable assignments, their transmittal to subordinates, and the time it takes to understand these directives and act upon them. It is important to realize that absolute speed is not the issue, rather is it the relative speed that is important. Thus, we gain as much from slowing down the enemy as we do in speeding up our C2. In fact, given the tradeoffs between absolute speed and quality, slowing down the enemy (via IW) carries with it some attractive benefits.We need to be more than a paper tiger. That is, we need the ability to actually execute the option selected. Having DBK certainly is a very big part of recognizing what needs to be done. But by the same token it is not sufficient to achieve this first necessary step on the road to option dominance. Perhaps the most important missing ingredient is the need to develop an appropriate response to the situation as it is unfolding. This requires the creativity and insight that only an experienced commander can bring to the battlefield.

The very same technology necessary to achieve DBK, namely information and communications technologies, may make it possible for us to operate inside the enemy C2 cycle. But the ability to push piles of data around the battlefield is not sufficient to allow us to operate inside the enemy's decision and execution cycle. We need to be able to design a more streamlined process than we currently have to satisfy the time-critical nature of this task. (This is considered a little later on). The kill-at-will capability assumed for the baseline analysis completes the picture and allows us to take advantage of the information dominance we have achieved.

If option dominance can be achieved, and we can demonstrate this capability to potential adversaries, then we may be able to preempt enemy actions and hence prevent this kind of extremely costly combat from occurring. In effect, we would effectively change the nature of conventional war.

C2 Implications

There are two major implications that the achievement of DBK has for our approach to C2. The first is that we will effectively move from a situation in which we are preoccupied with reducing the fog of war to the extent possible and with designing approaches needed to accommodate any residual fog that exists to a situation in which we are preoccupied with optimizing a response to a particular situation. In short, we will move from a situation in which decisionmaking takes place under "uncertainty" or in the presence of incomplete and erroneously information, to a situation in which decisions are make with near "perfect" information.

Decisionmaking in the absence of complete and accurate information is far more difficult than decisionmaking with perfect information. Therefore, many of the ways we approach command today are a direct result of finding ways to come to grips with the task of timely decisionmaking in the absence of adequate information, under conditions of extreme stress, and where the cost of error may be extremely high. Professional military education (PME), doctrine, and organizational structures have all been tailored to deal with this problem. The result is to concentrate on what is called "max a min" solutions, that is, on those focusing on avoiding decisions with large downsize risks in favor of decisions which are "optimal" by expected value standards.

There are other implications as well. These include an emphasis on strategy and tactics that require keeping considerable forces and resources held in reserve to deal with the unknown or unexpected. While DBK certainly does not eliminate risk or uncertainty from command decisionmaking, it does radically alter the balance of the situation. Accordingly, those command concepts, doctrine, organizations, and force structures that have been optimized over time to deal with the fog of war need to revisited to see how they might be better adapted to the realities of DBK.

The second major implication of having DBK derives from the conditions that must obtain if we are to be able to take full advantage of the opportunities provided by having this capability. The utility of having DBK is a function of both the timeliness of the response and the our ability to make the most of limited resources. These two prerequisites for success frame the C2 issues we need to address. At issue is the way we will distribute information and decision making. Without a doubt, we will need to finally break the umbilical chord between the command chain and the flow of information.

The Key Tradeoff: Speed v. Optimization

DBK gives us the opportunity to hit movers, blunt offensives with "massed fire" rather than "massed forces," and achieve option dominance. The desire to take advantage of this opportunity provided by DBK drives us to minimizing the decision and execution cycle -- going from seeing a target to destroying one. "Destroying" as used here includes physical destruction or "hard" kill as well as interruption, neutralization, and other aspects of "soft" kill. Running counter to this need for speed is the need for optimal resource allocation. Resource allocation is needed to ensure that the fire power available during a given period of time is allocated to targets with the highest priority (value) at that time. Resource allocation is also necessary to keep the costs of supplies and lift capability as low as possible. Thus, the desire to get ordnance on target rapidly comes into conflict with this need to efficiently and effectively allocate resources. This translates into C2 architectural tradeoffs. To minimize the decision/execution cycle, the path from the sensor to the shooter needs to be minimized -- if possible, to go directly from the sensor to the shooter. However, to make best utilization of resources, allocations needs to be made "globally,þ that is, over the entire battle space and in the context of an appropriate period of time. Thus, the decisionmaking process required to allocate resources needs to be able to "see the big picture" in order to determine overall priorities and the consequences of various allocations. Central to the future of C2 will be the nature of the tradeoffs made with respect to distributing information and decisionmaking.

The best way to distribute decisionmaking and information on the battlefield is, of course, a function of the mission, scenario, technical capabilities, and cost. However, we can be reasonably certain that, in the time frame for this analysis, that neither a completely centralized nor a completely distributed approach will be best. Why? First, providing DBK to all shooters would require prohibitively high bandwidth and hence cost. Second, hierarchical flows of information would be too slow to achieve the decision and execution cycle times necessary to maintain option dominance. Therefore, an inventive mix of horizontal and vertical information flows as well as a new approach to decision making will be required.

In terms of getting the right information to shooters in a timely fashion, the challenge will be to dynamically manage the flow of information from sensors to shooters along with targeting priorities and ROEs. This will involve a highly automated capability to establish virtual links (sessions) between selected sensors and weapons. These sessions would need to be dynamically managed in accordance with battle events and priorities. Here, again, a key tradeoff will need to be made; this time it boils down to a tradeoff between optimization with centralized control v. less than optimal allocations with distributed control.

Given the enormous complexity of the battlefield at the level of granularity of control needed for real-time targeting and prioritization, ways to effectively decompose a battlefield need to be explored. Creating what might be called "Information/ Resource Spheres" seems to be a promising approach. The concept of decomposing the battlefield into information/ resource spheres is designed to create manageable "areas" in which the distribution of information and decisions can be optimally distributed dynamically. These "areas" may not be solely geographically based. Each information/ resource sphere would contain all the information necessary for DBK within the sphere. Spheres would operate asynchronously. Forces within the sphere would need to be able to operate seamlessly, "organically joint" or integrated so that all communications, doctrine, and procedures worked together transparently. Each sphere needs a single commander who has command over all forces and resources necessary to counter the threat within the sphere. The creation of information/resource spheres is, in effect, a means to distribute workload in a way that tries to keep suboptimization to a minimum. Using spheres requires, of course, that an overall commander create spheres, collapse spheres, assign missions, ROEs, priorities, and resources to spheres and monitor their progress and situations.

Impact of DBK on C2

As noted, DBK moves us into a world where many decisions can be made with something approaching perfect information. Not only are these decisions far easier for humans to handle quickly while under stress, but these types of decisions become more like mathematical problems that are truly a "piece of cake" for computers running sophisticated applications software to handle. Computers do some things "better" than humans. Making "routine" decisions with near perfect information rapidly is one of those things. Given the very large number of decisions that will need to be made in near real time and the massive amounts of information that will need to be processed to support these decisions, not only can computers do the job, but computers are the only way the job can be accomplished.

Rather than diminishing the role or importance of the commander, the delegation of these decisions to computers (really "expert systems" that have been designed and tested by military experts) actually frees up the commander to devoted more energy to strategic issues and concerns. As a result, commanders will be able to concentrate their efforts on establishing mission objectives and priorities and in balancing assignments and resources. Perhaps even more importantly, it frees commander to devote attention to developing possible courses of action for consideration, a task that requires the creativity and experience that only they can bring to the battle.

The role of staffs will significantly diminish, however, provided that adequate processing power is available and appropriate expert systems have been developed and tested. Because many of the detailed tactical or logistical decisions will become automated, staffs will not be needed nearly to the extent they are now. There are some rather nice side effects to this consequence. First, the fog that is generated by staffs will be much reduced, and second, communications and processing resources utilized by staffs will also be reduced.

Edge of the Envelope C2

While by 2008 we will not yet be able to fully exploit the opportunities that are provided by DBK, we will be considerably down the road toward this objective. The edge of the envelope of C2 -- the C2 that makes optimal use of DBK -- while not achievable by 2008, is nevertheless instructive to imagine, providing us with a vision of the direction in which we are headed. This vision will not only help to focus our attention in broad terms on where we are going but will also enable us to see if there are unintended consequences or dangers associated with taking this path that need to be worked. DBK and the technology associated with the achievement of DBK will permit commanders to operate in the "Nintendo" style. With the view of the battlefield and resources literally at one's fingertips, a command will be able to, at the click of a mouse, obtain different views of the battlespace (varying in their focus and granularity) in order to be able to develop an assessment of the situation and in turn develop options. The commander will be able to explore the likely outcomes of various options and upon deciding on a particular course of action have the decision translated into appropriate orders and communicated to subordinates.

If the tempo of the battlefield permits, or if the sensitivity or importance of a particular aspect of the conflict warrants the commander's personal attention, a commander would have the ability to manage at a micro level as well. The operational and tactical levels of command would therefore be compressed into one in the "command console" and the systems that support it. To support this edge of the envelope C2, a number of automated capabilities would need to exist:

- Software that, given mission objectives and available resources, would prioritize targets
- Algorithms that, based upon the attributes of targets and weapons, would assign targets to weapons and provide for the virtual link between sensor and shooter
- Experts systems that could develop, in near real time, battle damage assessments. Planning tools that could allocate resources with total asset viability
- Software that could play out various options and determine and assess their outcomes.

A commander of the future would also be able to, with the help of automated decision aids, discompose the battle space into spheres that automatically parse mission assignments and objectives, as well as information and resources, in an appropriate fashion.

SUMMARY OF THE IMPACT OF DBK

Having DBK would have a dramatic impact on the way we approach C2. The role of commanders would be enhanced in a number of ways:

- The importance of a strategic vision would increase simply because, given DBK, such a vision would be far more likely to be "right" and hence less effort would be spent on "adjusting plans" or "replanning."
- Commanders would have a much greater chance of having their vision correctly implemented given the

automated processing and communications support provided.

- By freeing commanders from worrying about the fog of war and developing contingencies for a variety of different situations, commanders could devote more effort to thinking creatively about the best way to deal with a situation and to developing options.
- Commanders will be able to review proposed options both in greater detail and faster than ever before, thus further increasing the likelihood that options selected will be sufficiently well conceived to actually play out in the battle without significant alteration. However, commanders of the future will be required to have a greater understanding of technology and a greater facility to work with automated tools.

Organizationally, hierarchies will flatten to facilitate the flow of information and decisions while the role of staffs will be greatly diminished, their work being largely automated. Further, there will be an increased premium on interoperability to ensure that we get the greatest utility out of our resources. Technically, we will shift the emphasis from a reliance on bandwidth to communications connectivity and processing power and be increasingly dependant on "intelligent" software.

The changes in both C2 and in the form of warfare as we would prosecute it promise considerable economies. This leads to the conclusion that the investment necessary to move towards DBK is worth very serious consideration within DOD. The investment required is more than just R&D funds or system procurement dollars. It also involves a commitment to the kind of change in our organizational structures and doctrine that will allow us to both take advantage of the opportunities afforded by having DBK and the economics that are associated with a new approach to C2.

7

The Model of Information Based Warfare

Therefore, at times of revolution, when the normal-scientific tradition changes, the scientist's perception of his environment must be re-educated-in some familiar situations he must learn to see a new gestalt.

INFORMATION BASED WARFARE -THE NEW BATTLEFIELDS

Exiled to France, the Ayatollah Khomeni sought to maintain contact with the faithful. A cleric who espoused the return of his country to an Islamic theocracy-something: that many argued would move Iran back into the 16th century-the Ayatollah turned to 20th century tools to begin his crusade. Through the medium of cassettes, he began to record his message. After being mass-produced m 20th century studios, his 16th century message was smuggled back to Iran. Those tapes both planted the seed and inspired the flowering of a movement that brought Khomeni back to power m 1979.

For at least a decade, the American military had tinkered with devices for sabotaging enemy electrical systems. Some of the results were serendipitous. In the early 1980's, during a Navy exercise code-named Hey [Rube, long strands of rope chaff-glass filaments in which metal shards were embedded-had been dropped over the Pacific Ocean as part of a standard tactic to befuddle an opponent's radar. An unexpectedly skiff wind carried some of the chaff ninety miles to the coastline, where it got draped across power lines, shorting out transformers and causing power failures in parts of San Diego. The Navy quietly settled the damages- while carefully noting the effects of its unintended attack.

Information warfare has as many meanings as it has proponents, detractors and observers. Airpower theorists see it on the wings of Desert Storm; tank commanders see it in the American army's Force XXI; simulator designers see it in their virtual realities...and strategic-war planners see it as a way to lay waste to whole societies. Information warfare studies are proliferating within the American armed forces almost as quickly as the networks that carry them from desktop to desktop. The confusing planoply stems from the fact that the information revolution, whether it is in uniform or mufti, relies upon the fastest technology to do the oldest things. Thus it is always a peculiar mixture of the familiar and the shockingly new. In that war is all about strategies, command and morale, it has always been about information. All war is information war, and so every aspect of fighting wars in the information age can be called "information warfare" by someone. If information driven warfare means something new, it is the use of information as a substitute for traditional ways of fighting, rather than an adjunct to them. There are three ways that this might be achieved by:

- the high technology equivalent of brute force;
- subversion; and,
- a new form of deterrence.

For the purpose of this paper, we focus on the second element-subversion. It is our belief that because of the unique relationship between Americans and computers, IBW launched subversive acts-a prelude to, or the actual execution of "quiet wars"-may be accomplished.

The evolution and ultimate "blurring" of military and civilian sectors came about in large part because of the growth in hardware and software. It was not so long ago, in the early

1960's, that the Pentagon provided the market for sophisticated electronics. Today, it makes up less than 1% of that market. In many ways, the military is following the revolution, not leading it. In 1962 Paul Baran of RAND developed a concept that permitted the linking of computers from distant locations. It was designed to preserve the integrity of the military command and control network in case of a nuclear attack. In 1969, the Defense Advanced Research Projects Agency (DARPA) funded the first test of the concept, and the first node was installed at RAND. The test consisted of scientists from remote locations passing findings and research notes back and forth. However, a year later it was being used like a mail box for the users and it proceeded to grow rapidly in use. In 1983, the military part and the nonmilitary part grew apart and finally split, the nonmilitary section grew up into what is now called the Internet.

For the first time in our nation's history, technology is no longer the sole domain of the military. The speed of the growth and application of technology is clearly a concern for defense planners. While the US used some of the world's most advanced weaponry and technology in the Gulf War (much of which proved inaccurate) it also used a great deal of older technology, some of which dated back to the 1960's. As B.R. Inman and Daniel F. Burton Jr. note in their article "Technology and US. National Security, "the 8088 microprocessor used in the Patriot missile was developed by the Intel Corporation fifteen years ago." This technology is not competitive today.

Opening and Closing Pandora's Box

In the center of Strike the battleship's commander, Captain David S. Bill, Ferched in his high backed padded chair. Although he occasionally glanced at the screens above, the captain's attention was largely fixed on the men clustered around four computers lining the far bulkhead. Something had gone awry with the ship's Tomahawk missile system.. For reasons no one could fathom, the Tomahawk computers seemed confused, refusing to transfer the necessary commands from the engagement-planning console to the launch console. The resulting impasse_"casualty" in Navy jargon_meant the missiles could not be fired...On Wisconsin, where the scheduled launch was now just moments away, the men in Strike were running out of solutions...As the request for additional time flashed up the chain of command, an excited voice from one of the nearby ships crackled through Strike: "Alpha, alpha." This is the Paul F Foster. Happy trails." Happy trails: the code phrase for missiles away. Operation Desert Storm had begun without Wisconsin.

As the most technologically vulnerable nation, the US defense planners must recognize several concepts about the technical end of the IBW battlefield:

It must be assumed that everyone has access to technology, therefore the US is the most vulnerable to attack;

As the US's ability to wage IBW increases, so to do the IBW capabilities, and response capabilities, of other nation-states and non-state actors;

While at first glance it would appear that IBW is most effective against adversaries with like technological capabilities and infrastructure-the top end of the IBW target spectrum-it must be remembered that technology comes in two forms-high and appropriate-and it is the latter that will always defeat the former. Thus, the benefits of IBW in arena's of conflict as found in the Gray Areas are a target rich environment must be pursued alongside the force on force approach.

The technical realm of information based warfare can be split into two major areas: Netwar and Cyberwar. Netwar is the information related conflict between nations, societies, governments, or non-state actors with the targets being information systems and communications, and it consists of destruction of communications, acquisition of information, release of misinformation, and destruction or deletion of data. Cyberwar consists of militaries conducting their operations according to information based theories and principles. These terms can be broken down even further. Netwar can be broken into three main categories: Personal, Corporate, and Global.

We are constantly warned about the personal level of Netwar, we have passwords to computer accounts, never give our social security number over the telephone, and generally try to be careful about our own information. But protecting yourself from someone who genuinely wants to conduct information war against you is nearly impossible. Corporations are subject to a barrage of information security problems to an even greater extent. The stealing of company secrets is a new form of economic war that is plaguing many companies. It is also possible for one company to release false findings that indicate that a competitor has a poor or dangerous product. IBW spawned misinformation-a fertile area for denial and deception techniques-are very difficult to combat and correct. Finally, on the global level, Netwar can be waged against industries, economies, nations, or non-state groups. It ranges from intelligence and information leads, to the terrifying possibilities of terrorist groups breaking into such communications as an air traffic control system at a major US airport. The impact at the global level can be much more wide spread and all threatening than that of the personal or corporate levels of netwar.

On both sides of the war, Netwar and Cyberwar, the key to good protection and offence is good software to run the systems, encode the data, and peck holes in other's data. The vital link for the information and the technology is software, which relies heavily upon implanted logic. The newest and brightest theories and concepts of logic center around what is called 'fuzzy logic'.

The name fuzzy logic makes one think of a system that is inexact, but that is not the case, instead it has an infinite exactness. Fuzzy logic expands our normal computer principle of 0 or 1, true or false, and in the place of this is infinite degrees between 0 and 1. Fuzzy logic is used every day in the development of everything from smart washers to train systems in Japan. With a smart washer, you merely press a start button and the machine figures the cycle, how much detergent, and the water use; the logic train systems are smooth as silk, quick, and always on time. The theory started with a few paradoxes one of which is The Paradox of Theseus' ship:

When Theseus returned from slaying the Minotaur, says Plutarch, the Athenians preserved his ship, and as planks rotted, replaced them with new ones. When the first plank was replaced, everyone agreed it was still the same ship. Adding a second plank made no difference either. At some point, the Athenians may have replaced every plank in the ship. Was it a different ship? At what point did it become one?

At different points in time the ship was certain degrees the original ship, for instance when half the planks were replaced, it was the original ship. This same principle of degrees can be applied to many concepts around us, and what you end up with is a very exact and reliable process for computers. When you tie this concept into ideas such as artificial intelligence, you may obtain a computer that has the capacity to learn because it can start to work with more than 0 and 1.

Because of the importance of the technical tools of IBW-and their fragility-we list below the possible contents of an IBW techno "kit-bag":

Computer Viruses - A piece of code, or code fragment, designed to begin replicating itself when a host program begins to run. It's objective is to erase data, software programs, or memory in order to interrupt the action of the computer it infests. These can be loaded unwittingly by a user off the Internet or some other disk.

Worms - Instead of being just a code fragment, a worm is an entire program in and of itself. The code begins to replicate as soon as it touches a computer system, not dependent on the start of execution of any other program. Its aim is to eat up computer resources and/or delete data to result in a crippling effect on the host computer.

Trojan Horses - As the name would suggest, a Trojan horse is a program, or code fragment inside a program, that performs a function unbeknownst to the user. It usually performs a simple task on the outside, while unleashing a virus or a worm on the inside. It can also perform information retrieval while performing a task, leaving no trace.

Logic Bombs - Similar to a Trojan horse, a logic bomb is used to release a virus, worm, or complete some other secret task. These are usually planted by a programmer or system developer. This could be useful in US military strategy, instead of open bombs, the US could plant logic bombs to retrieve specific data from foreign users. This is plausible because many of the main software development in the world occurs in the US.

Trap Doors - The use of this is similar to a logic bomb. It is a secret way back into a system left by a programmer or designer. Unlike a logic bomb that executes, a trap door is merely an unknown security flaw. Chipping - This is the term for doing any of the above to the hardware of a system instead of to the software. One can build in circuitry to a chip that performs specific functions.

Machines and Microbes - Although one thinks of Star Trek and other science fiction when the subject of nanny machines comes up, it is actually a feasible plan. machines and microbes are tiny machines, like a small insect, that "eat" electronic circuits, oil, plastics, etc. If unleashed on a computer center, the result would be total shut down.

Electronic Jamming, HERF guns, and EM bombs- These are all forms of electronic signal jamming. One can jam communications, stopping computer information flow; shoot radio signals at an electronic target to shut it down with a High Energy Radio Frequency (HERF) gun; or send out a high powered electromagnetic pulse, an EMP bomb.

Hitch-hiking- This is a group of people, a subsection of hackers, that merely sit on the net and wait. They wait for any information and interesting code to go by and then hitch a ride with it, they follow and delete it, or they simply copy and steal it. Thinking in terms of closing Pandora's Box, the following techniques will have to be considered as an IBW operational security plan is built:

Firewalls - A limited gateway to the Interment from a company or group. Only passwords and certain configurations can get in, and everything is checked for viruses, etc. Only privileged personnel, or personnel with certain system configurations can get out. If implemented correctly they can be useful.

Encryption - This growing area of interest consists on coding data so that others can not place bombs in or around it or read the data. This is growing more difficult as hackers and other groups become more efficient at breaking the codes. This is one of the areas that fuzzy logic could come into serious play. If, at first glance, the foregoing appears to be merely a "laundry list," a reading of the following paragraph will surely prove sobering to the IBW planner:

The Defense Information Security Agency (DISA) conducts vulnerability studies of military and government computer systems. Their figures are truly alarming: 88% of defense computer systems are easily penetrated. Of the successful penetrations, 96% are not detected. Even worse, 95% of the detected penetrations are not reported or responded to. Even when an intrusion is detected, it is usually impossible to determine who did it. DISA studies indicate that there were possibly 300,000 intrusions into government computer systems in 1994 alone.

THE STRUCTURE OF SCIENTIFIC REVOLUTIONS

Whereas we had available for immediate purpose one hundred and forty-nine first-class warships, we now have two, these two being the Warrior and her sister Ironside. There is not now a ship in the English navy apart from these two that it would not be madness to trust in an engagement with that little [American] Monitor.. -The Times

The most recent steps in that evolution can be found in the Military Technical Revolution (MTR) which may be attributed to Soviet Military thinkers; and, a recurrence of what is called the Revolution in Military Affairs (RMA).

In the early 1980's the Soviets noted that "the emergence of advanced non-nuclear technologies was engendering a new revolution in military affairs. They were particularly interested in the "incorporation of information sciences into the military sphere" and in the idea of a "reconnaissance-strike complex. The events in the Gulf War convinced them of their hypothesis (comparative strategies). RMAs matter principally for two reasons. First, being second best may lead to catastrophic loss in future wars. Since the only objective benchmark for determining the relative effectiveness of forces (that is, success in combat) is unavailable in long periods of peace, there is great potential for asymmetries in combat effectiveness between militaries, observable only when the next war occurs. Secondly, as equipment life cycles, especially for platforms, steadily grow to encompass decades, many of the principal weapons systems of 2025 will likely be designed and built in the next few years. Since militaries are stuck with force structures they choose for long periods, it is more crucial than ever to think about them now, in peacetime, about the revolutionary changes in the nature of war and the about what will matter in winning wars in twenty or thirty years. Today with the United States arguably the only superpower for the foreseeable future, one might ask why this issue is especially pressing. Replicating the US force structure is clearly beyond the reach of all but a few other nations, even in the long term. This may not be relevant. Even small-to medium sized powers may be able to exploit specific technologies for significant military leverage in certain areas. The current rate of change suggests that state of the art in any technological context will be an extremely short-lived phenomenon, particularly with respect to the technologies that were key to the success of Desert Storm: space systems, telecommunication systems, computer architecture's, global information distribution networks, and navigation systems. Future revolutions will occur much more rapidly, offering far less time for adaptation to new methods of warfare. The growing imperative in the business world for rapid response to changing conditions in order to survive in an intensely competitive environment is surely instructive for military affairs.

The present RMA entails a fundamental change in who, how, and, perhaps even why wars are fought. It is driven not only by new technologies but by new operational concepts, new tactics, and new organizational structures. The impact of the current confluence of social, political, economic, and technological forces on American society and armed forces may equal-or exceed-what occurred during the 1960's and 1970's during the turmoil associated with the war in Vietnam.

The question that must be asked as we attempt to understand this RMA, is what were the results of change wrought by past Revolutions in Military Affairs? It has been suggested that accelerated interservice rivalries and over-reliance on management systems marked the last RMA, driven by the advent of atomic weapons at the end of WW II and the relatively stable and sparse defense budgets of the 1950's.

The current RMA is characterized by four types of changes:

- extremely precise;
- stand-off strikes;
- dramatically improved command, control, and intelligence;
- information warfare; and
- nonlethality

Many analysts see a number of benefits from harnessing the current revolution in military affairs and using it to build 21st century US armed forces:

- rejuvenating the political utility of military power;
- delaying the emergence of a peer competition;
- providing a blueprint for technology acquisition and force reorganization;
- and inspiring conceptual, forward-looking thinking.

Looking ahead, many believe that the current RMA will have at least two stages. The first is based on stand-off platforms, stealth, precision, information domination, improved communications, computers, global positioning systems, digitization, "smart" weapons systems, jointness, and use of ad hoc coalitions.

The second may be based on robotics, nonlethality, pyscho-technology, cyberdefense, nanotechnology, "brilliant" weapons systems, hyperflexible organizations, and "fire ant warfare."

Steven Metz and James Kievit of the Strategic Studies Institute argue that a cost /benefit analysis of the present RMA needs to be pursued. One the one hand, they argue that a case can be made that costs and risks of vigorous pursuit of the current RMA outweigh the expected benefits. These include the risk that:

- the current RMA will not generate increased combat effectiveness against the most likely or most dangerous future opponents;
- American pursuit of the RMA will encourage opponents or potential opponents to seek countermeasures;
- the current RMA might lead the United States toward over reliance on military power; and, vigorous pursuit of the current RMA might increase problems with friends and allies.

On the other hand, they argue that there are very pressing reasons for supporting the current RMA: it should bring significant increase in combat effectiveness against some mid-level opponents; a force built around stand-off, precision weapons and disruptive information warfare capabilities would be more politically usable than a traditional force-projection military; the RMA could augment deterrence; and, the United States may need to pursue the current RMA to avoid stumbling into strategic inferiority.

Lastly, they posit-and we strongly agree-that if policymakers decide to pursue the present revolution in military affairs, strategy, rather than technological capability should guide force development. The key question is: What do we want the future US military to be able to do?

Unfortunately one finds little discussion of the foregoing ideas in the DOD's recently completed "Bottom-Up" Review. Former Secretary of Defense Aspin initiated the review with the laudable goal of rethink the basis for US defense planning. It placed emphasis in many of the right areas: readiness, keeping forces for more than one regional war, acquisition reform. This review built a substantial consensus in the Pentagon behind the new force structure. Nonetheless, the review offers a classic example of military leaders planning to fight the last war. The report's proposed force for a single regional contingency-four to five Army divisions, four to five Marine brigades, 10 Air Force fighter wings, 100 heavy bombers, and four to five carriers-mirrors almost exactly the forces deployed in Operation Desert Storm. The review offers few thoughts on new technologies or techniques that might change the nature of war in coming decades.

Clearly, the challenge is to move beyond the last war-an undertaking that is fraught with peril and promise.

AN INFORMATION BASED WARFARE MODEL

We are pilgrims, Master; we shall go

Always a little further...."

-Inscription on the Clock, Bradbury Lines, Hereford, Home of the Special Air Service Regiment J. F. Flecker

We believe that it is instructive to review the Program of Analysis for FY 1996 as set forth by the Directorate for Combat Support, National Military Intelligence Production Center, Defense Intelligence Agency. Entitled, Intelligence Support to Infrastructure Warfare, the thrust of this paper is directed toward a new paradigm that is centered on the principal of attacking an adversary's infrastructure to degrade or deny mobility, support to combatants and leadership.

The paper sets forth valid arguments to support the thesis that to a large extent, recent advances in weapons and tactics were driven by the strategic objective of penetrating and rupturing the physical and psychological "centers of gravity" of the enemy warfighting capability. It is clear that new technologies have spurred an entire new generation of warfighting capabilities and, of equal importance, fundamentally altered the construct and performance of the modern nation-state.

Discrete centers of gravity are giving way to diversification and interdependence in the modern nation-state. Information is the raw material that fuels productivity and power. Critical systemic nodes in the dynamic flow of commodities-consumables, services, and information-are at the same time increasingly obscure, strategically important, and tactically vulnerable. Fine grain analysis [read Intelligence writ in large script] and precision targeting fin both the conventional and non conventional sense] of these nodes and their synergistic dependencies is the centerpiece of Infrastructure Warfare.

The primary elements of Infrastructure Warfare are:

- The nation-state as a System of Systems;
- Information as an Instrument of Power;
- Denial and Deception;
- Urban Infrastructure-The Operational Environment.

While the concept of Infrastructure Warfare is certainly a step in the right direction, we believe that this concept has several shortcomings that need to be addressed in order that it fully lead toward an answer to the strategic "bottom-line"-how do we win? We argue that the conflicts of the new world disorder will be largely fought on geography in the Third World (TW.) Driven largely by the chimera of the Gulf War, images of centers of gravity and smart weapons overshadow the tawdry back-alley settings in which actual conflict will take place in the future. In reviewing the "lessons learned" of recent wars in the Third World- where 95 percent of future conflicts will take place-a number of more accurate images appear:

First, the mix of forces facing each other has not been very different, regardless of the type of war being fought. Navies have been conspicuous by their absence or their modest role. Air forces have played a secondary role. Almost without exception, wars in the TW have been won or lost by ground troops.

Second, the type of war has not necessarily determined the tactics used; in fact, it has blurred the differences between them. Furthermore, as the frequent oscillations in tactics and strategy suggest, both irregular and regular armies in recent years have shared much in term of their ability to implement offensive doctrine. With the exceptions of campaigns involving an industrialized power, it seems that the defense has become the most effective form of warfare in the TW. With the exception of Israel and the war in Lebanon, none of the Third World combatants that have used an offensive doctrine has been able to effect a decisive breakthrough or cause the defenders to retire in disorder or retreat.

Third, the duration of recent wars have generally been protracted and have engaged large arrays of national and subnational forces. Most of the wars fought between regular lesser developed country army's have not been shorter.

Fourth, the involvement of external nation forces has been large. Of the wars fought between 1945 and 1976, 38 percent were fought with foreign participation. Lastly, because guerrilla wars pose particularly difficult challenges for governments, they represent a new and difficult form of conflict.

If the foregoing is correct, then we believe that the Infrastructure paradigm must address the Gray Area Phenomena (GAP). GAP is defined as threats to nation-states by non-states actors and non-governmental processes and organizations. The Gray Areas at once appear to be strikingly new and uncomfortably old. Simply put, they are the most critical issues confronting the world community as we enter into the Century. Just beyond the horizon of current events lie two possible futures-both of which look bleak. The first is the retribalization of large swaths of humankind by war and bloodshed: a Lebanonization of national states in which culture is pitted against culture, people against people, tribe against tribe-a Jihad in the name of a hundred narrowly conceived faiths against every kind of globalization and interdependence.

The second is being borne by the onrush of technical, economic, and ecological forces that demand increased integration and uniformity. The planet, it appears, is both falling apart and coming reluctantly together at the very same time.

The GAP consists of the following "arena's of conflict":

- Ethno-religious-nationalistic conflicts;

- Weapons proliferation-both conventional and nuclear, biological and chemical;
- Conflict over scarce resources;
- AIDS and other infectious diseases;
- The globalization of Organized Crime;
- Drug Trafficking;
- Economic Warfare and conflict over technology;
- Emigration; and,
- Famine.

The United States today is involved to some degree in each of the aforementioned arena's. While we strongly believe that traditional force-on-force warfare will always be with us, in the main, we sense that the present and future world situation more than makes the case for a strategy that encompasses the full-range of conflict supported by the appropriate technologies. Thus, we would add the Gray Area "arenas of conflict" to the DIA construct, and in so doing, move the ongoing debate to the new plateau of Information Based Warfare.

Tomorrow

We should be seeking tentative answers to fundamental questions, rather than definitive answers to trivial ones. — James Billington

Before framing a new definition and model for Information Based Warfare, we turn to a nonwestern look at information and warfare. Shen Weiguang, a writer who appears to be at the forefront of PRC IW theorists argues that: in a military sense alone, information warfare refers to both sides' attempt to gain the initiative of the battle through their control over information and flow of intelligence. With the support of information, both sides intend to comprehensively apply military deception, operational secrets, psychological warfare, and electronic warfare to destroy the enemy's information systems, block the flow of the enemy's information, and create false information to affect and weaken the enemies command and control capability. At the same time, they must ensure that their command and control system is not damaged in the same way by the opponent.

Further addressing the issues, Shen Weiguang illuminates a number of thoughts that cut to the heart of the concept of Information Based Warfare. He correctly argues that IBW in one sense is the "quiet battlefield," something we attempted to portray in our opening scenario.

Turning toward the concept of "centers of gravity" we feel that his descriptions of "attacks on the enemies cognitive and trust systems" perhaps better portrays the idea of attacking C2 and C4I nodes. This, he argues, is the main target of information warfare. The concepts of "hard attack" and "soft attack" with "soft damage" are noted as the two end-product manifestations of IBW; and, the concept of "war of structural damage" [read Infrastructure War] is thought to come into full play only when "it has absorbed the essence of information warfare."

Technology, he argues, does not determine superiority. It is determined by new tactics [in part this could be naval guerrilla warfare-PRC style] and "independent creations of commanders in the field. Information based warfare enables one to break with "traditional stylized engagement, " something we feel will give new impetus to the military arts.

Like a number of perceptive US thinkers, Shen Weiguang, has seized upon the Toffler' work to understand and further flesh-out the idea of "niche-warfare." And, he appears to understand that IBW will spawn special operating forces [differentiated from special forces] in the IBW setting. His comments about command and control are perceptive:

The operational target of information warfare lies in control rather than bloodshed;

The key to victory lies in human policy decisions rather than technology [hopefully a lesson learned and re-learned in the Naval War College games]; genuine advantage does not necessary lie in the leading technology but the leading ideas. History has given evidence to the fact when some new technology brings mankind brightness, a shadow is cast simultaneously.

Advanced electronic computers and information technology link society and the army to an integrated network; the result is very high efficiency and great fragility;

The input in grasping knowledge, costs far less than directly purchasing advanced weaponry [a Sun-tzuian slip, particularly in light of the fact that the PRC has taken this approach for years as it has covertly acquired primarily mid-level technology from the West, enabling them to jump the learning curve].

8

Digital War

Each age has seen war transformed by modern technologies and concepts. The Information Age promises to be no different. Some have called the Gulf War the first "Information War" - others have called it the last "Industrial Age" war. The power of information was clearly demonstrated in the context of traditional conflict. Information was leveraged to significantly improve the effectiveness of all aspects of warfare from logistics to command, control, communications, and computers, intelligence, surveillance, and reconnaissance (C4ISR). The effectiveness of the U.S. and its allies in the Gulf War has surely deterred potential adversaries from taking on our forces in the rather symmetrical manner that Iraq attempted and has stimulated thinking about other strategies for countering conventional forces. Digital war, enabled by advances in technology and its widespread adoption as well as the globalization of economics and commerce, is surely a strategy that potential adversaries are thinking about to achieve some of the objectives that have previously been sought by means of traditional warfare.

Digital war, a subset of what we call information war, involves non-physical attacks on information, information processes, and information infrastructure that compromise, alter, damage, disrupt, or destroy information and/or delay, confuse, deceive, and disrupt information processing and decision making.

Digital war intrinsically possesses in ultimate form some of the same characteristics that traditional military planners are striving for, including low-cost precision, standoff, and stealth. Digital war threatens the ability of a nation state's military to interpose itself between its population and "enemies of the state," thereby causing a loss of sanctuary. The importance of sanctuary can be inferred by our willingness to spend significant resources on air, sea, and missile defenses to provide our citizens with a workable sanctuary with respect to territorial intrusions.

Another characteristic of information attacks stems from the loss of sanctuary. Attacks of this sort, particularly when they consist of more than an isolated incident, create a perception of vulnerability, loss of control, and loss of confidence in the ability of the state to provide protection. Thus, the impact can far exceed the actual damage that has occurred. This non-linear relationship between actual damage and societal damage makes the problem of digital war a particularly challenging one because it creates a mismatch between rational defense responses and their effectiveness.

How does one respond to a serious set of information attacks? Responding with traditional military forces may be politically unacceptable or in fact, may be ineffectual. Currently there is no consensus, even among those in the defense establishment who think about these issues, regarding how to deal with such an attack. Given the potential effectiveness of digital war, particularly as an instrument of power for niche competitors and non-state actors, we need, as a society, to take this Information Age form of war very seriously. If we do not, and if we rely solely on traditional weapons and concepts of war, we may be building our own 21st Century Maginot line that can be flanked with the speed of light.

Inadvertent Robustness

There are some who have suggested that we are not as vulnerable to information attacks as has been claimed because the collection of our legacy systems provides a certain amount of inherent robustness and resiliency. They point to the overlaps and duplications in these systems and argue that it would be very hard for anyone to completely disrupt a given set of services.

They point to the lack of interoperability among legacy systems and the firewalls that are thereby created and argue that it would be impossible for attackers to get very far by penetrating the weakest systems and using them as launching pads for attacks on other systems.

They argue that our current legacy systems and their interrelationships are difficult (even for us) to understand, so it must follow that potential adversaries will also be confused.

Clearly there is some truth in each of these arguments. But this unruly collection of legacy systems also carries with it significant disadvantages. As far as security considerations are concerned, five points need to be made. First, this issue is not whether or not an attack could totally destroy or disrupt a particular system or type of service, but whether or not there could be sufficient damage to trigger the perception of a failure and result in panic behavior that could in turn create a significant national problem. Second, the redundancies in the systems are only partial and unplanned. Hence, they are neither complete nor reliable.

Third, our legacy systems, many having been designed and built with little or no attention to security, are difficult to protect and secure. Fourth, as the need for interconnectivity and interoperability increases, more and more systems are being lashed together with "work-arounds." These patches, in many cases, compromise security. Lastly, the lack of security that these systems provide is dampening the demand for services that could make operations more effective and efficient in many areas. Our current collection of legacy systems has other disadvantages as well. For example, the lack of interoperability wastes resources and impairs operations. Thus, it should be clear that the disadvantages of our current collection of legacy systems are not a blessing in disguise but rather the source of problems that need to be addressed so that we can take full advantage of the opportunities that information technologies can provide.

Formulating the Problem

The first step in tackling any problem involves developing an understanding of the possible environments that may be faced (or the "states of nature"), one's options, and the objective that is being sought. This requires an identification of the variables that are relevant, that is, those that can significantly influence the outcome as well as the subset of these relevant variables that are controllable, which form the basis for designing options. In a problem as complex as IW-D, working to formulate the problem accomplishes three things. First, it provides a useful framework for discussion. Second, it serves to keep the focus on those specific areas that are either unknown or in dispute. Third, it serves as a benchmark for measuring progress.

In this case, the states of nature correspond to the nature of the threat that will be faced vis-a-vis the vulnerabilities of our information infrastructure while our options correspond to the strategies we adopt and the actions we take to defend ourselves. The objective being sought corresponds to a level of infrastructure performance, its definition and measure being a major challenge in and of itself.

A good place to start is to try to develop an understanding of the nature of the threat, or more accurately the spectrum of relevant threats. This involves the identification of potential threats and the estimation of their likelihoods. Normally one would construct a set of states of natures that are mutually exclusive and collectively exhaustive so that a probability density function could be used. For the purposes of this discussion, the states of nature referred to correspond to potential threats grouped in some logical fashion to facilitate analysis of how well each defensive strategy deals with each of these threats.

Having an initial concept of the nature and range of potential threats, one can develop alternative defensive strategies and corresponding sets of action to counter one or more of these threats. A great deal depends upon what variables we believe we can and should control.

Each defensive strategy, with its corresponding set of actions, then needs to be analyzed with respect to each of the threats. The results of these analyses will be a characterization of the results or outcomes from pursuing each of the defensive strategies with respect to each of the threats. These outcomes, which are basically descriptions of results (e.g., number of penetrations and their consequences), then need to be translated into value measures that represent their impact. These costs and benefits provide a rational basis for determining an appropriate defensive strategy. Much will depend upon how we measure success. Given the central role that the threat topology plays in problem formulation, we will now turn our attention to examining this topology.

Threat Topology

The irregular nature of the space is meant to indicate that its boundaries are not well defined. Nevertheless, one can group threats in order of the seriousness of their consequences (from left to right). The consequences associated with a failure to counter a specific attack range, on the one hand, from isolated and limited consequences to, on the other hand, consequences of catastrophic proportions.

There are a relatively small number of threats that most everyone would agree have strategic implications and must be defended against with considerable vigor. Attacks against our systems that control and safeguard weapons of mass destruction (WMD) and our minimum essential emergency communication network (MEECN) clearly fall into this category. Others that fall into this category would include the information and communication systems associated with the National Command Authority (NCA), some of our command, control, communications and intelligence (C3I) systems, and some of our intelligence systems, particularly information regarding sources and methods. A review of other Government information and information systems would result in additional information and systems that should be added to this list.

Beyond those sets of threats that clearly fall into either the Everyday or Strategic categories, there are classes of threats that span the threat spectrum.

Attacks on our national, or for that matter international, infrastructure do not fall neatly into one area of the threat topology but in fact populate all three classes of threat. These attacks on our public safety, energy, financial, and communications systems and services have different implications and consequences depending on the specific nature of the attacks and the circumstances surrounding the attack.

The vast majority of attacks on infrastructure are by hackers whose motives run the full gamut from financial motives, to having some fun, or to more serious forms of antisocial behavior. While some of these attacks may have serious consequences in the form of significant losses of data, interrupted services, or stolen assets or services, only a small number of these lone perpetrator attacks are likely to have potential strategic consequences. This is not to say that it is impossible that some set of circumstances would result in the snowballing of one of these hacker attacks into a national security concern, but rather that this outcome is unlikely. However, infrastructure attacks can be quite serious if they are well planned and coordinated. Arguably this would require an adversary with seriousness of purpose and with some sophistication and organization. This kind of attack would be better named digital warfare rather than be included as part of the group referred to as hacker attacks. Depending on the level of sophistication of a digital warfare operation, its consequences could range from a "high-end" hacker attack to an attack with strategic consequences.

A key point to be made involves the chaotic nature of the transition between topological boundaries for infrastructure attacks. Chaotic behavior involves a non-linear relationship between input and output where prediction becomes extremely difficult if not impossible. Two distinct scenarios serve to illustrate the chaotic nature of infrastructure attacks. In the first case, a particular infrastructure attack may trigger a series of proximate consequences that are difficult to predict and that greatly magnify the effects of the attack. In the second case, a series of attacks will exhibit chaotic behavior when the sum of their consequences can not be determined by adding up their individual consequences, or when their cumulative effect far exceeds the sum of the individual effects of a series of independent events. These are not uncommon patterns. Valid scientific disciplines of complexity, catastrophe, and complexity theory have been developed because these patterns occur throughout nature.

MERGING LEVELS OF WAR

The American public's lack of stamina to endure a protracted conflict and their abhorrence of battlefield casualties requires quick, decisive, strategic results. It is the warfighter's quest for immediate strategic results that will force the restructure of the three levels of war. With the help of information technology, joint commanders of the Twenty-first century will be able to efficiently command and control geometrically greater battle spaces at a far greater tempo and confidence level. The amount of uncertainty will be less.

The virtually seamless flow of information from the lowest echelons--conceivably individual battalions, ships or aircraft--gives joint commanders a significantly increased knowledge base from which to coordinate, synchronize, and employ forces. This knowledge will be shared nearly simultaneous throughout the chain of command.

The force multiplying effect of shared information will be to achieve a greater coherence and unity of effort with significantly fewer casualties. Consequently, actions at every level will instantaneously effect the other and will have the affect of reducing the time between decisions. Furthermore, the trend toward more powerful weapon systems will give rise to tactical elements being employed more often in direct support of strategic objectives. Situational awareness will permit the conduct of simultaneous offensive operations allowing the capability to convert tactical success immediately into decisive strategic results.

In the pursuit of more decisive operations, a great shift in the power to make operational and tactical decisions at one echelon will occur. The desirability of this shift will depend on how senior leaders adapt to the greater responsibility. A goal of joint digitization is to provide a greater assimilation of more information into the warfighting process.

This implementation goal will ultimately expand the strategic level's span of control with the streamlining of the operational chain of command. Today, military organizations are generally sized by how much one commander can effectively control.

By design, each echelon's commander is better informed to make appropriate decisions concerning his responsibilities. During the late 1980's and early 1990's, an evolution in business management led by the integration of information systems caused an increase in the span of control for a typical senior manager; this subsequently resulted in a flattening of the management structure. Likewise, digitization will provide more senior leaders the information that will permit them to feel comfortable making more judgments that were traditionally left to operational and tactical commanders. As in business, digitization will cause an increase in the span of control at the strategic level and a subsequent greater centralization of command. In the future, digital technology may render our current structure obsolete.

A flatter structure may not be always beneficial. The disadvantage of centralization is the magnitude that each decision potentially has. Mistakes in simple judgment can lead to greater, longer lasting consequences. Since the influence of a strong commander permeates throughout, there may be cases where trusting a single individual's perceptions may be, in the end, very costly in terms of resources, lives, and continued public support.

Another important reason for the merging levels of war is that communication between all echelons is expected to shift dissemination and collection of intelligence, targeting, and other data from hierarchical to a non-hierarchical command structure.

Hierarchial Structure Non-Hierarchial Structure

This internetted command structure undesirably leads to an "diffused command authority." Even today there are indications of just how future technology can alter command approaches within the military. Electronic mail (E-mail) has created a formal, as well as, informal dissemination structure within the Department of Defense. The ease at which an individual can send a courtesy copy or a message to anyone, regardless of position, has placed unusual demands upon an organization's hierarchy. It is easy to interpolate how the future and its promise for "smarter" systems, which are better able to assimilate and display information, can change the traditional needs for hierarchical levels. What is not clear is the effect that these informal lines of communications will have on a command structure during times of conflict.

As technology increases the strategic echelon's span of control, there will be a predictable gravitation to coordinate tactical weapons at the highest possible level; thus, more pressure to flatten or merge the levels of war. Improved war-fighting capabilities which have increased the mobility, dispersion, lethality, and tempo will drive control measures at least to a joint theatre level. Centralized control is needed for synchronization of combat power in order to conserve assets, and prevent fratricide and civilian collateral damage. Weapon systems could be enabled or disabled remotely whether they are on a ship, land or aircraft. It will be possible to control tactical fires and the maneuvers of combat elements to optimize the direct obtainment of the strategic goal. These combat elements will be armed with far more sophisticated direct and indirect munitions with ranges that exceed line of sight. Military professionals saw just a glimpse of technology during Desert Storm. By Twenty-first century standards, Desert Storm will look antiquated, but it illustrates just how complex and how important synchronizing forces are in order to prevent friendly casualties and to insure decisive strategic results.

The significance for future military organizations is that traditional tactical and operational levels will have the same information and same battle space concerns. The need for separation based upon capability to command and control will likely cease to exist in the Twenty-first century. The overall disadvantages of this merging has yet to form. How the senior leadership adapts and structures the resulting organizations will determine the magnitude of the drawbacks.

Diminished Command Prerogatives

Like many problems, the solutions often have undesirable consequences. It is quite possible that digitization upon Twenty-first century military organization will be detrimental to the concept of execution at the lowest level and could lead to over control. With the shared vision resulting from digitization, every one within the chain of command could have access to the same situational information. Theoretically, everyone from the White House, the Joint Staff and CINC Staffs, down to the tactical levels could have access to the same facts. Potentially it could become normal for some operational and tactical level decisions to come from the White House or the Joint Staff. The United States military requires leaders that possess boldness and initiative to act on one's own judgment. These traits within our leaders make the U.S. military a formidable force. Digitization may unintentionally affect the relationship between echelons by limiting the organization's initiative, ingenuity, and inventiveness through constant monitoring by superiors.

No one likes to have someone looking over their shoulder as they work. Increased theatre awareness and the ability to automatically transfer databases will result in the expansion and availability of on-line information. This may very likely result in a great deal of second guessing by senior commanders and staff. Invariably during a crisis, a subordinate commander who is closer to the action will select a different course of action than that of the senior commander. Should the superior commander second guess and redirect the effort or sit on his hands and wait it out? The challenge for senior leaders in the future will be curtailing their inclinations and allowing subordinate leaders their prerogatives. When a commander thinks he has all the facts, allowing a subordinate his prerogatives by not interfering goes against the "zero defects" culture that permeates the military today; unfortunately, there is no evidence that the future culture will be any different.

Information technology will also find it hard to digitize what is in the commander's head and what he feels--the kind of intangible awareness that comes from being close and near the area of operation. Our forces will fight the way they train. There is a danger that factors that cannot be quantified will be disregarded and our commanders not near the action will be "partly conditioned" by the technical tools available to them. For example, during a peacetime exercise, based on intuition or other undigitizable information, a commander may want to deviate from a plan during its execution. How many times will a commander accept corrections or challenges, by a "all-knowing" higher commander or superior's staff. Echelons above may believe they understand and have the "correct" bigger picture and demand adherence to previously coordinated plans or only minor tweaks to an existing plan.

There are very few commanders, believing they have the right situational information, that can allow a subordinate to act contrary or independently to their expectations without at least making an inquiry. Sure, the subordinate commander could explain and defend his actions and even prevail; however, a sense of autonomy, pride and creativeness is predictably lost by a subordinate each time it occurs. It doesn't take many real-time corrections or constant challenges by a boss to stifle boldness and initiative. It might be hard for today's leaders to appreciate the loss of initiative and boldness caused by digitization, since they have had these traits nurtured into them throughout their careers. The concern should be about the generation of leaders who grow up with extensive and perhaps constant oversight and monitoring.

The Marines "Warfighting" manual, FMFM 1, has recognized this concern and has succinctly stated, "Equipment that permits over control of units in battle is in conflict with the Marine Corps's philosophy of command and is not justifiable." The digitization technology of the Twenty-first century, by obtaining massive situational awareness, may have the unintended consequence of permitting commanders too much control. The military services could be entering into a new era of electronic micro-management.

The pressure to micro-manage, to ask questions, and to second guess field commander's decisions will be very high. Consider a CINC or a Joint Task Force commander, with the military and civilian leadership in Washington D.C. and the media doggedly pursuing in "real time" their individual stories, demanding to know status and planned intentions. The pressures will be enormous for information. With instantaneous civilian global information networks, such as CNN and broadcast network news, our civilian population has become more addicted to war news. For the future, the "CNN war leads public and leaders to define political events in terms of the video clips and sound bites that compose TV news images." A causal effect of this coverage is that the available reaction time to events for civilian policy makers is going to decrease because of amplified public interest. The American people are going to demand more information from their senior civilian and military leaders. Accordingly, policy makers are going to want to know more and want to know it sooner.

The pressure upon senior military leaders to supply only the most accurate information and not to publicly embarrass themselves, as well as their civilian leaders, will be immense. The future joint leader and corresponding staff are going to be forced to make larger number of inquiries to satisfy the media and public. Situational awareness through digital technology will be the enabling technology for maintaining public support for the military, as well as keeping the political leadership from embarrassment.

A good counter argument might be that unintrusive electronic queries will be extensively used and the distraction will be very minor. This argument holds well, if the question is strictly qualitative in nature, is an acceptable answer, or doesn't require explanations. Unfortunately, it is more likely that one answer will precipitate several more questions that may or may not be available unobtrusively through an electronic data base. Digitization might inadvertently and unanticipatedly increase outside distractions through the answering of endless questions up the chain of command. On the positive side, it is easy to see how this kind of uncontrolled eavesdropping by a higher level staff can lead to better situational awareness and better serve a joint commander. Sadly, it is hard to imagine how unencumbered, direct access to planning and execution information by a superior and his staff, without the subordinate's personal spin, could have a positive effect on the hard-charging, self-motivated commander.

One could argue that the higher echelons will not be interested in information that is specific and in detail. It is more likely that the smaller Twenty-first century force structure will limit the options available to our senior leaders. Consequently, leaders will require more specific information in order to make decisions. For example, the Joint Staff is currently in the process of developing and fielding the first phase of the Global Command and Control System (GCCS). ADM Owens, Vice Chairman, Joint Chief of Staff was given a demonstration of the Global Status of Resources and Training System (GSORTS). While being impressed with its capability to easily understand air base and other readiness ratings, he indicated it would be nice to also receive the aircraft availability by individual weapon's load, including Precision Guided Munitions (PGMs), and by sensors in a particular area of responsibility. What is significant is not that the Admiral wanted to know this information, but how the information going to be used at the strategic level. What if the information is not as expected or quantifiably correct? Very few leaders like to be surprised, and with the relatively smaller force structure, specifics are becoming very important.

Another concern is whether our warfighters will be prepared for the avalanche of questions. It cannot be discounted that routine questions from higher echelons tend to increase exponentially in importance the farther down the chain of command they propagate. So the lower echeloned, smaller staffed, war-fighting organizations are less prepared to handle queries and are distracted disproportionately.

Often in discussions about digitization and automation, it is surmised that staff sizes will decrease in numbers. It is quite possible that staff sizes may need to increase--not decrease. The requirement for information is compounded by the problem that during peace there is a tendency to become over organized and more bureaucratic in structure. This tendency can be summarized as the "need-to-know everything" syndrome. The propensity to explain and track data is gradually taking up more of the commander's and staff's time. As our services become more complex, more records and information are required to be processed and the demand for support staff increases. Large bureaucratic staffs do not normally foster and facilitate initiative and boldness in subordinate organizations.

The military has already experienced the unintended consequences of automation when it comes to bureaucratic staffwork. Consider how the word processor has streamlined typing and the electronic mailing of documents and messages. As stated before, automated offices are able to effortlessly and with efficiency send documents and E-mail via Local Area Networks and, through MILNET, between organizations. These tools obviously save time through simplifying distribution, increasing information transfers between organizations, thereby decreasing the number of secretaries and military clerks. However, the demand for more usable information by senior decision makers has also increased, requiring staff officers to spend greater portions of their time typing questions and answers.

With the increase in productivity, automation has fostered an increase in reporting and information generation. It is true that reports and briefs are now written easily on computers, but organizations tend now to spend more time reworking letters and briefing charts to achieve limited gains in redrafts and minor formatting. The reworking does not necessarily result in better content but only ensures cosmetically perfect documents. The labor saving and time saving office computer has the unintended consequence of creating more work. Computers have increased the military staffs work load and have unintentionally required more staff, not less.

Increased Fragility

General Sullivan, Chief of Staff, Army, states technology driven battle space awareness "can provide us with lighter, more effective and more lethal weapon systems to offset our smaller force structure." But, one also must consider that as these force multiplying systems are effected by attritions of war, their corresponding impact upon the force is an equally multiplying loss. Digital technologies provide a tremendous capability, however, they must be weighted cautiously against their vulnerabilities.

The use of digital technology has consequences that are paradoxical in nature. While it is true that the implementation of more advanced sensor-to-weapon systems will give better situational awareness, help minimize fratricide and better focus combat power, they can also be our Achilles heel. There is the concern whether the new electronic systems will have the resilience to absorb shocks and withstand perturbations associated with the realities of modern war. The more advanced the equipment the more complex it becomes. Generally, the more complex the system, the less reliable, and the harder or longer it takes to repair.

A possible solution to the attrition issue is the use of redundancy in the digital architecture. Redundancy is not likely to protect the force as technology is being looked upon by our senior leaders to help mitigate the smaller force structure. It is a reality that the U. S. military will always be dependent upon finite amounts of specialized electronic equipment that will invariably not be easily replaced nor repaired.

There are other compounding effects of attrition, such as the digital technologies dependence upon reliable communication architectures. It is the dependence and reliance of electronically synthesized data from widely dispersed systems that makes communications the most vulnerable segment. The greatest threat to the entire digitization architecture is the lack of robust, redundant communications paths. For example, Desert Storm validated the notion that a CONUS based force projection strategy, with its anticipated tempo is dependent upon assured satellite communications for both inter- and intra-theatre communications irrespective of use on land or sea. Above the tactical level of war, it is anticipated for the Twenty-first century that medium data rates for the military, as well as civilian satellite systems, will be vulnerable to jamming by today's low cost technology. Since digital communications demands are going to be predictably greater than their capacity, there will be no redundancy nor unused capacity. Even today, it is doctrine not to normally keep communication equipment in reserve. Also, key communications equipment is subject to targeting through old-fashioned direct or indirect fires. An unsophisticated enemy sharp-shooter could easily fire a well placed bullet and take out the feed to a critical satellite or a microwave antenna. This would effectively disrupt the digital architecture with devastating consequences to the command and control process. Communications will be the weakest link for the future's dispersed digitized systems.

There is a trend growing within the U.S. military to use commercially available off-the shelf technology that is generally not designed to Military Standards nor for ease of trouble shooting. An unintentional result of using the less rugged commercial electronic equipment is it will require warfighting organizations to have near-by repairmen and large stocks within theatre of specialized electronic repair parts. Otherwise, replenishment could become a problem since strategic mobility will always be at a premium during a crisis.

Repair parts may not always be available. A CONUS based support structure assumes that the tempo at which critical items are used and destroyed will not exceed the rate at which they are being replaced. If tradition holds, then the military will keep electronic equipment beyond normal commercial applications. CONUS depots will have to have on-hand the repair parts since industry does not normally keep the production lines of specialized nor dated electronic designs operating. Leaders will need to take into account and understand the perishability and limited availability of electronic equipment.

Lack of timely repair could contribute to the increased fragility of the force. The advanced equipment of the future, whether it be built to commercial or military standards, will require a greater level of maintenance expertise. The philosophy of using built-in diagnostic and automatic check-out equipment does design complexity away from the operator; however, repair responsibilities dramatically shift to maintenance personnel. Repairing systems in the forward areas will be more difficult and there will be a greater tendency to evacuate equipment for repairs to the depots; thus increasing the time to repair. Based on complexity, it can be anticipated that digital electronic systems are going to have a much longer logistics tail than we have today.

Our force structure will likely have a critical shortage of qualified electronic technicians. Consider the same scenario of equipment damaged by a "low-tech" sharpshooter. What if the shooter decides to wait around to kill the skilled operator or maintenance person conducting the repair? Skilled repairmen will not be replaced easily. Maintenance personnel of the future will require more extensive and sophisticated training than today's technicians, since the systems will be more intricate. As the armed forces continue to compete against educational institutions and private corporations for the limited number of qualified 17-24 year-olds, it is going to be a challenge to keep qualified personnel skilled in electronics. Even the reliance on dedicated and first-rate National Guard and Reserve units is optimistic. Units meant to augment during national emergencies may not be able to keep operator and repair personnel up to warfighting standards.

The implication--"there will be time for training after the troops are assembled--is virtually over." It is not quantitatively known whether the rate of replacement of critical specialty skills will be able to keep pace, but one has only to look at where we are, traditionally short of technical specialists today. As during Desert Storm, it will be common for the Services to depend upon civilian technicians in forward deployed areas for maintenance and repair, due to the maintenance complexity of electronic equipment and the lack of qualified military personnel. It is possible that demographics, and sociopolitical educational realities, might just be the limiting factors of the Twenty-first century digitized force. The demand for "high-tech" personnel is going to go up--not down.

Another concern for the future is that we will depend more upon our allies for support. As the United States modernizes its forces with the latest electronic gadgetry, will our allies be willing to invest in the same kinds of equipment, or will we be willing to sell or give it to them' By digitizing everything from Command and Control to weapons systems, they might make it impossible to be electronically interoperable within a theatre with our coalition partners.

MILITARY INFORMATION TECHNOLOGY

Arabian sands had no safe haven for U.S. troops during Operation Iraqi Freedom. Dotting the barren Kuwaiti and Iraqi frontier, soldiers and airmen routinely found themselves targets of enemy rocket attacks and frontline probing actions.

Seasoned combat troops might expect such dangers, but not reservists in the 335th Theater Signal Command, who built, secured and maintained the American and coalition forces' IT networks. Firewalls and IDSes kept enemy hackers off their systems, but they relied on nearby Patriot batteries to keep Saddam Hussein's Ababil-100 missiles at bay.

It has been a year since U.S. troops pushed across the Kuwaiti border in their drive toward Baghdad. In the weeks leading up to the war and those tumultuous two months of heavy fighting, the network and security specialists supporting the combat divisions found that there are worse things than a bad day at the office.

"Everything is relative," says Tom Lantzy, a major in the U.S. Army Reserve who recently returned to his job as an infrastructure project manager for CocaCola. "If you've never been in a situation where someone is shooting at you, it may be that the server crash is the biggest problem you've ever dealt with."

Modern armed forces depend on high technology. Military intelligence, battle plans, troop movements and the availability of supplies are just some of the information that's converted into digital form and transmitted over cables, radio and satellites. Leave even a single crack and an enemy with access to computers and trained experts (hardly in short supply these days) could tap your entire command and control infrastructure. In other words, a breach could cost lives.

"Computer network defense issues and challenges in the commercial world and the military world are similar," says Lt. Col. Thomas Michelli, a Virginia National Guardsman deployed in Kuwait, where he oversees the Southwestern Asia CERT. "Except that the risks — mission-critical systems equal human lives — are much higher in the military world."

Marching Orders

The hurdles faced by the 335th dwarfed those of the civilian world, where mortar fire and missiles don't rain down. Creating and managing network systems — which link all U.S. units with those of 30 nations contributing troops or logistical support — was equivalent to integrating the complete IT systems for eight to 10 medium-sized corporations. The 335th rolled out the systems in just two months, an operation Lantzy estimates would have taken a full year in the corporate world.

"We moved more than 250,000 soldiers, Marines and coalition forces into a very small country about the size of Massachusetts," says Maj. Gen. Rip Dettamore, commander of the 335th and head of communications for all land forces in the Middle East.

Military units had to be plugged into the infrastructure that would connect them to their lifeblood — supplies, intelligence and instructions. Although there was a secure backbone for units already stationed in Kuwait, the 335th had to scale the infrastructure from 10 routers to approximately 600. Network bandwidth had to jump from 16 Mbps to nearly 200. Every unit needed a satellite link, IDS, router and other hardware and software.

The mission was immeasurably difficult because different services used different systems and standards. Even the various parts of the U.S. Armed Forces using the same equipment would configure them differently. Then, there was the need to integrate different databases and OSes to provide unified views of theater operations.

Another aggravating factor was that responsibility for critical IT jobs was split among different organizations because the total task was larger than the Army, the Air Force or the Marines could handle individually. For instance, the Army would install IDSes, but the Air Force would run them.

"I'm going to send this airman out, who is going to put in this new intrusion detection sensor, and you're going to have to reengineer the data package, maybe change the IP subnetting, which influences the way the routers work," Lantzy says.

While much of the equipment is off the shelf, important elements of the infrastructure are specific to the military and make securing the network easier. The Army uses one unsecured network that's connected to the Internet, and two closed satellite- and microwave-based networks for all critical information, as well as voice communications and video teleconferencing. Frequency-hopping and NSA Type-1 encryption are standard issue. All traffic and networks are protected with layers of firewalls, IDSes, proxy servers and tightly configured routers.

Hostile Environment

The climate was as hazardous and unwelcoming to the equipment as it was to the IT soldiers. In the first days of the war, the worst sandstorms in decades kicked up, leaving foot-deep drifts overnight and driving sand everywhere. Soldiers venturing into the open had to completely cover themselves to avoid getting burned by the blasting particles. The weather became a concern for the 335th, which had to keep shifting and blowing sand from tearing apart the infrastructure. "Opening up a server over there at a garrison base where it had been running a couple of months, the dust was an eighth of an inch thick, at least," says Lantzy. "It looked like somebody took the cover off and just poured it in there." Soldiers had to constantly clear out equipment with brushes and fans. In some cases, they improvised makeshift telecom facilities and data centers to protect equipment from the elements.

At first, in mid-March and early April 2003, the heat wasn't too bad in Kuwait, hovering in the 70s. Later, temperatures crept up to summer highs of 130 degrees. "You could be standing outside, and you felt that you had 2,000-watt hair dryers blowing in your face," says Dettamore. The 335th deployed air conditioning units to keep buildings, tents and shelters cool.

"You'd much rather be in the air conditioning taking care of the equipment than trying to sleep in a tent when it's 130 degrees," he laughs. "Given the two choices, it's no wonder that the equipment was clean."

Combat Conditions

Even with the occasional relief of cool air, the 335th had to keep systems up and secure under difficult conditions. Under the threat of chemical attack, Lantzy and his unit lived in their heavy protective suits for nearly two weeks. A rising and falling wail announced incoming missiles, and everyone at the base had to don a gas mask, boots and gloves. The sirens would give way to the whoosh of intercepting Patriots.

The threat of chemical-tipped missiles didn't stop the mission. IT specialists often had to work through the air raids, which presented their own challenges.

"It's hard to type," Lantzy says. "Most people use a pencil to type one letter at a time, because the gloves are so [thick] that you mash several keys at the same time. It's a very frustrating exercise." No matter the threat, the basic tasks facing corporate information security personnel were the same. IDSes and firewalls needed configuring, servers needed patching and AV needed updating. Soldiers of the 335th had to monitor attempts to breach the network. Their mission was complicated by the massive scale of their operation and the possibility that the next moment might be their last.

In one case, a server in one of the forward units hadn't installed a critical patch. When the command centre called, the unit said it would take a while to install the fix — its sysadmin had been wounded in a mortar attack.

All the work paid off, with uptimes on all equipment and systems exceeding 99 percent. Dettamore reports that not a single critical video teleconference or data link was lost during the war.

Coming Home

Things are quieter on the home front, and many of the veterans have a greater clarity of mind knowing that safety will always be more important than the latest Internet worm.

But their minds wander back to the desert. Some miss the adrenaline boost of near death and total commitment to a job. Newscasts also bring reality to their doorsteps.

"One of the guys we did some planning with was killed in November," says a subdued Lantzy. "They're your friends, your coworkers, and they're still over there, and there's still a threat."

9

The Drones of the Future Warfare

In November 2012, the U.S. Navy loaded an X-47B, officially labeled an "unmanned combat air system," aboard the USS *Harry S. Truman* for the drone's first carrier-based testing. The testing represents the beginning of developing successors to contemporary drones, which will be integrated into combat platforms like aircraft carriers. This signifies a remarkable break with current practices of operating drones in a strictly tactical, non-integrated capacity. Thus the X-47B illustrates the early stages of the U.S. military's long-term vision for drone warfare through the development of an unmanned combat aerial vehicle, or UCAV. Within this program the U.S. Air Force envisions a wide array of UAVs, from insect-like robots to tanker size pilotless planes, all of which are designed to perform the functions of traditional military aircraft while replacing the human pilot.

The Air Force's plan to develop advanced drones and integrate them into an increasingly autonomous platform is laid out in their roadmap for the future titled, "Air Force Unmanned Aerial System (UAS) Flight Plan 2009-2047." The Air Force envisions small-and medium-sized drones with lethal combat capabilities that would be almost unrecognizable compared to today's drone fleet. Today's medium-sized Reapers are set to be replaced by next generation MQ-Ma drones that will be "networked, capable of partial autonomy, all-weather and modular with capabilities supporting electronic warfare, close air support, strike, and intelligence, surveillance and reconnaissance missions."

The MQ-Ma generation will be supplanted by the MQ-Mb, theoretically capable of taking over even more roles once assigned to traditional fighter-bombers and spy planes, including the suppression of enemy air defenses, bombing and strafing of ground targets, and surveillance missions. These will fly more autonomously and be better linked-in to other drone platforms for cooperative missions involving many aircraft under the command of a single "pilot." Imagine, for instance, one human operator overseeing a single command drone that in turn holds sway over a small squadron of autonomous drones carrying out a coordinated air attacks.

The year 2047 is the U.S. Air Force's holy grail, "the capstone for its long term plan to turn the skies over to war-fighting drones." By then, the USAF plans to have MQ-Mc dominating the skies with futuristic hypersonic drones. It is possible that 30 to 40 years from now, the MQ-Mc will incorporate all of the advances of the current MQ-M generation while being equipped for mission platforms like aerial combat and missile defense.

THE INDELIBLE MARK OF AMERICA'S REMOTE CONTROL WARFARE

Nabila's favorite memories of her grandmother come from weddings. It didn't matter who was getting married – relative or neighbor – her grandmother, Mamana, was an active participant, owing to her matriarchal perch above their village. Mamana was as responsible as she was festive. An uneducated woman, she was the local midwife, and served as an impromptu primary care physician, even a veterinarian, when the need arose.

On a fall afternoon in 2012, Mamana called Nabila and a squad of her siblings and cousins outside to the family's okra fields, part of their sprawling garden in tribal Pakistan. It was about to be the Eid festival and the Rehman family needed to gather and prepare vegetables. Nabila, nine years old, had set to work when the drone fired its missiles. A dark plume of dust rose from the garden and mixed with acrid smoke. It spared Nabila and the other children the sight of their grandmother's mutilated corpse.

Her older cousins, all male, ran to help the screaming children. Nabila's hand and her arm were injured with burns and shrapnel. Her three-year-old brother, Safdar, who was watching the harvest from the roof of their home, had fallen to the ground, breaking bones in his chest and shoulders. The teenagers had gotten Nabila and some of the others out of the way when the second round of missiles hit, in what the CIA refers to as a "double-tap", to make sure it kills its targets.

Because US drone strikes are cloaked in secrecy, occur in remote or dangerous locales and target people presumed to be terrorists, Americans rarely hear from survivors or their relatives. But a theme emerges in interviews the Guardian has conducted with more than half a dozen drone survivors: the pain from the strike never ends, as the apparatus of secrecy renders closure unobtainable.

According to six people in Pakistan and Yemen who have lost their brothers, sons and grandparents to drone strikes, the strike lasts a moment and the consequences last a lifetime. Most of them have never told their stories to an American reporter. Some of them have theories about whom the US was targeting, while others are left guessing. The interviews were facilitated by the human rights group Reprieve and the Foundation for Fundamental Rights and conducted in translation.

The people are left impoverished, anguished and infuriated. Justice, let alone apologies, never arrives, even as a modest amount of blood money flows from the local governments. The United States, which styles itself a force for justice in the world, is to them the remote force that introduced death into their lives and treats them like they are subhuman, fit only to be targeted. At any moment, they fear, another drone could come for them.

The White House has said it will soon release of a tally of drone deaths. Relatives of the dead and survivors of the attacks expect little of it to include the truth, and doubt it will lead to the public apologies they desire – particularly since a senior aide to Barack Obama recently told the Atlantic that the president "has not had a second thought about drones".

The CIA would not comment for this piece. An Obama administration official said: "It is certainly not the case that lives of a certain nationality are more valuable to us than those of any other. What is true, however, is that the president has said ... that the American people need information to hold their government accountable. That is in part why we have been especially transparent when it comes to the deaths of US citizens."

Nabila's father, and Mamana's son, Rafiq ur-Rehman, took a different view. "If America kills any westerner, one of their own, white people, they apologize and compensate. But if it's Pakistanis like us, they don't care. In my opinion, America treats us worse than animals."

DECADE OF THE DRONE: AMERICA'S AERIAL ASSASSINS

Using the AfPak battlefield as a testing ground, the U.S. industrial-military complex has fine-tuned the most sophisticated high-tech weapon of the 21st century and has elevated warfare to the highest levels of cynicism. Operated through a screen from half a world away, unmanned drones slaughter indiscriminately great swaths of the civilian population while keeping U.S. lives safe. As Obama ponders his approach to the Afghan conflict, Joe Biden has already announced that he favours fewer troops as opposed to a significant increase in the use of assassination robots.

2010 is the last year of the new century and millennium and is the tenth consecutive year of the United States' war in Afghanistan and in the 15-nation area of responsibility subsumed under Operation Enduring Freedom. In early March

American military deaths in the Greater Afghan War theater – Afghanistan, Cuba (Guantanamo Bay), Djibouti, Eritrea, Jordan, Kenya, Kyrgyzstan, the Philippines, Seychelles, Sudan, Tajikistan, Turkey, Uzbekistan and Yemen – surpassed the 1,000 mark.

This year is also the tenth year of the first ground and the first Asian war fought by the North Atlantic Treaty Organization, which wages wars from and not to protect the nations of the northern Atlantic Ocean.

2010 is the tenth and deadliest year in Washington's use of unmanned aerial vehicles (drones) for targeted assassinations and untargeted "collateral damage."

Originally designed for battlefield surveillance and reconnaissance, albeit often to call in lethal military strikes, drones have been employed by the U.S. since 2001 to identify and kill human targets. The first "hunter-killer" unmanned combat air vehicle, the Predator, was used by the Pentagon in Bosnia in 1995 and later in the 78-day air war against Yugoslavia in 1999.

In 2001 Predators were equipped with Hellfire missiles and were deployed from Pakistan and Uzbekistan to launch attacks inside Afghanistan. The following year they were flown from the U.S. military base at Camp Lemonnier in Djibouti for the same purpose in Yemen.

The Predator and its successor, the Reaper, capable of carrying fifteen times more weaponry and flying at three times the speed, have been used for deadly attacks in Afghanistan, Iraq, Yemen, Somalia and with particularly murderous effect in Pakistan since the autumn of 2008. They are equipped with cameras connected by satellite links to bases in the United States.

In October Vice Admiral Robert Moeller, deputy commander of U.S. Africa Command, announced that Reapers, "capable of carrying a dozen guided bombs and missiles," were deployed to Seychelles off the eastern coast of the African continent to patrol the Indian Ocean.

Radio Australia ran a story on March 8 that stated "US President Barack Obama may have taken his time to decide on his Afghanistan policy, but he's also now become more of an enthusiast for drone missile strikes than his predecessor." In both Afghanistan and Pakistan as well as in Yemen.

Discussing a report by the New America Foundation, the station documented that deadly U.S. drone missile strikes on both sides of the Afghanistan-Pakistan border have been increased by 50 per cent since the Obama administration took over the White House a year ago January 20.

Citing the above-mentioned think tank, the *Radio Australia*report said there have been 64 drone strikes in South Asia in the past fourteen months compared to 45 under the George W. Bush administration between the invasion of Afghanistan in October of 2001 and January of 2009.

Bill Roggio, editor of the *Long War Journal*, was interviewed and said "there is an average five to seven strikes a month although in January there were 11."

He was further quoted describing the qualitative as well as the quantitative escalation of American drone warfare in Afghanistan and Pakistan: "The main drone is the 'Predator' which carries the 'Hellfire' anti-tank missile.

"The 'Reaper,' the older brother of the Predator, they made that so it could carry larger Hellfire missiles as well as it can carry, again, the 500 pound GPS (global position system)-guided bombs. So they're very, you know, this is sort of a revolution in air warfare."

The Reaper carries a thousand pounds of munitions and is also equipped for the Sidewinder heat-seeking air-to-air missile. Plans for adding Stinger air-to-air missiles are underway.

In terms of the human cost of Obama's 2008 Afghan war campaign pledge – "If we have actionable intelligence about high-level al Qaeda targets in Pakistan's border region, we must act if Pakistan will not or cannot" – at the beginning of this year Pakistan's influential *Dawn News* published an account of what that policy has meant to Pakistanis. In an article titled

"Over 700 killed in 44 drone strikes in 2009," the source, quoting Pakistani government statistics, wrote:

"Of the 44 predator strikes carried out by US drones in the tribal areas of Pakistan over the past 12 months, only five were able to hit their actual targets, killing five key Al-Qaeda and Taliban leaders, but at the cost of over 700 innocent civilians."

For each alleged al-Qaeda or Taliban member killed by missiles fired from U.S. drones "140 innocent Pakistanis also had to die. Over 90 per cent of those killed in the deadly missile strikes were civilians, claim authorities....On average, 58 civilians were killed in these attacks every month, 12 persons every week and almost two people every day." The dead may have been armed or unarmed, males or females, adults or children. What they have in common is that they were targeted based on "actionable intelligence" provided by someone on the ground, not necessarily a disinterested party. Last October, as the killing had begun in earnest, UN Special Rapporteur on Extrajudicial Executions Philip Alston warned: "My concern is that these drones, these Predators, are being operated in a framework which may well violate international humanitarian law and international human rights law.

"The onus is really on the government of the United States to reveal more about the ways in which it makes sure that arbitrary executions, extrajudicial executions, are not in fact being carried out through the use of these weapons." Undaunted, the U.S. substantially intensified the attacks.

This January China's Xinhua News Agency interviewed Pakistani political analyst Farrukh Saleem, who said that American drone missile attacks in Pakistan's Federally Administered Tribal Areas had increased from 17 in 2008 to 43 in 2009 with more than 70 expected to be delivered this year. Saleem was quoted warning that "Such attacks always trigger violence, suicide attacks and casualties in Pakistan. So more drone attacks mean more violence in Pakistan."

On the same day Senator John McCain was in the Pakistani capital of Islamabad and praised the drone attacks as "an effective part of the U.S. strategy." It was reported last December 17 that a U.S. drone strike had killed at least 20 people in Pakistan's North Waziristan Agency and on the 27th that 13 more were killed in the same region.

Since the New Year began the lethal attacks have only intensified. The following is not an attempt at a comprehensive account, but is gathered from assorted press reports. On January 1, it was reported that five people were killed and several more injured by two American drone attacks east of the North Waziristan capital. As to the identities of the slain, Reuters quoted a local security official as saying, "The bodies were burned beyond recognition. We are trying to determine their identity." The previous night two more were killed and several injured in another strike.

Reports continued to detail missile strikes and deaths in the nation's tribal areas.

January 3: Five more people were killed in North Waziristan in a drone attack.

January 6: At least thirteen were killed and eight wounded by two back-to-back missile strikes. "According to Pakistan's *Geo News*, a suspected drone fired two missiles at a house in the Datta Khel region in the first attack, killing seven people.

"Another strike occurred as local people began retrieving bodies from the rubble of the house, killing five people. The identities of those killed in the attacks were unknown."

January 8: Five were killed in a village in North Waziristan.

January 9: An American drone fired two missiles into a village, Ismail Khan, in North Waziristan which killed four people.

January 13: Thirteen people were killed in the village of Tappi in the same agency. "A senior security official confirmed the death toll, and said four missiles were fired from unmanned planes in the remote area."

January 15: Fifteen were killed in the village of Zannini in North Waziristan. Six were killed in the village of Bichi.

January 17: At least twenty were killed in the Shaktoi area of South Waziristan.

January 19: Six people were killed in the village of Booya in North Waziristan according to Pakistani intelligence officials.

January 24: Pakistani insurgents claimed to have shot down a U.S. drone in North Waziristan, one of eight drones seen flying over the area.

January 29: Between six and fifteen people were killed in the North Waziristan town of Muhammad Khel in a reported attack on the Haqquani Network by three American missiles.

February 2: The U.S. fired as many as eight missiles into four villages in North Waziristan, killing twenty nine people.

February 14: Five people were killed in a drone attack in the same agency. At least three others were wounded.

February 15: A drone strike allegedly killed a Chinese Uighur separatist leader in the same district.

February 17: A U.S. missile strike killed three and injured two victims in North Waziristan.

February 18: Four people were killed in a missile strike on a vehicle in the same agency.

February 24: At least thirteen alleged militants were killed in a U.S. drone attack in the Dargah Mandi area of North Waziristan.

March 8: An American drone fired five missiles into a house near Miranshah, the capital of North Waziristan, killing at least five people and wounding four.

Approximately 160 people have been killed in drone missile strikes in Pakistan in slightly over two months this year. If that pace continues, 2010 will be far deadlier than the year before: 960 to 700. If, as seems more likely, the amount of the attacks increases, the death toll will be even higher than the nearly 140 per cent increase the above extrapolation threatens.

Drone missile attacks are increasingly becoming the weapon of choice of the U.S. Central Intelligence Agency (as in Pakistan, Afghanistan and Iraq), the Joint Special Operations Command

(Yemen) and the Air Force, which as of last year had 195 Predators and 28 Reapers.

All indications are that they will soon have more. This year the Obama administration has sought from Congress $33 billion more for the wars in Afghanistan and Iraq "on top of a record request for $708 billion for the Defense Department next year."

With the new Quadrennial Defense Review, "The pilotless drones used for surveillance and attack missions in Afghanistan and Pakistan are a priority, with a goal of speeding up the purchase of new Reaper drones and expansion of Predator and Reaper drone flights through 2013."

A February 1 article called "China, Iran Prompt U.S. Air-Sea Battle Plan in Strategy Review," revealed that in line with the new Quadrennial Defense Review a "joint Air Force-Navy plan would combine the strengths of each service to conduct long-range strikes that could utilize a new generation of bombers, a new cruise missile and drones launched from aircraft carriers." As the U.S. is massively expanding its military buildup on the Pacific island of Guam, "The Army is building a missile defense system on the island and the Air Force is adding more drones."

In mid-January prominent U.S. senator Carl Levin called for "using drones to launch airstrikes" in Yemen, adding the demand for "everything from physical actions that could be accomplished in terms of use of drones or air attacks" to "clandestine actions." Regarding the strengthening of military ties between the U.S. and Yemen, a Russian news source disclosed that "Under a new classified cooperation agreement, the U.S. would be able to fly cruise missiles, fighter jets or unmanned armed drones against targets in the country, but would remain publicly silent on its role in the airstrikes."

In late January the *Wall Street Journal* reported: "The U.S. military's involvement in Yemen has already begun to grow....[T]he U.S. has increased the number of surveillance drones flying over Yemen, as well as the number of unmanned aircraft outfitted with missiles capable of striking targets on the ground, according to a senior U.S. official with direct knowledge of the deployments.

"Most drones operating outside of Iraq and Afghanistan are controlled by the Central Intelligence Agency, but the official said the drones operating over Yemen belong to the military's secretive Joint Special Operations Command."

The commander of Joint Special Operations Command until 2008 was now General Stanley McChrystal, chief commander of what will soon be 150,000 U.S. and NATO troops in Afghanistan. Drone missile assassinations and the indiscriminate slaughter of civilians that often accompany them are an integral component of his counterinsurgency strategy in South Asia. The qualitative escalation of drone attacks in Pakistan and Afghanistan began when McChrystal replaced David McKiernan as top U.S. and NATO-led International Security Assistance Force commander in Afghanistan last June.

In other parts of the world, the Pentagon is to contribute military drones for the Northern Coasts maneuvers in Finland this September, the "largest naval military exercise that has ever been seen in Finnish territorial waters." A resolution issued by the Finnish Peacefighters in Lapland last month mentioned "a program on Finnish TV about Unmanned Aerial Vehicles being tested in Lapland at the Kemijarvi Airfield. This actual training area stretches to the Russian border and follows the border for tens of kilometers.

"The strategy for Star Wars, which the US is developing, means that the pilotless plane is directed from a command center in Nevada, and follows the terrain and movements on a data screen thousands of kilometers away and maneuvers the drones. These drones have been used in Afghanistan and they have killed a lot of civilians." While Stanley McChrystal was commander of the Joint Special Operations Command the U.S. conducted eleven deadly predator attacks in Iraq in April of 2008. At the time "Defense Secretary Robert Gates prodded the Air Force to do more to rush drones to the war zone."

An American newspaper reported at the time that "Commanders are expected to rely more on unmanned systems as 30,000 U.S. troops sent last year are withdrawn. The military has dozens of Predators in Iraq and Afghanistan. In all it operates 5,000 drones, 25 times more than it had in 2001." Last December the government of Venezuela called on the world community to condemn incursions into its airspace by U.S. military drones operating from Aruba and from Curacao in the Netherlands Antilles. The type of drones that flew for several days over Venezuelan territory wasn't specified, but under both bilateral and NATO military obligations the Netherlands would not refuse the U.S. the right to station Predator and Reaper drones on bases in their Caribbean island colonies. The United States has not only increased its arsenal of unmanned aerial vehicles by twenty five times over the past decade, it has massively increased the range and lethality of its hunter-killer drones. A recent report disclosed that beginning in 2008 the Air Force Research Laboratory started to "build the ultimate assassination robot," described as "a tiny, armed drone for U.S. special forces to employ in terminating 'high-value targets.'" Formerly special forces teams were deployed or cruise missiles were fired to assassinate intended victims. In the case of the second and frequently the first the risk was that they couldn't be used twice.

Predator and Reaper drones return after missions and their supply of Hellfire missiles is replenished for further deadly attacks. They have become Washington's preferred 21st century weapons for perpetrating international assassinations.

DRONE WARFARE IN PAKISTAN

Drone warfare is now one of the most fundamental features of the U.S. battle against its enemies. Just don't ask anyone in the government to talk about it.

Since 2004, the United States military has fired about 270 missiles into Pakistan, killing thousands of militants, according to the U.S. government. Dozens of so-called high-value targets have been eliminated, like al-Qaida's No. 2, who was killed in an attack last month. But since the CIA runs these attacks, they are secret. As a result, no one in the government is supposed to admit they're happening.

"This is the least well-kept secret in the history of secrecy," says Peter Bergen, director of the National Security Studies Program at the New America Foundation, a think tank in Washington, D.C., which has compiled extensive data on the U.S. drone strikes.

"Everybody knows these are happening. Everybody knows the Pakistanis are involved in some way. Everybody knows we're doing it," Bergen says.

Dramatic Increase In Attacks

The drone strikes — part of a covert U.S. war in the northwest part of Pakistan — have changed the way the U.S. fights terrorism in the decade since the attacks of Sept. 11. Started under the Bush administration, the strikes into Pakistan have increased fivefold under President Obama. Last year, there were 118.

What accounts for the dramatic increase? According to former U.S. officials, the Obama administration made a decision to step up the drone campaign. The technology has gotten better — drones can now hover for days at a time. As a result, the strikes are working and key militant leaders are being killed. Peter W. Singer, director of the 21st Century Defense Initiative and a senior fellow in foreign policy at the Brookings Institution, explains: This is the least well-kept secret in the history of secrecy. Everybody knows these are happening. Everybody knows the Pakistanis are involved in some way. Everybody knows we're doing it.

Peter Bergen, national security analyst at the New America Foundation. "In a lot of cases, they'll track that target not just for minutes, but for hours or days, getting a pattern of life — who's coming and going from that compound, where are they? And then you get the strike," he says. And the strikes aren't just against al-Qaida's leadership. In 2008, the Bush administration broadened the campaign to include lower-ranking foot soldiers. They also started targeting groups that Pakistan saw as threats. The Obama administration did the same thing.

Risk Of Backlash

U.S. officials say the strikes are crucial to keeping al-Qaida off balance. But that tactical success comes at a cost. "There is the potential for backlash," notes Frances Townsend, who served as President Bush's homeland security adviser. "And in each case, you're making a policy decision about the potential gain versus those risks."

One big risk is that the attacks have fueled anti-American sentiment in Pakistan. Officials there have allowed the drone operations; but at the same time, Pakistan resents the U.S. for carrying out strikes on its territory. As a result, the U.S. and Pakistan are locked in a toxic marriage where neither partner trusts the other, but walking away isn't an option.

Former Director of National Intelligence Dennis Blair argues it's time to make the Pakistanis an equal partner in the strikes — putting "two hands on the trigger" — so they feel more invested in the outcome. There is another problem: civilian deaths. It's unclear how many innocent people have died in the strikes — between 50 and 300, depending on who's counting.

But Townsend says the secrecy of the drone campaign is a liability of sorts. Neither the U.S. nor Pakistan will admit the strikes are happening, which makes defending them almost impossible. "I do think there's an opportunity now for the administration to have, at least in a minimal way, some public discussion about the necessity of the tool, the care with which it is deployed, if we are to expect that the American people will continue to support such a program," Townsend says.

Need For The 'Knockout Punch'

For now, the U.S. government has no plans to ease up on the drone strikes, talk about them, or give Pakistan more say in how they're done. Far from it: A couple of months ago, a top security adviser to President Obama, Doug Lute, was asked about the drone strikes at a security conference. He said Osama bin Laden's death makes the strikes even more important. "So this is a period of turbulence in an organization which is our archenemy. This is a period, therefore, that all military doctrine suggests you need to go for the knockout punch," he said. Lute acknowledged that the U.S. does need a real partnership with Pakistan. But, he said, "I'm not ready to switch gears in the next six months when we've got a chance of a lifetime."

PAKISTAN: THE ORIGIN OF U.S. TARGETED KILLING

Since 2004 the CIA has been conducting aerial surveillance and targeted killings across Pakistan's Federally Administered Tribal Areas. But why 2004? It all centers around an important Pashtun figure: military commander Nek Muhammad. He was a "second generation" mujahedeen warrior who saw no necessary loyalty to Pakistan's ISI, who had aided his predecessors in the Afghan mujahdeen of the 1980s. Muhammad first fought in 1993 with the Afghan Taliban against the Northern Alliance. He later hosted fleeing Arab and Chechen fighters that moved into Pakistan in 2001 and 2002.

Under pressure from George Bush and the CIA's shadowy "global war on terror", the Pakistan military invaded South Waziristan in March 2004. The local tribesmen were furious, and attacks against Frontier Corps posts increased. Islamabad soon looked for a way out, and signed a peace deal with Muhammad in 2004, only a month after combat operations had begun.

This was a "deal" that greatly expanded Muhammad's power, and would ultimately lead to the formation of the Pakistani Taliban or TTP. But he soon reneged on his promise, attacking Pakistani soldiers. Islamabad was furious. And so it granted the CIA airspace for drone strikes. But there was one condition: Muhammad would be the first target. Moreover, the ISI insisted that they approve each and every strike, giving them control over the kill list, and small "flight boxes". Partly this was because Islamabad didn't want American drones poking their nose over its nuclear facilities or Kashmiri militant groups that were being trained for attacks against India. Muhammad was killed on June 18, 2004 and CIA and ISI officials agreed Pakistan would take credit.

"After the killing of Nek Muhammad in Pakistan...the CIA began to see its future: not as the long-term jailers of America's enemies but as a military organization that could erase them". (Mazzetti, 2013, p. 121).

The CIA's drone strikes are aimed at a number of militant factions in Pakistan. According to The New America Foundation the single biggest target has been the Taliban, followed by al-Qaeda and the Haqqani network—the latter, of course, is headed by the same family the CIA supported some decades earlier. According to the Conflict Monitoring Center, in 2011 alone the CIA fired 242 Hellfire missiles in Pakistan, and at a cost of $68,000, it meant the agency spent at least $16.5 million to kill 609 people.

Even after President Obama's 2012 admission that he was keeping the drone strikes "on a very tight leash", U.S. officials do not routinely comment on the CIA's program. Most drone strikes have taken place since U.S. President Barack Obama came to power in 2009, with the most prolific year of strikes taking place in 2010. This increase is partly a result of changes in the way targets are identified. Since 2008 the CIA began rolling out "signature strikes" against targets outside of named kill lists. In 2008, former CIA Director Michael Hayden lobbied Bush to relax drone targeting constraints further in Pakistan. No longer was a named target on a kill-list a legal prerequisite to attack. Instead, the CIA could now target individuals based on their 'pattern of life' or their suspicious daily behaviour. These 'signature strikes' use the same legal justification as the Presidential finding signed by Bush immediately after 9/11, and then re-signed by Obama in 2009, and they represent the apex of modern biopower and surveillance, honed and developed over decades.

Conclusions...and *the Rise of Drone Police*?

The development of the U.S. drone program was not simply a technological operation–it was a political process that required a series of fraught legal precedents to enable the Predator's post-9/11 rise.

The Rise of the Predator Empire is a story about people–about the engineering prowess of an Israeli engineer and the determination of an exiled Saudi national. But it's also a story about objects: about the technological capacities of the Amber, the GNAT, and finally the Predator drone–from the type of satellite data link used, to the sensing prowess of the camera, to the strength of the plane's wings. It's a story about legal objects called Presidential Findings that granted the CIA the ability to pursue its aggressive program in Afghanistan and then Pakistan. It's the story of how a technology came to embody a kind of secrecy; materializing a set of social relations and bureaucratic powers.

But above all, it's a story about geography—about the coming-together and assembling of all these objects in a distinctive time and space, from Vietnamese jungles to Pakistani mountains. And it's a story that is far from over, as the people still living under the hum and buzz of Predators know only too well. The rush to secure the U.S. homeland in the war on terror has stretched the Vietnam-era "electronic battlefield" across land, sea, and outer space. U.S. predators—both human and nonhuman—now surveil and strike a globalized battlespace in a project of *full spectrum dominance*. And it is this latter phenomenon that I wand to finish talking about.

We are now entering the "fifth stage" of drone warfare: *the age of the police drone*. This is period in which robots and drones will be increasingly used by the state not just against terrorists "out there" but against criminals back "at home".

The first decade of the war on terror saw U.S. military and CIA drones concentrated to the mountainous and remote geographies of Pakistan, and later Yemen and Somalia. In recent years, however, drones in and beyond the U.S. have been trialed by police force. Police forces are rapidly turning towards these robots for securing the economic insecurities of the contemporary urban landscape.

Crucially, police drones are not inert objects that simply "add" to preexisting forms of authority, but mediators that actively transform the very logics of state power. Unlike the helicopters prowling above the Los Angeles skyline, smaller drones that can pervade and saturate the urban volume complicate the very idea of *remote* surveillance.

The drone, and micro drone in particular, with its ability to swarm in the streets of densely packed urban environments, holds the potential for more *intimate* and invasive forms of state power.

This not only intensifies the coverage and mobility of existing state technology, but is fundamentally transforming them Currently, the Predator and Reaper class of military drones surveil the ground from up to a flight ceiling of 25,000 and 50,000 feet respectively. But a big trend in military and domestic robotics is to develop micro or "nano" drones that can range in size from a humming bird to an insect. Crucially, by going smaller, the geographies of state surveillance become more intimate.

Most U.S. police drones in existence today are variants of the small-scale quadcopter drones used by amateur hobbyists. Grand Forks sheriff's department in North Dakota, for example, owns four drones.

This includes the quadcopter Qube, developed by AeroVironment, as well as the U.S. military's most widely used fixed-wing drone, the hand-launched Raven. Moreover, advances in artificial intelligence are enabling small-scale nano drones to cooperate together in emergent, cooperating constellations called "swarms".

It is here that the specifics of a *dronified form of policing* are glimpsed. With an ability to swarm in roving robotic clouds, the (nano) drone holds the potential to pervade, saturate, and modulate the urban volume in a way that neither the helicopter nor CCTV can adequately perform. Nano drones would be able to move *inside* workplaces, or perch*inside* of homes undetected. These drones would be able to infiltrate a range of currently inaccessible urban micro-geographies.

Perhaps, in the cities of our future, many of the police drones will be weaponized. While attaching lethal missiles may appear a distant reality, what about Tasers? In 2015, North Dakota became the first state to legalize less-than-lethal weaponized drones: flying robots fitted with tear gas, rubber bullets, Tasers, or beanbags.

Whether this opens the door to other police forces remains to be seen. Additionally, non-state actors will disrupt the smooth running of the dronepolis while nonetheless feeding its power.

Recently, police in Tokyo established the first "drone squad" tasked with capturing nuisance drones flown by the public, as well as patrolling important government buildings. This atmospheric securitization followed a 2015 incident when a drone carrying a radioactive substance landed on the Japanese prime minister's office. Such a landscape of ultra-secured government and corporate headquarters fitted with anti-drone shields and patrolled by police drones might very well be a permanent feature of our future urban landscapes.

SHAPING THE FUTURE

Currently the United States has more or less a monopoly on drones, which will not likely last any longer than the American monopoly on nuclear weapons did after WWII. Drone technology is already proliferating, suggesting that the United States is not the only country that understands the future strategic significance of drones.

Modern military powers such as Germany and India have announced plans to acquire combat drones, while several other countries have growing UAV capabilities, most notably the Chinese, Iranians, and Russians. Of these three countries, China poses the most significant threat in terms of UAV capability.

China is fast developing tactical unmanned aerial vehicles capable of supporting ground, sea, and air forces with similar capabilities to American platforms. According to a 2013 report by the Project 2049 Institute: In a worrisome trend, China has ramped up research in recent years faster than any other country... It displayed its first unmanned system model at the [annual] Zhuhai air show five years ago, and now every major manufacturer for the Chinese military has a research centre devoted to unmanned systems.

The report, which said "the military significance of China's move into unmanned systems is alarming," suggested that China could "easily match or outpace U.S. spending on unmanned systems, rapidly close the technology gaps and become a formidable global competitor in unmanned systems."

Two Chinese drones that closely resemble the American Reaper and Predator UAVs were unveiled at the Zhuhai air show in China in November of 2012. The Chinese arsenal also possesses a larger drone that Western experts say is modeled after the American RQ-4 Global Hawk. The proliferation of armed drones in other nations is indicative of the platform's increasing strategic significance as countries recognize UAVs as a valuable war fighting tool that will play a vital role in future conflicts.

Paralleling the proliferation of drone technology as well as the rapid pace of American drone capabilities is an organizational shift that symbolizes the growth of the UAV role within U.S. military force structure.

The Air Force is beginning to recruit separately for drone programs since the type of individual operating a drone is extremely different from those piloting fighter jets both mentally and physically. A new talent pool is drawing on a generation that has grown up surrounded by technology and therefore has a greater aptitude for dealing with unmanned systems. The move to identify new skill sets represents a profound cultural change within the Air Force and U.S. military as a whole. The growth of the RPA community and its integration within the Air Force indicates a larger organizational shift within the military to embrace the rising RPA platform.

Further evidence of the drone's strategic evolution within the military is a growing tension between the Department of Defense and clandestine drone operators. In a *National Journal* article, journalist Michael Hirsh argues that current CIA

Director John Brennan thinks that, "the drone program has run its course as a CIA operation" and that moving the a program to the Department of Defense (DoD) is the way of the future. A proposed transfer of the operational network to the DoD would unify the command and control structure of targeted killings and create a uniform set of rules and procedures. According to *The Daily Beast* reporter Daniel Klaidman, the move could potentially toughen the criteria for drone strikes, strengthen the program's accountability, and increase transparency, as the military would have operational control over targeting.

Lethal missions would take place under Title 10 of the U.S. Code of Laws, which outlines the role of the armed forces, rather than Title 50, which outlines the legal authority for intelligence activities and covert operations. This possible organizational modification represents the growth of the program from a simple tool of counterterrorism to assuming a broader role within the U.S. military and defense community.

Will drones lead to more war in the future? Or a "space race" within drone technology, leading up to a world filled with drone warfare on all sides? It has been argued that virtual technologies make it easier for democracies to wage war because they eliminate the risk of blood sacrifice that once forced prudence. Indiana Congresswoman Susan Brooks wrote in *The Washington Post*:

> Drones will not reduce conflict. Their very ease of use will tempt nations, our own very much included, to engage in automated conflict. The problem with automated conflict, however, is that it doesn't stay automated. People die in drone wars, just like they died from the automation of arrows when the crossbow was invented. War machinery has a terrible capacity to tempt us to think it's something else.

Proponents of this line of thought argue that technology disengages the public and instead turns war into something merely to be watched and not weighed with great seriousness. Without public debate or risking troops, the decision of war may reflect a nation that does not care due to the lack of lives invested in a conflict. Others have dismissed the idea that drone weaponry by itself will subtract humanity from warfare. Human psychology and human emotions are still a primary driving force behind wars, and technological advances have not substantially curbed that element of warfare in the past. He argued:

Despite the nearly century-long prevalence of airpower, we have not become numb to war. Airpower, drones included, has not erased emotion from war because war is a complex mixture of irrational forces, chance, and rational policy. And as long as humans are involved in conflict, these forces will continue to exert themselves on the theory and practice of war.

Thus, rather than drones determining the frequency of future conflicts, they will likely define its characteristics. As unmanned systems become more prevalent, militaries will be more likely to use force, but also will be less willing to conduct operations that expose soldiers to danger. As a result, the experience of going to war is changing.

Humans are increasingly functioning "on the loop" of combat systems, overseeing the autonomous actions of vehicles rather than participating directly. Simultaneously, advances in artificial intelligence will enable systems to make combat decisions without necessarily requiring human input. Such weapons seem advanced, but represent just the beginning. "There has been a game change in weaponry over the last several years," Peter Singer and Thomas Wright say, "with a new generation of advanced technology that moves the point of critical human decision, both geographically off the battlefield and also, increasingly, chronologically away from the time of kinetic action."

New UAV technology will be like every other in initiating a new evolution in military platforms and doctrine. However, unlike previous military "revolutions," Peter Singer writes that "the introduction of unmanned systems to the battlefield doesn't change simply how we fight, but for the first time changes who fights at the most fundamental level. It transforms the very agent of war, rather than just its capabilities." He goes on to say, "In the dismaying history of war machinery, armed drones are a game-changing technology, akin to gunpowder, the steam engine, the atomic bomb, opening up possibilities that were fiction a generation earlier but also opening up perils that were unknown a generation ago."

Therefore, while drones currently present a narrow tactical benefit, they posses tremendous potential that could spur the U.S. military to an onset of a decades-long technological transformation in warfare that will be defined by the strategic use of unmanned aerial platforms. UAV technology could spur a paradigm shift in the nature of warfare, comparable to the introduction of mechanization and airpower in WWII.

Bibliography

Ahuja, Vijay: *Network and Internet Security*. Academic Press, Inc.: Boston, 1996.

Atkinson, Rick: *An Army at Dawn: The War in North Africa 1942–1943*, Henry Holt, New York, 2002.

Bajpai, G.S. : *On Cyber Crime and Cyber Law*, Serials Publications, Delhi, 2011.

Bernauer, Thomas: *Genes, Trade, and Regulation: The Seeds of Conflict in Food Biotechnology*, Princeton, Princeton University. 2003.

Bradley, John. *Learning to Glow: A Nuclear Reader*. Tucson: University of Arizona Press, 2000.

Buzan, Barry & Eric Herring: *The Arms Dynamic in World Politics*, London: Lynne Rienner Publishers, 1998.

Chandler, David G: *The Campaigns of Napoleon*, Macmillan, New York, 1966.

Citino, Robert M: *Blitzkrieg to Desert Storm: The Evolution of Operational Art*, University Press of Kansas, Lawrence, 2004.

Clausewitz, Carl: *On War*, Michael Howard and Peter Paret (trans and ed), Princeton University Press, Princeton, 1989.

David S: *Understanding Information Age Warfare*, CCRP Publications, Washington DC, 2001.

Dery, Mark. *Escape Velocity: Cyberculture at the End of the Century* . Grove Press, 1997.

Duffy, Christopher: *The Military Life of Frederick the Great, Atheneum*, New York, 1986.

Garrelick, Renee. M.I.T. Beginnings: The Legacy of Nuclear Metals. Concord, MA: Nuclear Metals, Inc., 1995.

Gast, A. P. : *The impact of Restricting Information Access on Science and Technology* Retrieved October 1, 2008.

Gibson, James N. *Nuclear Weapons of the United States: An Illustrated History*. Atglen, PA: Schiffer Publishing Ltd., 1996.

Hasan-Askari Rizvi, *Chemical Terrorism and South Asia,* Albuquerque, NM: Sandia National Laboratories, February 2003.

Hoffman, Bruce: *Inside Terrorism and Internet Crime,* New York: Columbia University Press, 1998.

Jones, W.H.: *Government and Politics of India Military,* London, Hutchinson, 1971.

Kumar, Raj : *Weapons and Military Technology,* Sumit Enterprises, Delhi, 2009.

Laliberte, S. : *Security by Example Defend I.T.* New York, Addison Wesley, 2004.

Norris, James A.: *The First Afghan War 1838-1842,* Cambridge, University Press, 1967.

Paul Buis : *Internet Security: Professional Reference.* New Riders: Indianapolis, 1996.

Paul T Augastine: *Combating Cyber Crime,* Crescent Pub, Delhi, 2007.

Posen, B.R.: *The Sources of Cyber Crime,* Ithaca, 1984, Cornell Univ. Press.

Rosen, P.: *Societies and Military Power: India and its Armies,* Ithaca, Cornell University Press, 1996.

Rothenberg, Gunther Eric: *The Art of Warfare in the Age of Napoleon,* Indiana University Press, Bloomington, 1978.

Singh, Y.K. : *Cyber Crime and Law,* Shree, Delhi, 2005.

Verton, D. : *Black Ice: The invisible Threat of Cyber-terrorism,* New York: McGraw-Hill/Osborne, 2003.

Winkler, Allan M. *Life Under A Cloud: American Anxiety About the Atom.* New York: Oxford University Press, 1993.

Index

M

N

O

P

R

S

T

W

❑❑❑